ON ROMAN RELIGION

On Roman Religion

*Lived Religion and the Individual
in Ancient Rome*

Jörg Rüpke

Cornell University Press
Ithaca and London

First published 2016 by Cornell University Press
Printed in the United States of America

Library of Congress Cataloging-in-Publication Data

Names: Rüpke, Jörg, author.
Title: On Roman religion : lived religion and the individual in ancient
    Rome / Jörg Rüpke.
Other titles: Cornell studies in classical philology. Townsend lectures
Description: Ithaca ; London : Cornell University Press, 2016. |
    Series: Townsend lectures/Cornell studies in classical philology |
    Includes bibliographical references and index.
Identifiers: LCCN 2016017486 | ISBN 9781501704703 (cloth : alk. paper)
Subjects: LCSH: Religion—Social aspects—Rome. | Rome—Religion. |
    Experience (Religion)—History.
Classification: LCC BL803 .R84 2016 | DDC 292.07—dc23
LC record available at https://lccn.loc.gov/2016017486

Cloth printing   10 9 8 7 6 5 4 3 2 1

To Richard Gordon,
colleague, teacher, and friend

CONTENTS

Acknowledgments

The publication of the Townsend Lectures is a wonderful opportunity to thank my hosts, the Department of Classics at Cornell University, and above all its chair at the time of my visit, Charles Brittain, and my personal hosts, Eric and Suzanne Rebillard. I am also grateful to all the members of the department and students in the seminar who engaged with my ideas and critically discussed methods and evidence: Annetta Alexandridis, Ben Anderson, Tad Brennan, Caitlín Barrett, Nicole Giannella, Kim Haines-Eitzen, Sturt Manning, Hayden Pellicia, Verity Platt, Pietro Pucci, Courtney Roby, Barry Strauss, and Michael Weiss. Last but not least, I am grateful to Katrina S. Neff, who managed all the administrative arrangements related to my visit. I remember with gratitude the wonderful atmosphere and the many compelling conversations, in addition to the hours left free for working on my notes and revising my arguments.

Even cursory readers will note that the thrust and details of my earlier arguments have developed significantly. The book has benefited from subsequent discussion with further colleagues, above all in the ever innovative, stimulating interdisciplinary context of the Max Weber Center of the University of Erfurt and the Kolleg-Forschergruppe "Religious Individualization in Historical Perspective." Here, I must mention Clifford Ando, Eve-Marie Becker, Jan Bremmer, Martin Fuchs and Antje Linkenbach, Knud Haakonssen, Bettina Hollstein, Dietmar Mieth, Martin Mulsow, Bernd Otto, Rahul Parson, Hartmut Rosa, Veit Rosenberger, Jutta and Markus Vinzent (with special thanks for his criticism of chapter 8), and Katharina Waldner. The lectures and the book built on research conducted within the project "Lived Ancient Religion Questioning 'Cult' and 'Polis Religion'" (funded by the European Research Council within the Framework Programme 2008–13 under agreement no. 295555), and would not have taken the shape it has without the constant exchange within the team. Many thanks go to Christopher Degelmann, Valentino Gasparini, Maik Patzelt, Georgia Petridou, Rubina Raja, Katharina Rieger, and Lara Weiss. I am even more grateful to Richard Gordon, a member of this team, but much more a friend and teacher whose influence I felt so deeply when reading the final version. This book is dedicated to him.

I owe much to the careful reading of the final manuscript by Alice Brigance. She edited my English and her critical reading helped improve the argument in several places. She did a marvelous job. I thank Maik Patzelt for preparing the indexes. My final thanks go to Peter Potter and the staff at Cornell University Press for their benign and efficient engagement with the author and the careful production of the book. The readers provided important criticism and invested hope. I hope not to disappoint them.

INTRODUCTION

Ancient Mediterranean religion is traditionally viewed through the lens of public religion. It is regarded, that is, as the religions of political units (usually city-states) that are part and parcel of civic identity. Given the local roots and immobility of such public political religion, the movable elements were conceptualized on the patterns of modern religions, but termed "cult" for their organizational deficits and openness to pluralism. These cults were centered on a deity, whose "essence" (in German, *Wesen*), "nature," or "personality" defined the character and function of the cult on a transregional scale. Much of twentieth-century scholarship on ancient religion was invested in locating, identifying, and classifying the evidence for such cults, and there was a clear focus on the supposed distinguishing mark of many "other" religions, that is, the plurality of venerated gods. "Idolatry" and, more recently, "polytheism" were terms central to this procedure.[1] These cults were seen as being coordinated within a

---

1. See Schmidt 1987; Ahn 1993; Gladigow 2002; Rüpke 2012d.

pantheon,[2] an organized system of gods of different "powers" or "fields of competence."[3] That which, in the writings of intellectuals such as Hesiod or Marcus Terentius Varro, was probably above all an attempt to order a world of competing images and narratives and to transform religion into knowledge[4] became the dominant framework of late ancient, premodern, and even contemporary interpretations of ancient Mediterranean religion. Within this framework, individual religious competence would be the ability to address the most relevant deity in the most appropriate way, to properly formulate names and epithets.[5] Modern historians of religion carefully distinguished between gods and goddesses that were venerated in proper cults and those that were merely the inventions of poets. This may make use of Varro's distinction between *theologia poetarum* and *theologia civilis*,[6] but it certainly distorts it.

The ontological model implied in such analyses gives priority to the gods, and it is still gods that form the grammatical and logical subject of many statements about the history of religion. They develop, move, arrive, demand cult, and reveal themselves. Monographs on individual gods or their veneration are still a genre current in the historical study of religion—presupposing that there is a coherent "idea" or "experience" (to enlarge the list given above) behind the use of a single specific name to address a divine entity in different contexts. Where names are not attested, iconographical identifications made by the modern observer easily fill the gap.

A growing strand in scholarship has resisted this framework without opting to describe ancient religion as a belief system on the blueprint of Christian dogmatics; that is, these works are not mustering theology, anthropology, cosmology, eschatology, and eliminating "religious practices" (those that were official as well as those deemed "popular" as an indication that they do not conform to dogmatic definitions and are therefore to be rightly regarded as marginal, if not irrelevant). Instead, ritual has been

---

2. Rüpke 2003c; more generally Rüpke 2007a, 16–17; cf. Athanassiadi and Frede 1999; Rüpke 2003c; Pongratz-Leisten 2011.

3. See Rüpke 2005b for the Roman use of such metaphors.

4. See Rüpke 2005c, 2009b, 2014b on Varro.

5. Belayche et al. 2005b.

6. See Rüpke 2005c.

established as a cornerstone of religion, if not a synonym for it, at least for antiquity. Sacrifices and festivals are regarded as the religious grid that was superimposed on urban and rural reality, establishing sacred time and space, religious calendars, and religious landscapes.[7] Architecture (even if minimal) and fixed religious roles, frequently taking the form of priesthoods, gave permanent visibility to these ritual structures. Time-honored traditions, occasionally even in written form (or sometimes supposed to have existed in written form), as in the case of the Roman *libri sacerdotum*,[8] shape and preserve this type of "cold" religion. Following the lead of the introductory account of John Scheid and the two volumes of Mary Beard, John North, and the late Simon Price, I have myself published a medium-sized account of "Religion of the Romans."[9]

I invoke this model only to discard it along with other trends in early twenty-first-century scholarship. We have learned to see the authorial agenda and discursive quality of our literary sources as part of religion proper and to detect the situational and expressive, that is, performative, character of many rituals.[10] Though it may be predominantly practice, ancient religion is practice that is reflected in discourse, and discourse itself frequently assumes the form of religious practices. It is on that basis that Robert Parker held his Townsend lectures in 2008 "On Greek Religion," and that I myself had edited a *Companion to Roman Religion* not much earlier.[11] In 2012 I was able to publish a monograph that demonstrated how processes of rationalization shaped and modified religious, and above all ritual, practices in the period of the Roman Republic.[12]

The invitation to the Townsend lectures in fall 2013 gave me the opportunity, for which I am deeply grateful, to advance my previous work on ancient religion. *On Roman Religion* will add the perspectives of lived

---

7. See Cancik 1985; see also J. P. Brown 1986; Alcock and Osbourne 1994; Steinsapir 2005 for the concept of "sacred landscape"; Salzman 1999; Wescoat and Ousterhout 2012; cf. Rüpke 1995, Feeney 2007b, Rüpke 2011b for calendars.

8. Sini 1983; Scheid 1994; Beard 1998. See Rüpke 2003b for the role of this postulate in the history of scholarship.

9. Scheid 1998c, 2003; Beard, North, and Price 1998; Rüpke 2007a.

10. For literature, see Feeney 1998; Beard 1986, 1991; Rüpke 2012e, 2012i. On performance, see, e.g., Anonymous 1999; Bierl 2001; Hofman 2004; Pelikan-Pittenger 2008; Rodriguez-Mayorgas 2011. Beard 2007 combines both aspects.

11. Parker 2011; Rüpke 2009a (1st ed. 2007).

12. Rüpke 2012a.

ancient religion and individual appropriation to the study of Roman religious institutions and ritual. The concept of appropriation, fundamental to my interpretation of lived religion, is taken from Michel de Certeau and refers to individual, everyday action.[13] The individual is not seen as somebody who simply acquires and reproduces established or normative ways of thinking or acting; instead, hegemonic as well as alternative options are evaluated, selected, and transformed for the individual's purposes. Hence, the individual's actions are strategic, even subversive. These individual ways of living are not merely petty variations of societal norms. It is only through manifold individual appropriations that norms and traditions are reproduced, hence continued and modified at the same time.[14] I do not mean to deny the limited range of options available to many, in particular the nonelite people in ancient (and contemporary) societies, but this change of perspective invites us to pay more attention to individual variations in religious behavior, resistance to and rejection of certain practices, and the consequences of these over time. Our interest is not in the immutability—claimed rather than proved in most historical cases—but in the fluidity of ritual and other religious traditions.

Lived religiosity, "lived religion," as reformulated by urban anthropologist Meredith McGuire,[15] is a concept helpful for further developing the notion of individual appropriation and reformulating it as a new paradigm in the analysis of Roman religion. Instead of inquiring into how individuals reproduce a set of religious practices and the intellectual tenets of a faith,[16] religion is to be reconstructed as everyday experiences, practices, expressions, and interactions; these in turn constantly redefine religion as practice, idea, and community. The very different, strategic, and (if necessary) even subversive forms of individual appropriation are analytically confronted with traditions, their normative claims, and their institutional protections. Thus the precarious state of institutions and traditions comes to the fore. These are as much means of expression and creativity for their inventors and patrons as they are the spaces and material of experience and

---

13. In general, Certeau 2007; for the term "appropriation," see Füssel 2006.
14. Lüdtke 2009.
15. McGuire 2008; for the adaptation to ancient religions, see Rüpke 2012c. For the preference of "religion" over "religiosity," see Rüpke 2015b.
16. Stausberg 2001.

innovation for their users and clients. Lived ancient religion thus offers a framework within which we can address the whole range of religious practices and conceptions, not as sets of fixed rules or beliefs, but as a permanently changing field of individual actions, inceptive traditions, monumental examples, and incoherent assumptions. Lived ancient religion is as much about variation or even outright deviance[17] as it is about the attempts and failures to establish or change rules and roles and to communicate these via public authorities or literary discourse. It is such roles and rules, their variations and limits, and their establishment and communication to oneself and others that constitute the material under consideration in *On Roman Religion*.

I am quite aware that a decision to foreground "individuals" in a study of premodern religion might encounter immediate criticism. The general image of religion, Roman religion in particular, as a rigid ritual system seems not to allow for significant individual variance and even less, to stress my point, for systemic individual variance. Furthermore, the framework of civic religion has been reaffirmed by its principal advocate, John Scheid,[18] who has greatly shaped and advanced my own thinking. Hence, in my first chapter, "Individual Appropriation of Religion," I concentrate in a rather elementary manner on the question of individuality in religious matters. Is this a concept that is applicable to ancient societies at all? Or do I base my whole enterprise on a mistaken anachronism? I must, first of all, ensure that I have not been led to implausible historical claims by the hegemonic character of present day individualism: We ought to be individuals!

Roles shape the possibilities for individual appropriation as a strategy for action.[19] Thus, special attention must be paid to the appropriation of roles and role variation among religious specialists, a general term that I prefer to "priest" and "priesthoods," which denote a much smaller range of religious roles.[20] "Religious specialist" encompasses: short-term religious roles such as dedicators; annual roles such as the magistrates that were frequently responsible for the performance of the most important public

---

17. See Rüpke 2016a.
18. Scheid 2013.
19. For the concept of role, see Emmet 1966; Sundén 1975; Sterbenc Erker 2013.
20. For the concept of religious specialist, see Rüpke 1996b; see Rüpke 2008 for an application.

rituals and the elected heads of religious colleges; and unlimited or even permanent roles such as magicians, public priests, prophets, interpreters of dreams, healers, and writers of religious texts. Chapter 2, "Individual Decision and Social Order," focuses on the roles of religious specialists, in particular on priestly roles in the late republican period. These are typically determined by career patterns and family prestige; individual proclivities are scarcely evidenced within the numerous different Roman priesthoods. At the same time, we do occasionally observe strange, highly individual behavior. This chapter traces these late republican cases and balances them against the social expectations—both the more and the less obvious—that informed individual actions.

The following chapters will concentrate on individual ritual practice. Chapter 3, "Appropriating Images—Embodying Gods," proposes reading a text of the Augustan poet Propertius as a reflection on dedicatory practices and individual appropriations of images. The enormous malleability of the resulting divine figure is among the most interesting results of this analysis. This chapter fundamentally questions the usual understanding of dedications as primarily a means of establishing and continuing specific "cults."

Chapter 4, "Testing the Limits of Ritual Choices," once again turns to the Propertian oeuvre, with attention to its imagination of individual magic practices and how this is informed by contemporary discourse and practice. Magic is imagined in the poems as a traditional and widely available technique, a legitimate option within certain limits. At the same time, the role of the user of magic is shaped by technical considerations and the agency of objects in magical procedures.

Can the practices and experiences of lived ancient religion be identified beyond those that are described and imagined in a discourse that sought to denounce certain practices as extreme? This is the opening question of chapter 5, "Reconstructing Religious Experience." Again, I take a text from the early empire as a point of departure: in this chapter it is Ovid's commentary on the Roman *fasti*. I search this text for traces of individual appropriation and the spaces within which this was possible. Ovid construed a reader who was interested not only in religious knowledge but also in the emotional registers appropriate to participation in religious performances.

Evidently, writing was an important part of many Roman ritual practices from the late republic onward. It offered new spaces and media for the individual appropriation of ritual, in performance and in later more reflective contexts. Chapter 6, "Dynamics of Individual Appropriation," reviews this relationship within a number of ritual settings. Contexts for the interplay of reading and ritual performance in the late republican and early imperial periods include the taking of auspices, ritual banquets, the festivals of the Arval Brethren, and domestic rituals. The invention of rituals—fictitious rituals, that is—is also discussed.

Against this background, in chapter 7 I explore the notion of "Religious Communication" more systematically, before it concentrates on the role of inscriptions accompanying dedications in communicating individual situations and interests both to the gods and to a wider audience. Religious communication is special in its insistence on its vertical dimension, which at the same time allows for very specific and often highly visible horizontal, interhuman communication. Against the background of the enormous growth of the epigraphic habit until the early third century, this chapter treats lived religion in the imperial period.

More narrowly focused, chapter 8, "Instructing Literary Practice in *The Shepherd of Hermas*," considers the interplay of supply and demand in religious writing as it relates to an early second-century text, *The Shepherd of Hermas*. It is the growth of the text itself and particular features of its contents and style that suggest an interest both in communal reception and in individual reading. This is confirmed by findings that illustrate the history of the text's transmission and reception. Taken together, these observations suggest that we read this as a process of long-term, reflective religious individualization.

The brief conclusion concentrates on the basic agenda of this book: Roman religion not as a set of cults, one of many localized "religions," but as a regional and temporal segment of lived religion in antiquity, serving individuals who employed religion as a resource for many a purpose, who tried to find their places in and beyond traditions, or who tried to define those very traditions for successful communication with the divine as well as with their unquestionably relevant human contemporaries.

1

INDIVIDUAL APPROPRIATION OF RELIGION

Any attempt to think about ancient Roman religion needs to start two millennia later. In religious studies it has become a matter of course to look at religion, not only from the perspective of religious communities and religious traditions, but also from the viewpoint of the individual. The latter is true in two respects.[1] First, religion today seems to have become primarily the business of individuals who shape their personal religiosity (some say "spirituality") by selecting from a broad spectrum of religious options, whether these be in the form of religious groups and organizations, or doctrines and practices encountered in mass media (in a book, for instance, or on the Internet). Second, the individual seems simultaneously to have become ever more the thematic focus of religion, not just as the bearer of expectations concerning an individual afterlife, personal "well-being," and "spiritual welfare," but also as the practitioner of specific rituals and religious training, and as the subject of spiritual experiences.

---

1. Krech 2011, 163. The following builds on Rüpke 2012h.

Such diagnoses of the "privatization of religion"[2] have gained currency in a variety of studies over the last decades, specifically as diagnoses of the present state of religion,[3] and "individualization" is, needless to say, regarded as a characteristic feature of the modern age far beyond the sphere of religion. Meanwhile, it has become apparent that the notion of religious individuality as the exclusive and superior property of the "Western world," which privileges itself with the term "modern," is also open to criticism.[4] Such critiques have taken the form of pointing out the historical absurdity of claims to singularity, or of embracing a counterstereotype that elevates Eastern collectivity over supposed Western individuality.[5]

The conceptual association of modernity with religious individuality has obstructed the investigation of comparable phenomena in earlier periods. Consequently, individuality has received limited consideration in the examination of the dynamics of religion throughout history and in ancient, pre-Christian religion in particular. The religions of great individuals, the religions of poets and thinkers, and the role of the founders and reformers of a given religion have, of course, received much attention.[6] This was and is largely due to the nature of available sources, which has favored such interest: it is often the literary products of single authors that are handed down in complete or extensive form, whereas verbal communication within and between groups and their members lacks evidence, as is also typically the case regarding testimonials for the reception of the aforementioned texts. By and large, it is the "great individual" who has won the attention of observers, historiographers, and authors of letters. Yet it is precisely the deficits inherent in such access to isolated figures that have prompted much critical comment during the last fifty years or so; for all their value, a political history based on big men, a history of ideas based on geniuses only, and a history of religion that concentrates on the testimonies of these major figures have limitations that, since the turn of the twenty-first century, have become visible.[7]

---

2. See Dawson 2006; Rüpke 2016b.

3. E.g. Knoblauch 1999, 189–202; Aupers and Houtman 2008.

4. M. Fuchs and Rüpke 2015; M. Fuchs 2015.

5. Cf. Asad 1973, 1983.

6. A classical study with regard to Roman religion is found in the concluding chapters of Altheim 1953. Cf. van den Bruwaene 1937; Goar 1972; Speyer 1989; Stepper 2003; Schmid 2005; Orlin 2007.

7. See, e.g., Gladigow 2005, 29–39; Mulsow 2012, 11–36.

From the same period onward, approaches are interested in religious experience,[8] in religion as communication,[9] or in the social or cognitive genesis of religious knowledge.[10] But such perspectives have scarcely been used in considering the role of the individual, the distinction between individual and society within that cultural phenomenon that I here address as "religion," or the history of religion. This is all the more astonishing because in many cultures religion represents a central instrument of individuation, by individual prayer, vows, or methods of confession. Much of the archaeological evidence for religion from Mediterranean antiquity has been produced in the course of, or in response to, individual religious action. Religious individuality has been concretized in our very sources, in the form of durable institutionalizations and the media of religious communication.[11] In this chapter I intend to highlight the possibilities and problems of an approach to the history of religion that makes use of individualization and individuality, concepts that have been and continue to be used liberally as stereotypes of auto-description and ascription.

Marcus Tullius Cicero, in his accounts and discussions of Greek philosophical positions, coined the term *individua* as a translation of the Greek *átoma*.[12] In his paraphrase of the Platonic *Timaios*, Cicero employed this word to distinguish between the indivisible and divisible matter used by the creator god to form the human soul (*animus*).[13] Seneca later used *individua* for indivisible material connections and for indivisible goods, such as peace and liberty.[14] By the end of the first century AD the application of the term had been extended to very strong bonds of friendship or love.[15] Within philosophy, the dominant discussion remained fixed around the question of whether individuals regarded as first substances (Aristotle) or

---

8. Jung 1999; Ricken 2004; Taves 2009, 2010.

9. Tyrell, Krech, and Knoblauch 1998; Rüpke 2001; Malik, Rüpke, and Wobbe 2007; Stavrianopoulou 2006; Pace 2009; Rüpke 2015b.

10. Berger and Luckmann 1967; Lawson 2000; Whitehouse and McCauley 2005; Rüpke 2012e.

11. See chapter 7.

12. E.g., Cic. *Fin.* 1.17.

13. Ibid., 21.

14. Sen. *Dial.* 1.5.9; *Ep.* 73.8.

15. Tac. *Ann.* 6.10; Apul. *Apol.* 53; *CIL* 8.22672.

as generalities (Plotinus) should be given ontological priority, leading to an understanding of individuals as clearly, demonstrably separate beings, easily illustrated by human individuals, but never restricted to human and superhuman rational beings.[16]

As far as I can see, neither the questions associated with the growth of individuality through the development in time and space of a single human being (individuation) nor the issue of communication between separate individuals (and hence the social dimension of any concept of individuality) became a matter of debate in ancient texts. Unlike the discussions of the nineteenth and twentieth centuries, ancient discourse did not the treat difference and distinction between persons as central concerns. Hence the problem of individuality in antiquity.

Today, the term "individual" is so frequently employed that it is easy to overlook the difficulties involved in using it in a historical inquiry to set an individual apart from society and to draw a distinction between individual behaviors and the norms of social conformity. In short, "individual" has now become a normative concept: one should be an individual, and of course the individualism of today is the result of a process of individualization that categorically distinguishes the Western modern age from the non-Western world, as from the ancient world, geographically as well as culturally.

This turn has consequences for those writing the history of religion. In regarding "Western" premodern cultures, the concept of a polis religion or a civic religion (that is, the identity of the religious practices of a political unit and their functions within the whole of religion),[17] or the concept of the religious unity of medieval Europe[18] is exactly the opposite of the self-description of modern societies implied by the secularization thesis: in contrast to the collective and public phenomenon that was premodern religion, contemporary religion is mainly found in individual forms up to the point of being "invisible,"[19] if its fundamental decline is not taken for granted anyway.[20]

---

16. Rüpke 2013d, 9.
17. See Rüpke 2007a, 5–38 and Kindt 2012, 12–35 for criticism.
18. Köpf 1993; Borgolte 2001; Auffarth 2009.
19. Luckmann 1967.
20. E.g., Bruce 1999.

A Conventional History of Individualization

The history of the development of "modern" religious individualization has been reconstructed and dated in very different ways, but the following points are generally made: according to the narrative current already in the nineteenth century, the individual is a product of the Renaissance, during which the revival of pre-Christian antiquity had made it possible for the first time to escape intentionally from one's own tradition. Thus new and groundbreaking philosophical, aesthetic, linguistic, institutional, and religious alternatives laid open, or even organized and practiced, critical distance toward traditional society.[21] This entailed the renewed establishment of Platonism besides and above Aristotelianism, the upgrading of everyday languages, the vernaculars, to written languages (Italian in addition to Latin, for example), the foundation of academies, and the outlining of ideal states. If paganism became not just an aesthetic form but also a real religious alternative,[22] we could here identify a tradition of religious individualization that would be enlarged by late medieval practices of religious piety. Later, in the sixteenth century, the Reformation made religion definitively the object of individual choice (however sanctioned in practice) in parts of Europe (and later the Americas) and created space for the individual.

The following period displayed a paradox that is characteristic of the individualization processes: the institutionalization of religious individuality brought about new norms and limitations, brought about deindividualization. The two phenomena, individualization and institutionalization, are difficult to disentangle. Down into the eighteenth century the processes of confessionalization sharply defined group limits and assured the internalization of specific denominational norms; they did not create religious options freely available to any historical individual. Because of the interaction of individualization and institutionalization, the specification of religious individualization in a given period typically remains spongy for us, or it is based only on isolated textual evidence, for example, the

---

21. E.g., J. J. Martin 2004.
22. This remains controversial; see Stausberg 2009.

descriptions of human rights in the philosophical discourse of the European Enlightenment, notoriously difficult to place in a history of *religion* of the last centuries.[23]

Facilitated by the normative idea of the individual, self-separation from other (particularly Asian) cultures has affected scholarship on the history of religion in a comparable way.[24] Admittedly, the French Indologist Louis Dumont rightly diagnosed Indian processes of religious individualization in the phenomenon of ascetic abnegation. His starting point was the assumption that in traditional societies individualism could appear only in a clear opposition to society. In India, this took the form of extraworldly oriented individuals.[25] However, pace Dumont, Indian individualism did not in the long run reshape society since it did not lead to theocratic radicalization of the social order, as in Europe. Here, religious authority (church and pope) initially superseded the more worldly powers. The later religious freedom of the individual was then established within the very institutions of a posttheocratic society.

Many other authors, by contrast to Dumont, have allowed their imaginations to be dominated by the Orientalist stereotype of Asian despotism and collective protagonists such as "castes." This has even led to the insinuation that in certain non-European, contemporary, but so-called premodern cultures, individuals lack even the capacity for formulating any opposition of interests between "themselves" and "society." This idea at least has been successfully criticized by anthropologists, who do not deny the phenomena of individual personhood.[26] Recent work on the religion of premodern and pre-Christian antiquity, usually characterized as "collective," has produced similarly limited results. But extensive ancient discussions about religious deviance and attempts to legally standardize religious behavior attest to the perception and acknowledgment of pervasive religious individuality practiced in quite different forms.[27] It is on evidence such as this that I here intend to build.

---

23. Cf. Joas 2013.
24. Cf. Seiwert 2009, 106.
25. Dumont 1986, 26.
26. E.g., Spiro 1993; M. Fuchs 2015, 340.
27. Rüpke 2011c.

Problems and Benefits of Using Individuality
as an Analytical Concept

A critique of the Western intellectual self-image, with its assumption of the
exceptional individualization of the "modern age," might seem to suggest
that we discard altogether the concepts of individual and of individuality,
of individuation (the biographical process of fully acquiring a member's
role in a society)[28] and individualization (the social structural process of institutional or discursive changes allotting more space for individuality) in
the history of religion. Such a course is not, however, recommended by the
very different configurations of individuality I have outlined in the preceding section. The polemical stamp of "individuation" and "individualization" helps steer our attention toward phenomena that have received too
little attention within the usual collectivizing perspective. Of course, it is
necessary to clarify these concepts along with their complex associations by
differentiating forms, types, and phenomena, and by verifying such incipient typologies with the help of further material; examples will be given in
due course. First, however, we must examine the concepts more carefully.

    In everyday speech, individuality is an idea that marks distinctions and
differences: the differences between a human being and others, but even
more so, those between a human being and the society in which she or he
lives. The concept has two dimensions: first, an objective dimension. "Individuality" addresses differences between individuals and between individuals and societies to the point of deviance and societal rejection; a deviant
individual's actions are judged to violate generally binding norms. Second,
less dramatically, individuality can be understood as the perception and
practice of choices. Here, the norms of a tradition and a group do not determine actions as "individual." Understood as such, individuality can even
be perceived within mass phenomena. Differences between individuals can
even result from the fact that each individual combines different social roles
and represents different intersections of different overlapping networks.

    At this point, we should revisit the ideas of the sociologist Georg
Simmel.[29] He associated the historical development and distribution of

---

28. See Musschenga 2001, 5 for these terms.
29. Simmel 1917.

individuality with an increase in the number of social circles touched due to the increased density of contacts in towns. One could develop the follow-up hypothesis that phenomena of individuality can be found in towns and urban centers rather than in villages and face-to-face communities. As a consequence, ancient Rome would be an especially interesting case. With regard to social hierarchy, individuality should then be most pronounced among local elites, who are embedded in supraregional communications. It should also appear among immigrants rather than in small stationary populations. All this without denying the banal individuality that is the genetic property of every human.

This last sentence points to a fundamental problem: At what point are differences simply expressions of variability without consequences? At what point do they make a difference for the relationship of the individual to society at large? Such variations do not necessarily impede the reproduction of society or successful socialization, that is, the biographical integration of a person into society. As a consequence of this difficulty in evaluating objective differences, the criterion for individuality is frequently located in the sphere of subjectivity: thus, a significant individuality would be ascribed only if the agent, the subject, enters into a relationship to her or his Self and reflects upon his or her difference compared to the group, traditions, or the various obligatory roles. It is by contrast to all these norms and situational variations that the individual would then attain identity and coherence. Such concepts of the self can be further combined with different concepts like "soul" (frequently employed in antiquity)[30] or "inner being" (hardly employed in antiquity).[31] Imagined communication with the divine or the perceived presence of the divine within or for oneself would be of great importance in the religious stabilization of such subjective individuality.[32] Historical sources, however, only rarely attest to such processes.

A solution might seem to be provided by the contents of source material for historical inquiries, but (as I will show) this "evidence" happens to be rather problematic. One could, obviously, make the diagnosis of

---

30. Bremmer 1983, 2002.
31. Markschies 1997.
32. See Rüpke and Spickermann 2012 and Rüpke and Woolf 2013 for examples.

individuality dependent on its explicit textual confirmation. Already in antiquity, starting with Plato, philosophical reflections on the Self played an important role.[33] Important lines of such thought can be traced from the philosophy of the Hellenistic schools of the Stoics and Epicureans, through the biblically inspired ideas of Jewish thinkers of the Hellenistic epoch (particularly Philo of Alexandria and Flavius Josephus), into Middle and Neoplatonic philosophy (and its reception in Christianity).[34] These reflections, however, are frequently interested, not in a single, unique person, but rather in a generalized individual.[35] What seems to be an interest in the situation of the individual turns out to be a reflection on duties that arise from clearly defined social positions.[36] At the same time, apparently conventional behavior does not force us to assume a lack of reflexivity. Traditional behavior might be a conscious choice, as fundamentalist movements demonstrate quite sufficiently. How can we solve this dilemma?

Ancient reflections on the generalized individual lead to an impasse. Could autobiographical texts that offer reflections more intimate than mere narratives of events provide a solution? The late ancient bishop Augustinus has, for example, time and again been identified as the locus of the beginning of autobiography and individuality.[37] But this criterion for a qualified individuality is also problematic. The assumption that an autobiographical reflection grants an unaltered or at least privileged access to the individual, since the object and subject of the examination are identical, is in itself a topos of the typology of modernity.[38] From a literary perspective, autobiographies are, furthermore, constructions of a self that are offered by the author and not simple undisturbed glimpses into the psyche of the subject. The self thus produced is first and foremost a literary fiction. The only empirical datum is the fact that such fictions are composed and read—and this is indeed an interesting characteristic of the respective epoch or discursive space.

If access to past individuality via textual subjectivity therefore proves difficult, ancient discussions of objective individuality, as described above,

---

33. E.g., Brakke, Satlow, and Weitzman 2005.
34. Arweiler and Möller 2008.
35. Gill 2006, 2008.
36. Gill 1988.
37. Misch 1969.
38. Radke-Uhlmann 2008.

do not open any ideal way either. Simple deviance is insufficient an attestation of greater individuality (and hence individualization), even if it indicates intentional individual variation and discourses about the legitimacy and limits of socially accepted variance.[39]

Consequences for Historical Research

Some results from research on the present age are helpful in this situation. In an examination of religious behavior and religious convictions in the United States of America, Richard Madsen has shown that individuality is not a general feature of "modern" religion but has itself the character of an option. "Individuality" as a framework of interpretation as well as a form of behavior is primarily located among mobile members of the white middle class. For these persons individuality is affirmed by their own religious commitments and the social consequences of these.[40] Individuality is not an arbitrary option, though; it carries a hegemonic character. It is a lifestyle that is dominant and endowed with the claim to dominance in the eyes of the entire society.[41] This insight should be taken into account whenever analyzing biographical processes in which individuals acquire "individuality" as full members of their society. Such a process of "individuation"—as I would term the biographical development of a single human being from a point of view that supplements the perspective of socialization—is a process of appropriation. It is dependent on ideals that are communicated and on realities experienced through these perceptual filters. It is also dependent on there being space available for individual lifestyle and experiences of difference. Of course the latter in turn influence communication and perceptions.

This has important consequences for the analytical use of the concept of individuality in my approach, but also generally for historical disciplines such as classics, history, and the archaeology of religion.[42] It seems less fertile to examine specific situations and persons for the existence of a religious individuality. What might be described as individuality in each

---

39. Rüpke 2011c.
40. Madsen 2009, 1279–82.
41. Ibid.
42. For archaeology of religion, see Raja and Rüpke 2015.

case encompasses different phenomena; these range from unusual combinations of different divinities through ritual innovations and competitive donations to reflections about one's own relationship to traditional behaviors. It is an empty claim to insist that all these phenomena are simply different expressions of the very same feature, "individuality." Such a claim is merely the result of a theory of modernization that demands a uniform scale of individuality as a yardstick of modernization.

If, on the other hand, one understands individuality primarily as a concept of differences, it is necessary to analyze the space between collective and individual protagonists as well as how the individual structures this space. One might start by locating the forms and variables in processes of individuation. The description of individuality then is informed by differences in individual behavior and the social necessity to justify choices that are made, or the simple existence of such justification, even if it concerns conformity or traditional actions. For example, an ancient person might pursue animal sacrifice despite philosophical criticism of this practice.[43] Whether or not different forms of such individuality strengthen each other and become long-term institutions or reproducible models or discursive formations that are subject to transmission is historically contingent and can be examined under the heading of "processes of individualization."[44]

Again, it is an empty claim that such processes are uniform and unidirectional. Late antiquity saw reflections about individual religious alternatives and real choices. At the same time, the period was marked by increasing legal standardization and violent enforcement of local religious conformity. Past processes of individualization are not incipient forms or precursors of "modern" individualization, nor is modern individuality categorically different from such premodern forms of individuality. Once more, this is not a plea for renunciation of the concept. Its use enables comparison between epochs and cultures[45] and thus offers new interpretative frameworks. Such a revision is desperately needed in the study of a period characterized by a scarcity of coherent sources, a field in which the counterstereotype of collectivity has too often been imposed onto the evidence.

---

43. Cf. Stroumsa 2008.

44. M. Fuchs 2015.

45. For discussion of the ancient Mediterranean, ancient and present-day India, and early modern and modern western and central Europe, see M. Fuchs and Rüpke 2015.

Religious Individuality in Antiquity

I will briefly review some of the most interesting areas of individual appropriation of religion in antiquity, singling out three classes of activity, each consisting of at least two subclasses.[46]

Structural Individuality in Ancient Polytheism

It is comparatively easy to detect how individuals combined gods according to their situational or role-specific needs in different fields. Domestic cults and the collections of statuettes at house altars comprise the first specific area of study under this heading. When viewed statistically, the results for specific places or regions are not very surprising.[47] The predominance of certain divine signs (that is, gods) is easily explained by reference to typical functions or local traditions.[48] And yet, the specific pattern, the combinations of gods and materials, and the different age and provenance of statuettes and images of any particular household show the very individual character of each collection.[49]

In antiquity, the choice was not made from a catalog. Objects handed down from older members of the family found their place beside those that were newly purchased, selected from local producers or merchants. Local public cults were very influential, but this type of formation was occasionally supplemented or even supplanted by knowledge derived from texts or personal travels. The archaeological finds—comparatively rare, as the easily transportable items were usually removed when the inhabitants left their place—are the synchronic image of a long biographical, perhaps transgenerational, process. These selections were, of course, influenced by the selections of others, those who had significant relationships to an individual, and even more so by publicly accessible documents of dramatized selections (that is dedications, votive offerings, and inscriptions in temples), or even by participation in such rituals.

---

46. More extensively in Rüpke and Spickermann 2012; Rüpke 2013c; Rüpke and Woolf 2013.
47. See, e.g., Cicala 2007; Bassani 2008; Fröhlich 1991; Kaufmann-Heinemann 1998.
48. Van Andringa 2009, 265–69.
49. Ibid., 265; Bodel 2008, 261.

Publicly accessible sanctuaries consequently offered a second sphere for religious action. As we learn from Aelius Aristides (AD 117–after 177), one could even be drawn into ritual proceedings unintentionally. Aelius was admonished by Asclepius to go into his sanctuary, offer sacrifice, put up dedications, and distribute sacrificial shares to all present,[50] certainly a nice surprise (or an expected form of dining?) for the latter. Children would learn such rituals from participating, for instance, by forming choirs to perform hymns.[51] Individuation was a social process, just like socialization. To conform is as much a matter of learning as is to understand the extent of one's personal competence and legitimate difference.

Not every vow and dedication was a crisis ritual, and many "crises," moreover, were normal and frequent, such as illness, crop failure, childbirth, or emancipation of slaves. And yet individual competence in ritual performance was universally recognized. Inscriptional details about familial or occupational positioning vary widely in degree of detail, and we see the invocation of gods that were unknown locally. In order to define situations, divine help was invoked as precisely as possible; innovative combinations and, even more so, innovative names were created. At Carthage, for example, we find a single instance of a juxtaposition of Juno, Minerva, and Bellona with a Diana Caelestis Augusta. Dedicants might simultaneously address deities as distant as Sicilian Venus Erycina and the Thracian hero,[52] thus attesting individual variation rather than standardized practices.[53] One might call this a *cult pragmatic individuality*. Again, however, we should not think of these as isolated actions. What we find are perhaps also, at least partly, the results of priestly consultation and artisans' knowledge. It is the very individual "confessional inscriptions" from Lydia and Phrygia that most clearly demonstrate the close collaboration of clients and priests within the context of a sanctuary.[54]

---

50. Aristeid. *Hieroi Logoi* 2.27. See below, chapter 7.

51. Aristeid. *Hieroi Logoi* 4.43; see in general Leeuw 1939 and Brelich 1969.

52. Rives 1995, 186–93, pointing to *Corpus Inscriptionum Latinarum* 8.999, 24528, and 24518 and *Inscriptiones Latinae Africae* 354.

53. Ibid., 190–92.

54. See Petzl 1994 and the interpretations of Belayche 2006, 2008.

Intensification of Religious Practices

Even leaving theoretical atheism as a very rare choice aside,[55] there was more to public rituals than participation or nonparticipation. The space available for participants was quite limited; many altar-bearing platforms in front of Roman temples could accommodate only a few dozen people. Following Krautheimer, Ramsay MacMullen has suggested that there were perhaps only around 4,500 places within titular churches in late fourth-century Rome.[56] As a consequence, decentralized rather than centralized rituals might have mobilized the largest number of participants.

Again, phenomena of intensification can be found in two areas. Complex cults and religious organizations were dependent on a division of labor, including servile butchers and writers, musicians, priests, and children as assistants. Although—as in the case of the magistrate required to lead a procession—many roles were defined by their associated social prestige and political functions, and thus hardly serve as witnesses of specifically religious individuality, yet we also know of a number of very peculiar appropriations of such roles, which led to conspicuous changes in lifestyle. For instance, at Rome in the late third century BC, a higher frequency in the loss of priestly offices is observable. This will be dealt with in detail in the following chapter. Changes in behavior after becoming a *flamen* or even the suspension of military operations are known from the early second century BC. Given the lack of alternatives, religious roles and honorific positions must have been even more important for women and *liberti*, and these often comprise the single element of characterization on the tomb inscription of such people.[57] This could be termed *expressive individuality*. In several cases it is evidenced in the collection of historical *exempla* composed by Valerius Maximus in the early thirties of the first century AD. Exceptional behavior of the past becomes exemplary behavior of the present.[58]

---

55. Obbink 1989; Winiarczyk 1990; Auffarth 1997.
56. MacMullen 2010, 597–98.
57. E.g., Rüpke 2008, no. 471; P. Aelius Malcus Tector, *CIL* 6.2256 = *ILS* 2090; see also nos. 361, 365, 464, 466 etc.; Rüpke 2006b.
58. See Mueller 2002, 148–174; Rüpke 2016c.

Bust of a female priest from Antioch, veiled and adorned with jewelry.
First half of second century AD. Mainz, Römisch-Germanisches
Zentralmuseum, inv. O.39017. Courtesy of RGZM.

"Elective cults," institutionalized options,[59] have been treated under the assumption of standardized behavior in recent scholarship. However, we do not have any statistics about the frequency of their meetings. Occasional dramatic rituals of change of status (such as the sham execution of a mithraicist-to-be in a fresco in a Mithraeum at Santa Maria Capua Vetere)[60] probably did not correspond to a high frequency of interaction within the group. Frequent meetings cannot be excluded, but sequences of votives and remnants of meals[61] do not offer corroborative evidence. Furthermore, as already indicated, the verification of individual choice and subjection to behavioral norms were two sides of the same process of institutionalization.[62] Virtuosi roles, as seen among Christian monks, are scarcely paralleled in other cults, but some diviners and some philosophers prove exceptional, even as religious agents, as illustrated by Apollonius of Tyana.[63]

Visionary Individuality

Here I point to individual revelations and the biographies of authors. Thousands of inscriptions, often in the very reduced form *ex visu*, "from a vision," attest to dreams and visions in which gods appeared, spoke, and gave commands. Formulas and atypical formulations are both in evidence. The large number of deities thus credited is astonishing, more than a hundred according to Gil Renberg.[64] Individual religious action, usually dedication, is legitimized by pointing to individual communication with a deity. Such a strategy is known on a larger scale from the aforementioned venerator of Asclepius, Aelius Aristides.[65] In his case, far beyond incidental legitimization, it is the autobiography as such that results from the transmission of a divine message.[66] The production of the text is a drama in itself.[67] Divine intervention is made plausible by the detailed narrative

---

59. See, e.g., Bonnet, Rüpke and Scarpi 2006; Casadio 2006; Bowden 2010; Gordon 2014.
60. Gordon 2015b, 201.
61. See, e.g., Schäfer and Diaconescu 1997; Marten 2015, 171–72.
62. See North 1994.
63. Demoen and Praet 2009; Hahn 1989.
64. See Renberg 2010.
65. See, for instance, *Hieroi Logoi* 4.45–46.
66. See *Hieroi Logoi* 2.4; Petridou 2015.
67. Petsalis-Diomidis 2006, 201.

construction of the author and his individuality. John of Patmos was the first to use the term "apocalypsis" for a revelatory genre and the first author of such a text, giving himself an individual face and autobiographical history. At Rome, a person addressed as Hermas in his text, *The Shepherd of Hermas*, followed these lines, causing his audience to witness even his sinful thoughts and the reproaches they earned from the revelatory figure. I will return to this text in the final chapter.[68] Following models of Hellenistic authorial self-presentation, Hermas, Aristides, and later Augustine create their divine interlocutor and hence a dialogue in order to open a space for narrating their own individuation, their own becoming a specifically religious individual.

Such texts were intended for recitation in institutionalized discursive spaces, meetings of religious groups as described above. The complex interaction of individualization and institutionalization as two interrelated processes are visible here. But temples, the regular infrastructure of ancient religions, should not be forgotten as places for religious individuality. Astonishingly, many texts and regulations concern individual differences if not deviances in the use of these sacred spaces and their resources (divine presence primarily in the form of divine images),[69] as we will also see in a later chapter.

Methodical Consequences

Certain consequences must be accepted if one wants to use the idea of the individual (and individual appropriation of religion) and that of individuality in religious studies to counter the claim of uniqueness in descriptions of "modern" religiosity. These begin with the choice of the objects of research: the focus is on individual practices, on life-cycle rituals in their importance not only for the constitution of communities, as Victor Turner has emphasized,[70] but also for the process of individuation. Family or individual religious practices in the domestic sphere (which can encompass areas outside the house, such as burial grounds) accrue. Religious activities,

---

68. See Osiek 1999; Rüpke 1999, 2003a, 2013b.
69. Rüpke 2010c.
70. Turner 1982.

from common banqueting and prayer to shared dedications in different social and urban spaces and in changing groups, must not be viewed as solidified or permanent, or as well-organized "cults" and "religions," formulating and achieving far-reaching normative claims and identities. Instead, they must be analyzed with regard for their temporary and situational character, with regard for the many roles that were involved and the widely diverse strategic interests of the participants. Through the lens of individualization, religion is as much a traditional system of symbols as it is a strategic option for an individual.[71]

71. See Rüpke 2015b.

2

INDIVIDUAL DECISION AND SOCIAL ORDER

Exercise of individual choice and detraditionalized behavior are among the basic phenomena of individualization. We find examples of these that merit a detailed analysis already in the Roman Republic of the third century BC. Among the attested variety of apparently normal official and priestly careers from the third until the first century BC, there are some examples of individual interpretations of traditional priestly roles that seem surprising and are often unique. These cases have been interpreted as evidence for the fluid character and adaptability of so-called sacral law,[1] but I would like to analyze them anew. They merit our interest and attention as they point to a somewhat neglected aspect of late republican religion: the influence of patrician origin.[2] With regard to what the Romans called "public priests" (*sacerdotes publici*), the cases I will discuss illustrate the basic mechanism of individual agency within structures defined

---

1. Rüpke 2005d, 1569–86 (with regard to the prosopographical entries, the German and the English version of Rüpke 2008 are equivalent).
2. Baudry 2006, with reference to his not-yet-published thesis.

by social order and tradition. As a consequence, these instances not only offer examples of individual appropriation of religion but also highlight a structural trait, that is, the complexity of processes of institutionalization, by casting new light onto another sacerdotal group, the priestesses of Vesta.

Reinterpretations of Priestly Roles

The events that form the basis of my considerations[3] can be organized into three groups: first, those that concern ritual mistakes by *flamines maiores*, members of the larger pontifical college who were individually responsible for the cult of a specific deity. Second, conflicts about the question of whether these Flamines should be allowed to assume an extraurban office. Third, the case of a priest who, by reinterpreting the regulations of his priesthood, justified interrupting his duties in an extraurban office.

In monthly routine rituals at the Ides and in some annual rituals, a priest known as the Flamen Dialis was active at Rome. As the two other *flamines maiores*, namely the Flamen Martialis and the Flamen Quirinalis, this office was named after a god (in this case Jupiter, in the others, Mars and Quirinus respectively), but his duty was not restricted to the cult of the eponymous god. All the *flamines maiores*, but in particular the Flamen Dialis, were subject to various regulations. Evidence for these regulations in the antiquarian tradition is concentrated or even projected on the Flamen Dialis; the writer Aulus Gellius offers the most detailed list in his *Noctes Atticae*.[4] The penalties for noncompliance were, without exception, harsh: the Flamen Dialis would therefore have been in permanent danger of losing his office. All the more astonishing, then, is the fact that the number of historically documented instances of removal from office is very low. The most comprehensive source for these is offered by a short passage in the *Memorabilia* of Valerius Maximus:

Consimili ratione P. Cloelius Siculus, M. Cornelius Cethegus, C. Claudius propter exta parum curiose admota [deorum inmortalium aris uariis temporibus

---

3. The following resumes and develops arguments found in Rüpke 2012g.
4. Gell. 10.15.

bellisque diuersis] flaminio abire iussi sunt coactique etiam. at Q. Sulpicio inter sacrificandum e capite apex prolapsus idem sacerdotium abstulit . . .[5]

By the same logic Publius Cloelius Siculus, Marcus Cornelius Cethegus, and Gaius Claudius were summoned and even forced to resign from the Flaminate because of a careless presentation of entrails. But an apex that fell down during the sacrifice snatched the same priesthood from Quintus Sulpicius.

Parallel traditions for two of the four persons named by Valerius Maximus suggest that the list is organized chronologically:[6] Plutarch states that Marcus Cornelius Cethegus was forced to resign in the year 223,[7] and according to Livy, Gaius Claudius, one Flamen Dialis, experienced the same fate in the year 211.[8] The explanation offered by Livy (*Quod exta perperam dederat* "because he had offered the entrails incorrectly") corresponds to that given by Valerius Maximus, who might have referred to Livy for this information. The passage in Plutarch attests the fact that Quintus Sulpicius must be placed chronologically within this list. His forced resignation due to loss of the apex identifies Sulpicius as Flamen Dialis since it was this Flamen that was forbidden from appearing in public without his headdress.[9] The event belongs to the same period as the withdrawal of Cethegus and must, therefore, be dated to around 223.[10] Since there was only one Flamen Dialis at a time, the contemporary Cethegus must have been Flamen Martialis or Quirinalis;[11] I assume the same for his probable predecessor Publius Cloelius Siculus.[12]

These cases, all appearing within a very short period of time, can be characterized as signs of radicalization due to external pressures; exacting observation of the performance rendered the office precarious. Should

---

5. Val. Max. 1.1.4–5. Perhaps the Horatian verses *hinc apicem rapax / Fortuna cum stridore acuto / sustulit hic posuisse gaudet* (*Carm* 1.34.14–16) refer to this incident and not (as supposed by most of the commentaries on Horace) to some unknown contemporary or to mythical accounts of fallen kings (e.g., Wili 1948, Oksala 1973 for the former and Nisbet and Hubbard 1970 for the latter).

6. Klose 1910, 27–28.

7. According to Plut. *Marcellus* 5.3–4.

8. Livy 26.23.8; Rüpke 2005d, no. 1159.

9. Gell. 10.15.17.

10. Rüpke 2005d, no. 3176.

11. Ibid., no. 1317.

12. Ibid., no. 1272.

we invoke the envy of rivals competing for the extremely limited number of available posts as an explanation? Without doubt, competition was an important factor in both political and religious innovation during the republican era and later.

The second set of cases, however, does not support such an interpretation. Already in 242 BC, we find conflict concerning a Flamen. Aulus Postumius Albinus was both Flamen Martialis and at the same time a magistrate, namely a consul, who wanted to leave Rome in order to attend a theater of war. The Pontifex Maximus opposed this and Albinus was forced to remain in Rome.[13] Comparable cases followed. According to Livy,[14] Quintus Fabius Maximus Verrucosus "Cunctator" interrupted the consular elections of 215 when the votes of the *centuria praerogativa* went to—along with a fellow applicant—the Flamen Martialis, Marcus Aemilius Regillus. Fabius pointed out the difficulties that a Flamen would have performing his consular duties in warfare. He was not, however, able to have Aemilius excluded unequivocally.[15]

This pattern of conflict continued: Gaius Valerius Flaccus initially had to argue for his right to a senate seat and magisterial offices. However, he finally occupied the offices of *aedilis* and the urban praetorship.[16] We will return to Flaccus below. In general, the treatment of such problems showed a remarkable flexibility. Rules were easily modified to accommodate specific personal circumstances and political situations. When, in the election to the aedileship, Gaius could not take an oath as Flamen Dialis,[17] this handicap was overcome by having his brother swear the oath in his place.[18] This workaround did not solve the fundamental problem of the incompatibility of this priesthood with the magistracies and their political and military duties. In 189, the newly elected praetor Quintus Fabius Pictor was forbidden from leaving the city and had to resign himself to the urban praetorship.[19] The Pontifex Maximus and consular colleague Publius Licinius Crassus Dives Mucianus denied the assignation of a province

---

13. See Livy, *Per*. 19; Val. Max. 1.1.2; Rüpke 2005d, no. 2817.
14. Livy 24.7.12.
15. Rüpke 2005d, no. 525.
16. Ibid., no. 3393; Livy 27.8–10, 31.50.6–9, 39.45.2–4.
17. Plut. *Quaest. Rom.* 44; Paul. Fest. 92.25 L.
18. Livy 31.50.6–9.
19. Rüpke 2005d, no. 1599; Livy 37.51.1–7.

to the Flamen Martialis Lucius Valerius in the year 131 BC.[20] We even find a similar configuration of opposition in the imperial period. In AD 22, as a result of augural and pontifical objections, Servius Cornelius Lentulus Maluginensis, Flamen Dialis and suffect consul of AD 10, was prevented from becoming proconsul of Asia.[21]

These disputes have been interpreted as conflicts between two "systems," a political and a religious set of rules, and as the political mobilization of antipatrician sentiment.[22] A common denominator cited in these interpretations is the serious political hindrance attendant on the assumption of such a priesthood. Another set of incidents are, correspondingly, also assigned to such political machinations: from the beginning of the second century BC, male members of the elite could be, for the first time, appointed to a priesthood against their will. Gaius Valerius Flaccus was subject to such an appointment in 209, but with unexpected and even long-term success; Flaccus proved himself an excellent Flamen Dialis.[23] This did not always turn out well: in 180, an attempt to appoint Lucius Cornelius Dolabella against his will to the office of Rex Sacrorum (perhaps previously occupied by his father) failed.[24] An attempt to appoint an ailing member of the Cornelii Scipiones, one Publius Cornelius Scipio,[25] to the office of Flamen Dialis in the year 174 seems to have had the same result.[26] Likewise, it is frequently questioned whether Gaius Iulius Caesar actually was interested in the position of the Flamen Dialis, an office for which he was nominated but never occupied, and which was not filled by anybody else during his lifetime either.[27]

The final type of individual action sheds some doubt on the generalizability of the political interpretation offered above. In March 191 BC (republican calendar) the Salius Publius Cornelius Scipio Africanus

---

20. Rüpke 2005d, no. 3395 and 2236 (PM); Cic. *Phil.* 11.18.

21. Rüpke 2005d, no. 1349; Tac. *Ann.* 3.58–59 and 71.

22. See the discussion in Simón 1996, in particular 195–206. For conflicts about the rules in general, see Lundgreen 2011.

23. Rüpke 2005d, no. 3393; Livy 27.8.4–10; Val. Max. 6.9.3.

24. Livy 40.42.8–11.

25. Rüpke 2005d, no. 1371; *ILS* 4; Livy 41.28.7 (with *praenomen* Cn.).

26. Simón 1996, 199.

27. Ibid., 212: "era demasiado joven para una elección autónoma que, admás, le imponia fuertes constricciones en la vida pública y privada." See my argument to the contrary in Rüpke 2005d, no. 2003.

interrupted military operations in Asia Minor for the duration of the urban Roman rites of the Salii and ordered a break in his army's march for thirty or thirty-one days.[28] He offered as an explanation that, on the days on which *ancilia moventur* (that is, when the Salians in Rome were dancing and moving the shields), Salii could not march on in the field.[29] Obviously Scipio exercised a quite individual and subjective interpretation of his role, radicalizing religious rules beyond established practice.[30] However, this should not be thought to undermine the following systemic explanations.

Patrician Priesthoods

It is no coincidence that the events mentioned above occurred within the decades before the *lex Villia annalis* and during an epoch that was highly interested in the systematization of the official career path. This effort to clarify the character of public offices was also extended to religious roles, *sacerdotia*. But what is striking are the restrictions placed on holding various offices simultaneously. Not only are these measures surprising, but they seemed to fail or to work contrary to intention.

Older research in particular has stressed that the incidents we have discussed are located in a field of conflict between patricians and plebeians. The relevance of this social distinction in the religious arena is illustrated by the *lex Ogulnia* of 300 BC. This legislation established that the large colleges should have a majority occupation of at least 50 percent plebeians while simultaneously preserving a patrician minority of nearly 50 percent. This principle was not only maintained within all the old colleges but was also applied to the staffing of the newly founded college of the Tresviri Epulones in 196.[31] Publius Manlius was, presumably, a patrician alongside two tribunes of the plebs.[32] It might be supposed that this put an end to the

28. Polyb. 21.13.7–14 (with regard to Herakleides of Byzantium). According to most editors, the text has a lacuna (Causabonius 1609; Buettner-Wobst 1904; Paton 1926).

29. Livy 37.33.6–7: Stativa deinde ad Hellespontum aliquamdiu habuerunt, quia dies forte, quibus ancilia moventur, religiosi at iter inciderant. idem dies P. Scipionem propiore etiam religione, quia salius erat, diiunxerant ab exercitu; causaque et ipse morae erat, dum consequeretur.

30. See Rüpke 2010d for this argument.

31. For the immediate (religio-)political context, see Rüpke 1995, 319 and 330.

32. Rüpke 2005d, no. 2342; Baudry proposed this hypothesis.

tension between patricians and plebeians, as it forced members of both orders to cooperate and removed the patrician monopoly on certain religious
activities. And yet it actually attests to the ongoing relevancy of the social
distinction. Furthermore, certain offices remained inaccessible to one of
the two orders: the curule was exclusive to plebeian aediles, and no plebeian could become a Flamen Dialis or a Rex Sacrorum.

With regard to the cases discussed above, we should also take into account the introduction (even if modified) of direct elections of the Pontifex
Maximus in the second half of the third century.[33] This was followed by
what was presumably the first selection and direct election of a plebeian
for the office of Curio Maximus in the year 209.[34] From the time of the
reorganization of the priesthoods under the *Lex Ogulnia*, if not before, the
authority of the Pontifex Maximus grew constantly, so that he came to
play a decisive role in virtually all pontifical and related questions. From
243 until 221, Lucius Caecilius Metellus was the first known plebeian to
fill this office. It was during his period of office that the conflicts discussed
above arose (241–221). The next plebeian Pontifex Maximus, for the years
213–183, was Publius Licinius Crassus Dives. It is during his priesthood
that most of the remaining conflicts that I will examine occurred.

We must take a step back, as the historical context of these conflicts is
not without interest. First, Rome encountered the problem of the ongoing
administration of provinces far from Rome. This problem was completely
new for the city: it had not existed until the end of the First Punic War
and, in its aftermath, the creation of the provinces of Sicilia and Sardinia.
The solution to this was legislation forbidding long-term absence for the
exclusively patrician priesthood of the Flamines (maiores) (and, of course,
the Rex Sacrorum). This policy, put in place during the second half of the
third century BC, endured despite repeated individual protests. The second area of conflict concerned the most significant characteristic of Roman
priesthoods, the fact of lifelong appointment. The requirement for rigor-
ous observation of ritual details as a precondition for remaining in office
fundamentally endangered this conception of priesthoods. It is this topic
that was picked out as a central theme in discussions from the first century

33. The election was performed in a meeting (*comitia*) of seventeen out of thirty-five *tribus*
(drawn by lot; see Cic. *Leg. Agr.* 2.16–18).

34. Livy 27.8.1–3.

BC and later regarding the exile of augurs.[35] Although the failure of any effort to develop a systematic process for ousting priests from their offices is shown by the fact that we know of no further cases after the 220s, the memory nevertheless lingered and carried political force. When Livy talks about the fact (in the case of Gaius Valerius Flaccus) that a positive change in the character of Flamines led to a resumption of the supposedly old custom of granting this priest a senate seat, a privilege that had been lost due to the *indignitas* of earlier Flamines,[36] then one could relate this to the events of the 220s, if one assumes historicity.

When Crassus succeeded the patrician Metellus and became the second plebeian to occupy the office of the supreme pontiff, he opened another area of conflict by imposing forced appointments. It is worth examining instances of such compulsion closely. In the aforementioned case of the plebeian Gaius Valerius Flaccus in 209 BC, Livy does not emphasize the resistance of the candidate (a fact that one might, but need not, infer from the wording *coacti flaminis*), but rather refers to his poor reputation among his cognate relatives, possibly indicating that there was resistance to the appointment. The case of Flaccus should be viewed alongside another appointment, one that remained undetermined, namely that of the Rex Sacrorum. It is highly probable that Marcus Marcius had been appointed the first plebeian Rex Sacrorum by the first plebeian Pontifex Maximus during the late 240s or 230s. Unfortunately, there is no extant literary report of this process.[37] When Marcius died in 210, the office remained unfilled, and after a vacancy of two years—pointing to conflict and debate—only patricians were appointed whenever the office again became vacant. Finally inaugurated in 208, the Rex Sacrorum Gnaeus Cornelius Dolabella had only been Monetalis before; he was young and remained in the office for twenty-eight years.[38] The first plebeian Curio Maximus had also been chosen in the year 209. The appointee, Gaius Mamilius Atellus, attained a praetorship soon thereafter, in 207 BC.[39] His praetorship, to be precise, was

---

35. For example, for Sulla, see Rüpke 2005d, no. 1390 with further literature.

36. Livy 27.8.7: *huius famae consensu elates ad iustam fiduciam sui rem intermissam per multos annos ob indignitatem flaminum priorum repetivit, ut in senatum introiret.*

37. Rüpke 2005d, no. 2368.

38. Ibid., no. 1322.

39. Ibid., no. 2334.

related to the administration of the province of Sicily. The importance of the local dimension, the tie with Rome, is illuminated by the distribution of priesthoods. Potential absence from Rome (due to a lack of frequent ritual obligations) made it acceptable that a plebeian fill such a priesthood.

In the year 205, a vacancy appeared when the Flamen Martialis Marcus Aemilius Regillus[40] died after attaining the consulship. In 204, a successor was found in Tiberius Veturius Philo, brother to the consul of 206 and perhaps already of advanced age, since it is probable that he was succeeded not long after the turn of the century.[41] The lack of offices Philo had held, his age, the vacancy (the precise length of which cannot be determined, as the turn of the year is our only evidence)—all these conditions signal conflict about filling the office. If Philo's successor, Publius Quinctilius Varus, was identical with the praetor of the year 203, he would have been of a very advanced age when he died as Flamen in 169 BC; it seems more reasonable to conjecture that a son of his was chosen, one who was appropriately young but attained no other office despite the possibilities afforded by his familial status.[42] A routine procedure seems to be at work here, visible also when the young Scipio was appointed Flamen Dialis in the 180s or in the attempt to appoint Dolabella as Rex Sacrorum; he was, after all, the son of the deceased Rex Sacrorum. Given this pattern, Dolabella's rejection of the office should be interpreted as idiosyncratic, hardly systemic. Like the forced resignations of the 220s, the forced appointments and the disputes over the quality of the appointees occur within a relatively short period around the year 210. Both types of activity are centered around controversial individuals and demonstrate a new awareness of individual qualities and differences. At the same time, in systemic terms, it was the conflict between patricians and plebeians that brought these new notions of personal fitness to the fore.

The practice of forced appointments should not be thought to suggest that the offices of the Flamínates were dreaded. Although young persons, practically children, were nominated, these were also regularly candidates that showed considerable promise in terms of a future political and military career. Considering his pedigree, the nomination of

40. Ibid., no. 525.
41. Ibid., no. 3481.
42. Thus ibid., no. 2868.

the young Julius Caesar to the office of Flamen Dialis could be classified with the latter group. And there is much that suggests that this was not without reason: these offices must, in fact, have been sought after. Evidently, the exclusively patrician offices, the great Flaminates, the Rex, even membership in the Salii conferred significant privilege and prestige. These positions offered an entire lifetime of public prominence with their unusual dress (to be worn even outside larger ritual performances), with the right to a curule chair and a lictor, and with their frequent appearances in public; these priests were frequently active in the political and religious center of the city. All this stands in a clear contrast to the other priesthoods—with terms of just a month or a year—that were open also to plebeians.[43]

The *sodalitas* of the Salii admitted a considerable number of patricians to an early priesthood that was characterized by a short period of office. In the case of the Salii, it is likely that it had become common practice already in the late republic to leave the priesthood on achieving higher official offices or another priesthood that conferred great prominence in the imperial era. The prosopographical material offers no corroboration, and the case of Furius Bibaculus, who was already praetor and remained a Salius, even seems to speak to the contrary.[44] We need not, however—against the background of the cases reviewed so far—generalize such an example, evidently considered worthy of individual mention in what must have been contemporary sources. Traditions of dealing with priestly offices were subject to divergent individual appropriations and interpretations. Instead of a radical break and a mass eviction of priests from their Salian priesthood under Augustus (as a part of his attempt to grant access to priesthoods to large numbers of his followers), it is easier to assume that the basics of republican practice were continued into the imperial period. This hypothesis is supported by the twofold nature of Augustus's course of action: he increased the number of patricians and the number of the Salii at the same time. Before the Augustan era, there is no evidence for differentiation between the Salii Palatini and the Salii Collini, nor for the higher status of the former.

---

43. See Rüpke 2005a on the limited visibility of other priesthoods.
44. Rüpke 2005d, no. 1781; Val. Max. 1.1.9.

Excepting loss of the economic potential of provincial offices, the restrictions placed on the major priesthoods were definitely tolerable. Moreover, the individual privileges described above could begin as early as two decades before consular age. Who would exchange an associated professorship directly after high school for the mere hope for a chair at the age of forty-five? We should not imagine that the importance of these priesthoods was limited to their potential to advance one's political career.

Again, these individual interests had a systemic aspect. Several questions present themselves: What (in the uniform nobility of the republic since the third century) legitimized the disproportionately large representation of patricians in high offices, particularly the consulate? What legitimized their monopoly on certain procedures, such as the interregnum? And finally, what justified the Julian-Augustan expansion and promotion of the patrician order with its enormous array of distinct careers? Evidently, the special religious roles of the patrician order formed the hardest argument for these privileges (irrespective of the perennially controversial issue of the auspices),[45] and the argument for the special religious role of patricians was conveyed through the few exclusively patrician priestly offices. Only the aforementioned patrician priesthoods were permanently and unmistakably visible. The election of a priest, just as the election of consul or another magistrate, required public knowledge of the status, patrician or plebeian, of the candidates, in order to assure the correct overall composition of a given priestly college.

Transposing Religious Rules across Genders

The visibility and the exceptional quality of the patrician religious offices are also apparent in their inclusion of women, a practice not found in the priesthoods available to plebeians. This needs no argument in the cases of the Reginae Sacrorum and the Flaminicae, the wives of the great Flamines. For the Salii, however, we are dependent on a very weak tradition. Fay Glinister has shown that the *Saliae virgines* in a quotation of Cincius in the

---

45. In addition Livy 10.7.9–10.

lexicon of Festus refers to patrician girls in their sacerdotal capacity.[46] If the parallelism between the Rex and the Flamines holds true for the Salii also, Cincius's use of the term *conducticiae* (referring to female Salii) might be a deliberate linguistic reference to the expression *in matrimonium ducere*, a term that was applied, of course, to the marriage entered into *per confarreationem*. It is important to note that this form of marriage was also open to women of plebeian origin, who were thus made patricians.[47]

The topic of women calls attention to an obvious gap in my presentation of the evidence thus far, and it offers a further argument for interpreting Roman religion as a historical phenomenon subject to constant modification. There was another lifelong priesthood with high visibility: the Virgines Vestae, the vestals, persons who were excluded from all political offices on account their gender. While male priests have entered the historical record by virtue of their appointment, in the case of the vestals it is more often than not their removal from office—in the horrifying ritual of being buried alive—that has brought their names into the literary tradition. This is true from mythical times down to the late antique corpus of letters of Symmachus, in which he continues to make the detection of unchaste vestals a task of the pontifical college, one of the few remaining at the end of the fourth century.[48] Hildegard Cancik-Lindemaier has shown that the threat of lawsuits on account of *incestus*, frequently resulting in death sentences, was a basic feature, the *conditio humana* so to speak, of the six-headed college of Vesta. This was a danger for which other legal privileges did not fully compensate.[49]

The issue here is the precariousness, the vulnerability of sacerdotal status construed mainly as a consequence of (alleged) infringement of ritual prescriptions; it was this state of insecurity that Lucius Caecilius Metellus, as a plebeian Pontifex Maximus, tried in vain to introduce among the patrician Flamines maiores when he enforced the penalty of divestment of a priesthood for the mere loss of a headgear during a ritual. For a period of more than half a millennium this vulnerability so construed was imposed

---

46. Fest. 439.18 L; Glinister 2011.
47. Thus Baudry, following my suggestion in Rüpke 1990.
48. Symm. *Epist.* 9.108–9 and 147–48. See Wissowa 1923.
49. Cancik-Lindemaier 1990, 10; for the political dimension of the lawsuit of 114/3 BC, see Cancik-Lindemaier 1990, 8. For the ritual construction of the burial, see Schultz 2012.

much more forcefully on the Vestal Virgins, the priesthood dwelling at the heart of the city.[50] Therefore we should now investigate the status of the vestals. Answers, I claim, are to be found not in the latest monographs,[51] but in prosopography. Plebeian names, twelve (with any certainty) of the seventeen names that are known, dominate the republican period, starting with the mythical names.

The temporal distribution of the exceptions is interesting. The earliest is an Aemilia, made vestal around 205, who in 178 served as Vestalis Maxima and in a wondrous way relit the fire that a younger vestal had, in her carelessness, allowed to dwindle.[52] This Aemilia[53] has been considered a patrician since Friedrich Münzer identified her as the oldest daughter of the later Pontifex Maximus Marcus Aemilius Lepidus.[54] The assumption that the anonymous younger delinquent vestal was also patrician[55] is completely unfounded. The patrician status of Claudia, the daughter (or sister, according to a less probable tradition) of the triumphator and consul of 143 BC, Appius Claudius Pulcher, is secure.[56] The vestal Aemilia executed in 114 might well have been patrician;[57] it would be unusual to find a plebeian Aemilia in such a position by the late second century. However, this argument applies in no way to the vestal Fabia, accused of *incestus* with Sergius Catilina but acquitted in the year 73.[58] This half sister of Cicero's wife Terentia could quite probably have been a plebeian; distinguished patrician family branches hardly offer themselves for identification in this period. If Fabia was plebeian, the only possible patrician would be removed from the circle of the Virgines Vestales, the composition of which is completely known for the late seventies: for Popillia, Perpennia, Fonteia,

---

50. See the documentation in Arvanitis 2010.

51. Wildfang 2006; Schultz 2006; Mekacher 2006; Takács 2008; Bätz 2012. Cf. Saquete 2000, 120–22, who repeats the older *status opinionis* in assuming an opening for plebeians as a consequence of the *lex Ogulnia* of 300 BC.

52. Rüpke 2005d, no. 490 listing the sources; the dated account of Livy (Livy *Per.* 41; Obseq. 8) quotes no names.

53. Rüpke 2005d, no. 507.

54. Münzer 1920, 173–76; 1937, 199–203.

55. Saquete 2000, 64; followed by Rüpke 2005d, no. 130.

56. Rüpke 2005d, no. 1152.

57. Ibid., no. 491.

58. Ibid., no. 1577.

Licinia, and Arruntia, the remaining five of this period, we can exclude such a status with certainty.[59]

Virgines Vestales were, therefore, plebeians presumably until the end of the third century BC and again, unquestionably, in the first century. It might have been due to the activity of the Pontifex Maximus Crassus, already discussed above, that the first exception occurred at the end of the third century. Toward the end of the second century, perhaps with the execution of Aemilia in the year 114, we cease to find any examples of patrician vestals. This observation is corroborated by legislation from the following period. For example, the *lex Papia*, recorded by Gellius in the second half of the second century AD, systematically laid out rules regarding this priesthood. Gellius catalogs norms: at what age, from what kind of family, by what rites, ceremonies, and observances, and under what conditions a Vestal Virgin was "captured" by the Pontifex Maximus. He describes the legal privileges she was granted immediately upon being chosen, and he states that, according to Labeo, neither was she lawfully heir of an intestate person, nor could anyone be her heir, in the case that she died without a will. He continues:

Sed Papiam legem inuenimus, qua caueretur, ut pontificis maximi arbitratu uirgines e populo uiginti legantur sortitioque in contione ex eo numero fiat et, cuius uirginis ducta erit, ut eam pontifex maximus capiat eaque Vestae fiat. sed ea sortitio ex lege Papia non necessaria nunc uideri solet. nam si quis honesto loco natus adeat pontificem maximum atque offerat ad sacerdotium filiam suam, cuius dumtaxat saluis religionum obseruationibus ratio haberi possit, gratia Papiae legis per senatum fit.[60]

Yet there is a Papian law, which provides that twenty girls be selected from the people at the discretion of the supreme pontiff, that a choice by lot be made from that number in the assembly, and that the girl whose lot is drawn be 'taken' by the supreme pontiff and become Vesta's. But that allotment in accordance with the Papian law is usually unnecessary at present. For if any man of respectable birth goes to the supreme pontiff and offers his daughter for the priesthood, provided consideration may be given to her candidacy

---

59. These names are known from the list of participants in the inaugural dinner of the pontifical college in 70 BC (Macrob. *Sat.* 3.13.11).

60. Gell. 1.12.11–12.

without violating any religious requirement, the senate grants him exemption from the Papian law.

The law limits the Pontifex Maximus's absolute right in the determination of the *virgines Vestae*. He is obliged to prepare a list of candidates including twenty names—one cannot otherwise understand the phrase *pontificis maximi arbitratu uirgines e populo uiginti legantur* (11)—from which one name is drawn by lot in a public meeting (*contio*), as a future vestal. The text suggests that the names of the fathers of the candidates were on the lots. The girl was then made vestal by the Pontifex Maximus's ritual "capture."

A conflict regarding whether patrician women could be made vestals is already suggested by the nomination of the patrician Aemilia by the plebeian chief pontiff, and if one seeks more definitive evidence for such a dispute, one could find it in a detail that, with no connection to the context, Gellius mentions shortly before his treatment of the Papian law. It was permitted to sisters of vestals as well as daughters and fiancées of different priests, to decline the office:

> . . . eam cuius soror ad id sacerdotium lecta est, excusationem mereri aiunt; item cuius pater Flamen aut augur aut XV uirum sacris faciundis aut VII uirum epulonum aut Salius est. sponsae quoque pontificis et tubicinis sacrorum filiae uacatio a sacerdotio ista tribui solet.[61]

> But they say that one whose sister has been chosen to that priesthood acquires exemption, as well as one whose father is a Flamen or an augur, one of the Quindecimviri sacris faciundis, one of the Septemviri epulonum, or a Salian. Exemption from that priesthood is regularly permitted also to the betrothed of a pontiff and to the daughter of the tubicines sacrorum.

The exemption of daughters of Flamínes or Salii implies that it was not priests per se but primarily patricians that were concerned, even if Gellius's wording avoids explicit mention of this status. This concentrates the choice of vestals on plebeian families. The superiority of patricians is demonstrated to all *ex negativo* in every lawsuit against the vestals, and the

---

61. Ibid., 1.12.6–7.

systemic exemption of patricians from the danger of losing their religious qualification again contributes to the adscription of special status.

Let me return to the cases of the end of the third and beginning of the second century BC. We see innovative behavior not only on the part of the plebeian Pontifices Maximi; we also find among the patricians individuals who interpret a priestly role not in the traditional way (as a lifelong magistracy with some ritual tasks) but as a specifically religious role, as a Salius for instance. Both case types demonstrate highly individual behavior. It seems that the actors intended to problematize the relationship between their priestly and political offices or to privilege a specific religious obligation over a political role. In each case they did this by asserting the obligation of perfect religious performance. Basic, however, to these individual attempts to further develop given roles was a shared conviction: the religious framework of the Roman polity was to be provided by its patrician members in particular. Even the elite's "civic religion" was not available in equal part to all noble citizens. In the emperors' postconstitutional state[62] this inequality was even further highlighted by the extensive ennobilization of supporters through the endowment of patrician status and by Augustus's reorganization of patrician priesthoods like the Salii. With regard to the priestesses of Vesta, the combination of these trends entailed further accusations and sentences. The limitations on individual appropriations of this religious role were clearly drawn more tightly.

---

62. I take this concept from Alfred Schmid: Schmid 2005, 54–64.

Appropriating Images — Embodying Gods

In the introduction to this book, I outlined the concept of lived ancient religion. In its application to contemporary social analysis, the concept of lived religion does *not* address how individuals replicate within their biography a set of religious practices and beliefs already institutionalized by some "official religion"—or, conversely, opt out of adhering to tradition. Of course, given the relationship of individuals to tradition, such a definition of lived religion could, in principle, work for an ancient context that was religiously pluralistic, or in a mono- or oligo-confessional society. But because clearly distinct religions did not begin to be formed until late antiquity, as I have argued elsewhere,[1] the perspective of lived ancient religion focuses on the actual everyday experience, on practices, expressions, and interactions that relate to religion. As such, religion is understood as a spectrum of experiences, actions, beliefs, and communications hinging

---

1. Rüpke 2010b, 2015a.

on human communication with superhuman or even transcendent agents, usually conceptualized as gods in the ancient Mediterranean.[2] Ritualization and elaborate forms of representation are employed for successful communication with these addressees.[3]

Of course, such practices are not entirely discretionary. For the purposes of historical research, the existence of religious norms, of exemplary official practices, and of control mechanisms and enforcement should be taken into account. It is precisely such institutions and norms that tend to predominate in the surviving evidence. In analyses of the interplay between the individual and tradition, the concept of "appropriation" plays a key role.[4] The specific forms of religion-as-lived are barely comprehensible in the absence of distinct modes of individual appropriation (to the point of radical asceticism and martyrdom), in the absence of cultural techniques (such as the reading and interpretation of mythical or philosophical texts, rituals, pilgrimages, and prayer), and in the absence of the various media employed in the representation of deities within and outside of sanctuaries.

The notion of agency implicit in the notion of appropriation (far more so than in that of "reception") is not unproblematic, if one forgets about its structural dimension. Agency is an attribute ascribed to a subject within a context of structures, but these structures are themselves the product of (repeated or modified) individual acts.[5] With respect to the normativity ascribed to teachings, traditions, practices, and narratives in the field of religion, the description of how ideas are adopted and the specifics of processes of reception are of particular importance. Cultural-theoretical and historical-anthropological accounts of appropriation often clash with the models found in religious symbolic systems where transcendent entities are acknowledged as norm-setting agents. Jupiter teaches Numa how to sacrifice in Roman tradition; Apollo is asked to give oracles on theological and ritual matters at Claros. It is this disjunct that leads me to a text wherein a god both formulates such norms and simultaneously illustrates their appropriation. Of course, it would be just as problematic to

---

2. Rüpke 2015b.

3. See below, chapter 7.

4. Certeau 2007; Lüdtke 2009.

5. I follow the notion of agency as developed by Emirbayer and Mische 1998. For such a relational view, see, e.g., Dépelteau 2008. For a radical critique of agency, cf. S. Fuchs 2001.

generalize an individual instance (hardly ever representative in a method-
ologically plausible way) as it would be to rely on elite descriptions of mass
behavior—which is, of course, standard practice in the historical critique
of sources. To make full use of the model of lived ancient religion, scat-
tered evidence should be contextualized and interpreted by relating it to
individual agents, their use of space and time, their formation of social co-
alitions, their negotiation with religious specialists or providers, and their
attempts to make sense of religion in a situational manner and thus render
religion effective.

First, however, I should add another preliminary observation, vital to
our understanding of the claims and complaints of the god who speaks
in the text: in many modern accounts of ancient gods they are accorded
ontological priority, thus following a mode of thinking that is imputed to
ancient agents. Representation of a god is, by this view, a secondary activity, albeit one that has become the subject of increasing academic interest.[6] According to a systemic view of ancient religion, the central concern
of representation is similitude; for those interested in the cult pragmatics
of lived ancient religion it raises different questions. Religious communication with the unseen must first medially construe their addressees and
second hide their constructed character.[7] The religious actor must control
the selected deity and emphasize its power and whimsy at the same time.
Both tasks would be facilitated whenever the actor were able to refer to
traditions of beliefs and canons of representation, but these would need
to match the relevant situation, the availability of resources, the strategic
aims of the agent, and all the other social and material constraints, in
short, the extent and the limits of her or his agency.[8] Three-dimensional
statues of gods held a special position within the media available to
achieve these purposes. It is the form of a human or at least partly an-
thropomorphic body that gives a maximum of person-like qualities and
individuality to the figure before the religious actor. It is to such statues
and the practices associated with them that I will turn in the final part of
this chapter.

---

6. E.g., Stewart 2003; Mylonopoulos 2010; Rüpke 2010c; Pirenne-Delforge and Prescendi 2011.

7. For this mechanism in sacrifice, see Belayche 2011; Naiden 2013.

8. For the concept of agency, see Emirbayer and Mische 1998.

Propertius, *Carmen* 4.2

The material to be investigated in this chapter is a text by the Augustan poet Sextus Propertius (54/47–before 2 BC). Propertius won fame by publishing a book of elegies on the theme of his love (or that of his male persona) for a fictitious Cynthia, with both characters as members of the upper echelons of society. The poems also dwell on the political context of the civil wars preceding the sole rule of Caius Iulius divi filius Caesar, called Augustus from 29 BC onward. Interspersed among the love elegies are poems that deal with the cruelties of Augustus's subjection of Etruria and Umbria (the region of the poet's birthplace, Assisi). During the second half of the first century BC, the cultural and political unification of Italy was an ongoing and still-painful process, invoked by all the poets dominating the literary circles of Rome, who issued from the different Italic regions.[9] Propertius was a very careful observer of politics and of the society of his time, and he had access to the immediate circle around the *princeps*. Book 4, an addition to the earlier poems in books 1–3, brings religion center stage, from the opening poem onward.[10]

Propertius 4.2 has held a degree of prominence in histories of Roman religion due to its references to topography and early Roman history.[11] However, as far as I can see, this text, which has a god speak about himself in the first person, has never been the subject of an analysis interested in ritual or modes of religious representation and appropriation of gods. One might read it as a contribution to the ancient controversy about the status and power of images of divinities, a controversy that has generated much interest in previous decades, as noted above.[12] My analysis, however, will be focused on the practices through which the image is addressed and their consequences. This is relevant for our understanding

---

9. See, e.g., Feichtinger 1991; Rüpke 2009d, 123–24; and Günther 2012 for the civil war context; on Assisi, see Newman 1997, 54–99 and Cairns 2006, 4–14.

10. For very different approaches, cf. Burck 1966; Gurval 1995; Edwards 1996; Fox 1996; Newman 1997; Janan 2001; Keith 2008; Lowrie 2008; W. R. Johnson 2009; Rüpke 2009d; Cristofoli, Santini, and Santucci 2010; O'Rourke 2010; Bettini 2012; Lentano 2012.

11. For example, Latte 1960, 191.

12. Gordon 1979; Scheer 2000. I leave aside the stimulating, but also limited, discussion on ancient regimes of seeing, much furthered by Jaś Elsner (e.g., Elsner 1995; Platt 2011, 386-393; Francis 2012).

and even for the constitution of a text that is among the most disputed in Latin poetry. As it turns out, my readings are extremely conservative. The text presented is much closer to the pre-twelfth-century archetype than those of all modern editions. Evidently, this poem presents a good example of a hermeneutical circle that begins with faulty expectations regarding cultural (and, in this case, specifically religious) patterns, and thus arrives at the necessity to alter a transmitted text even where it is inherently acceptable and hardly the result of misunderstandings on the part of copyists.[13]

Our poem begins the careful sequence of interspersed aetiological and erotic elegies contained within Propertius's relatively short fourth book. It is preceded only by a pair of programmatic elegies, which call for and subsequently criticize aetiological poetry on Roman topics (4.1 and 4.1a).[14] Review of all possible contemporary references has led to a general agreement that the book was composed in or shortly after 16 BC. The dense network of motifs (such as *unus* and *una puella*) and the well-organized range of subjects indicate that many of the poems were composed specifically for this book, and were edited or at least finished by the poet himself.[15] As a whole, they put into practice what is asserted in the very first elegy: "I will sing rituals and gods and the old toponyms."[16] In the ensuing poems, a variety of speakers are found in locations of ancient ritual in the center of Rome. They are interested in antiquarian details and provide aetiological explanations for various phenomena.[17] Erotic poems appear at regular intervals. Evidently, Propertius is pursuing his initial poetological deliberations on the appropriate subject of elegy, as formulated in 4.1a and b. One might read the whole book as a metapoetic discourse. If I neglect this dimension, as my analysis is directed toward Roman religion, I do not negate it. The existence of this strand does not, however, diminish the relevancy of Propertius's observations on religious practice. Rather, it

---

13. For a methodological discussion of the problem with regard to Roman religion, see Rüpke 1998b.

14. On which see Rüpke 2009d with further bibliography.

15. Hutchinson 1984.

16. *Sacra diesque canam et cognomina prisca locorum*, 4.1.69.

17. See the map in Welch 2005, 16; for *signum Vertumni*, see ibid., 39.

supports a critical reading that is focused on the media portrayed within the text.

The poem also participates in a discourse—important to the poets and the Italic peoples at large of Propertius's generation and the previous one—on ethnicity after the bloody civil war of the forties:[18] What did *Romanitas* constitute for inhabitants of the Italian peninsula? How Italic was Roman culture? How many *patriae* did a Latin-speaking Italian at Rome have? Etruscans and Oscans are agents mentioned in the Vertumnus poem, while the speaker of the introductory elegy of the fourth book had defined himself both as an Umbrian and at the same time as a "Roman Callimachus" (4.1.63–64). This discourse is prominent in the antiquarian contents of our elegy; it has dominated, as mentioned above, the religio-historical interpretation of the text.[19] Nevertheless, it will be disregarded in the following.

I start by presenting the text, mostly following the rather conservative edition of Gregory Hutchinson, but without his transposition of verses. James Butrica's evaluation of the textual tradition and Stephen Heyworth's edition built thereon have not been neglected in their contributions to determine the archetype and its problems.[20]

> Qui mirare meas tot in uno corpore formas,
>   accipe Vertumni signa paterna dei.
> Tuscus ego et Tuscis orior, nec paenitet inter
>   proelia Volsinios deseruisse focos.
> haec me turba iuvat, nec templo laetor eburno:
>   Romanum satis est posse videre forum.
> hac quondam Tiberinus iter faciebat, et aiunt
>   remorum auditos per vada pulsa sonos:
> at postquam ille suis tantum concessit alumnis,
>   Vertumnus verso dicor ab amne deus.   10
> seu, quia vertentis fructum praecepimus anni,

---

18. See in general Farney 2007; Whitmarsh 2010; W. R. Johnson 2009, 67–68; for ethnicities in Roman religion, see Rüpke 2014a.

19. Recently Cairns 2006, 281–85; Gibson 2007, 68, n. 72.

20. Hutchinson 1984, 2006; Butrica 1984; Heyworth 1986, 1995, 2007a, 2007b.

Vertumnmi rursus creditur esse sacrum.
prima mihi variat liventibus uva racemis,
  et coma lactenti spicea fruge tumet;
hic dulces cerasos, hic autumnalia pruna
  cernis et aestivo mora rubere die;
insitor hic solvit pomosa vota corona,
  cum pirus invito stipite mala tulit.
mendax fama, vaces: alius mihi nominis index:
  de se narranti tu modo crede deo.   20
opportuna mea est cunctis natura figuris:
  in quamcumque voles, verte, decorus ero.
indue me Cois, fiam non dura puella:
  meque virum sumpta quis neget esse toga?
da falcem et torto frontem mihi comprime faeno:
  iurabis nostra gramina secta manu.
arma tuli quondam et, memini, laudabar in illis:
  corbis in[21] imposito pondere messor eram.
sobrius ad lites: at cum est imposta corona,
  clamabis capiti vina subisse meo.   30
cinge caput mitra, speciem furabor Iacchi;
  furabor Phoebi, si modo plectra dabis.
cassibus impositis venor: sed harundine sumpta
  fautor plumoso sum deus aucupio.
est etiam aurigae species Vertumnus et eius
  traicit alterno qui leve corpus equo.
sub petaso pisces calamo praedabor, et ibo
  mundus demissis institor in tunicis.
pastor me ad baculum possum curvare vel idem
  sirpiculis medio pulvere ferre rosam.   40
nam quid ego adiciam, de quo mihi maxima fama est,
  hortorum in manibus dona probata meis?
caeruleus cucumis tumidoque cucurbita ventre
  me notat, et iunco brassica vincta levi;
nec flos ullus hiat pratis, quin ille decenter
  impositus fronti langueat ante meae.

---

21. I follow Heyworth's conservative treatment of the transmitted but superfluous *in imposito* (Heyworth 2007b, 439).

at mihi quod formas unus vertebar in omnes,
    nomen ab eventu patria lingua dedit.
et tu, Roma, meis tribuisti praemia Tuscis,
    unde hodie Vicus nomina Tuscus habet,   50
tempore quo sociis venit Lycomedius armis
    quoque Sabina feri contudit arma Tati.
vidi ego labentes acies et tela caduca,
    atque hostes turpi terga dedisse fugae.
sed facias, divum sator, ut Romana per aevum
    transeat ante meos turba togata pedes.
(sex superant versus: te, qui ad vadimonia curris,
    non moror: haec spatiis ultima creta meis.)
stipes acernus eram, properanti falce dolatus,
    ante Numam grata pauper in urbe deus.   60
at tibi, Mamuri, formae caelator aenae,
    tellus artifices ne terat Osca manus,
qui me tot docilem potuisti fundere in usus.
    unum opus est, operi non datur unus honos.

                      (Prop. 4.2)[22]

You who wonder at the many forms I have in a single body, learn the features that from the days of your forefathers have distinguished the god Vertumnus. I am Etruscan, and come from Etruria; but I don't regret having deserted the hearths of Volsinii in time of war. The crowd here pleases me; nor do I take delight in a temple decorated with ivory: it is enough to be able to see the Roman forum. Once Tiber made his way past here, and they say one could hear the sounds of oars striking the shallows. But after he gave up the pool to his nurselings, thanks to the turning of the stream I am called the god Vertumnus; (11) or again, because we pluck the first-fruits of the passing year, the rite is believed to belong to Vertumnus. It is for me the early grape changes colour as the bunches redden and the hairy ears of corn swell with juicy fruit; here you see sweet cherries, here plums in autumn, and the mulberry ripening on a summer day; here the grafter his vow with a garland of fruit, when the pear has borne apples on a reluctant stock.

---

22. The translation is Heyworth's (Heyworth 2007b, 590–91), restored, however, to the sequence of the verses as transmitted and printed above. Likewise, differences in the reading of the Latin text in lines 34, 48, and 57 are rendered.

(19) Lying rumour, be quiet: you are a false witness of my name; reader, you should believe only what the god tells about himself. (21) My nature is suited to all forms: turn me into whichever you like, I shall be at home in the part. Dress me in Coan cloth: I shall become an easy girl;[23] and who would deny me a man when I put on a toga? Give me a scythe and press my brow with a twist of hay: you will swear my hand has been cutting grass. I bore arms once, and, I remember, I was praised in them. I was a harvester, equipped with the weight of a basket placed on me. Sober I go to court; but when a garland has been put on, you will shout that wine has gone to my head. (31) Surround my head with a turban: I shall steal the appearance of Iacchus; I shall steal Phoebus's, if only you give me a plectrum. With nets placed on me I hunt, but when I've taken up a [limed] reed, I am the god who favours the capture of feathery fowls. Vertumnus is also the image of a charioteer, and of the man who nimbly transfers his body from one horse to another. Under a cap I shall catch fish with a rod, and I will travel as a spruce pedlar with my tunic trailing. A shepherd, I can bend myself to the crook, and also carry roses in baskets amidst dust.

(41) Why should I add what I am most famous for, that the choicest gifts of horticulture are in my hands? The dark-green cucumber, the swollen-bellied gourd mark me out, and cabbage tied with light rush. Nor does any flower spread wide in the meadows without first elegantly drooping, placed on my forehead. But because I alone changed into all kinds of shapes my country's tongue gave me my name from the result, and you, Rome, granted a reward to my Etruscans thanks to which Tuscan Street has its name today. (51) What time the Lycomedian came in allied arms and crushed the Sabine arms of fierce Tatius, I myself saw battle lines slipping, weapons dropped, and the enemy turn their backs in ignoble flight. But, father of the gods, may you ensure that the toga'd Roman throng passes before my feet for all time.

(57) (Six lines remained to be performed; I do not delay you who hurry to answer bail: this is the finishing line of my circuits:) I was a maple stump, fashioned by a hastening sickle, a poor god in a grateful city before the days of Numa. But, Marmurrius, divine sculptor of my bronze form, may the Oscan earth not wear away your artist's hands, you who had the ability to cast me to be taught so many roles. It was a single work; not single is the honour given to it.

---

23. That is, a prostitute (see O'Neill 2000, 268).

Copy of a statuette of a libating *genius centuriae* with mural crown and cornucopia, bearing a revised dedication: "in honor of the divine [i.e., imperial] house" (*CIL* 13.7748). Mid-third century AD, from the Saalburg castle. Photo by J. Rüpke, used by permission of Archäologisches Landesmuseum Baden-Württemberg.

Changing and Being Changed

The poem is witty and fascinating from a number of perspectives. Nevertheless, my reading, which will be given in some detail, is interested only in the narrator's view on lived ancient religion. On the whole the text presents itself as an inscription, addressing every possible passerby. Such a communicative technique is known from many epigraphical texts. Who, however, is the speaker? My first contention is that it is the god himself. The speaker establishes a distance between himself and the statue by his speaking of a body (*in . . . corpore*, 1) and of a statue (*signa . . . dei*, 2). Thus a difference is established; the god who introduces himself by the name of Vertumnus possesses a body and a statue (or statues).[24] The god is not co-extensive with the statue, as is stressed in a later passage where reference is made to an earlier wooden image (59): identity is constituted in the continuity of the god, not that of the statue. Likewise, the god is not identical with or bound to his place; verses 3–4 indicate that the speaker has been in other places before Rome: he "left," that is, was previously in, Etruria among the Volsinii. Perhaps even a third distinction is referred to. The divine subject preceded his naming; he is earlier than his name: *mihi . . . nomen ab eventu patria lingua dedit* (47–48). Here, we should note that "fatherly language" is somewhat ambivalent in the mouth of an Etruscan immigrant, as it refers to the Latin etymology made explicit in this distich. In sum, the identity of the god is the identity of a subject who is able to remember and narrate change as change encountered by himself. Under these circumstances, the fact that he knows of the change of the course of the Tiber only from hearsay (*aiunt*, 7)—this is the first of the poem's etymologies Vert-amnis, "turned river"—implicitly questions the correctness of an etymology that is not backed by his own experience. In another passage, that which refers particularly to unsuitable dedications, the assertion "I remember" (*memini*, 27) affirms the identity I propose.

It is not etymology that defines the god, but ritual. Various agricultural products adorn the god from summer to late autumn. The variety of fruits is

---

24. I follow Hutchinson (2006, 89 ad loc.) in rejecting the interpretation of *signa* as mere indicators (as does Cairns 2006, 281). These lines define the topic of the poem; they do not initiate argumentation regarding ethnicity.

stressed as much as the different seasons (11–18). Transposing these verses, as has been suggested recently by Heyworth,[25] would destroy the link between the immediately preceding etymology based on *annus*, "year," and the elaborate description of seasonal offerings. It would also eliminate the carefully maintained distinction between agriculture here and horticulture later.[26] The specific dedications that the god lists are pronouncedly individual. The grafter who harvests apples from a pear tree (17–18) is the most extreme example. Nevertheless, all these practices could be summarized as *sacrum*; it is recurrent ritual that is described. A generation earlier, Marcus Terentius Varro had mapped highly specialized deities onto functions or rather fields of competence in the fourteenth book of his *Antiquitates rerum divinarum*.[27] At first, this poem also seems to suggest such areas of competence. After all, the Forum Holitorium, the urban market of vegetables, was not far from the statue's position during Propertius's time.

I follow the transmitted text in preserving *Vertumni . . . sacrum* (12).[28] *Sacrum* is the aspect of cult that provides the raison d'être of the god at Rome. From a different perspective, *sacra* is that which is due to the god. Again, *sacrum* implies regularity. This regularity, however, is not a precise and detailed repetition of a ritual script. Instead, it is based on habits and beliefs, the range of variation of which is described in the verses that follow. There are no written documents, no *lex sacra* affixed to the open sanctuary.[29] The rules are rules that are presumed by visitors. The reading *vulgus* instead of *rursus* in verse 12 is an old conjecture, an attempt to define the subject of such assumptions and beliefs; *populus* is a younger proposal.[30] Both miss the point of the whole poem. It is not Propertius but modern scholarship that restricts heterodox beliefs to a particular (lower) social stratum, "popular" or "folk religion."

After amply illustrating it, the god himself opposes the etymology based on *annus* with a forceful *mendax fama*, "lying rumour" (21). It is surprising

---

25. See, however, for example, Heyworth 2007b, 438.

26. Overlooked also by Syndikus 2010, 313.

27. See Rüpke 2005b and 2007a, 59–61.

28. The conjecture *Vertumno* (dative) of Ayrmann is followed by Hutchinson (2006, 91), who argues that mere usual practice could hardly define the ritual in a sufficient manner.

29. On such rules for the performance of ritual in sanctuaries in the Latin world, see, e.g., Ennabli and Scheid 2007–2008.

30. Thus Hutchinson 2006, 91, who suggests that the etymology is the content of the belief.

that the god distances himself from what he had conveyed as the reason for the practices described over six lines, but the text takes pains to restrict the criticism to the etymology, *nominis index* (22). The offerings derived from commercial agriculture are very similar to what is later described as gifts supplied by gardening, by horticulture, *de quo mihi maxima fama est*, "what I am most famous for" (41). But Propertius's speaker is not contrasting correct and incorrect practice. In both cases the rationale behind the offerings is, epistemologically speaking, a matter of *fama*, "rumor." We are far from knowledge or prescripts. Any truth claim could be related only to the accuracy of the etymology itself. Ritual action and theological reflection about the god's identity fall asunder.

In a long chain of examples (23–46), the discrepancy between ritual practices and theological deliberations increasingly comes to the fore. This is hardly consistent with an idea of ancient religion wherein individuals are religious actors who carefully try to select and reproduce the most effective cult from the broad public (and sometimes private) range of available sanctuaries and sets of ritual practices associated with a particular god (frequently referred to as "the cult of Apollo," "the cult of Venus," and so forth). What is presupposed in Propertius is a basic mode of communication with deities via dedications. As Marcel Mauss has pointed out in his groundbreaking reflections on giving, the gift is an element in a strategy to define addressees in terms of their status and their relationship to donators.[31] This is relevant for the ancient practice of prayer accompanied by dedication and for that of the vow promising dedication. Within the asymmetrical communication between the hierarchically inferior mortal and the powerful god, who is visible only in mediated form, these practices were able not only to represent the initiator before an audience and attract the latter's attention, as relevance theory suggests,[32] but also to help define the elusive recipient.[33] Therefore, the temporary donations arising out of situational decisions by individual agents and viewed by others momentarily on the one hand, and permanent attributes on the other, are thus

---

31. Mauss 2002, on which see Moebius and Papilloud 2006.

32. For the basic tenets of relevance theory, which does refer to religion, see Sperber and Wilson 1987; Wilson and Sperber 2002, 2012.

33. For this characteristic of religious communication, see Rüpke 2007b, 73–88, and the next chapter.

part of one and the same continuum; the two are hardly separable when applied to an image in a public space. It is only the later, distant observer who can draw a distinction between a contingent and temporary votive, which could be lost without any long-term effect on the one hand, and a conceptual and permanent element of an image, the loss of which might result in the end of a cult on the other. The contemporary observer would have to apply external norms to arrive at such judgments. I claim that it is the very purpose of the Propertian poem to deny the existence of such extramaterial norms.

The examples given by the text are adequate to such a strong claim. The first distinction involved is a norm regarded as fundamental in Roman religion, that is, the category of gender. Whether Vertumnus is male or female is subject to the dedicator's decision. *Fiam*, "I shall become," and the rhetorical question "Who would deny?" (*quis neget*, 23–24) illustrate the factuality of a temporary change that instantly becomes normative. The location of the statue (and hence the poem's putative setting) in a "red-light district" of Rome[34] makes this even more pointed.

The strong tone is continued. In the following distich "you will swear" (*iurabis*, 25) is used, where a much softer wording such as *crederes* "one would believe" could have sufficed. The implications of these lines extend far beyond ephemeral appearances. To imagine that the statue itself could have "been cutting grass" a moment ago (26), inverts the relationship between what is seen and what is merely imagined, heightening the factuality of the imagination; it is the immobility of the statue that seems to be deceptive. The challenge now becomes to truly believe that the figure is a motionless statue rather than to enliven it in one's imagination. The immovable has a moved past.

The following verses problematize the credibility of such a past. The claim that the god had gloriously carried weapons needs confirmation by the god's own memory—I have already pointed to this instance of *memini* (27). This is supplemented by the much more plausible memory of having been a harvester by virtue of receiving a basket. I need not stress here that the position of the martial reference in the hexametric line and of the peaceful memory in the pentametric line is also part of a poetological

---

34. O'Neill 2000, 273.

discourse, referring to the problem and rejection (*recusatio*) of epic panegyric in earlier books.

The following contrast, "sober" (*sobrius*, 29) in court and drunk (*clamabis capiti vina subisse meo*, 30) at a party, shifts the sphere of the statue's animation into physiological details. As no dedicatory objects are named, I suggest that what might be indicated here are different media of religious representation. The text perhaps refers to transportable statuettes, such as were used in domestic contexts and brought to court appearances. This might also explain the reference to Vertumnus as a charioteer and expert horse rider, expressed by the term *species*, "image" (35). Statuettes of the god appeared in such forms and were used on such occasions.

The figures of a horseman and soldier do not cohere with any possible single "function" of the god. Propertius's use of past tenses in 27–28 (*tuli, eram*) underlines how contingent and situational such configurations were. The identity implied here is not a theological proposition, but merely a remembered biographical identity.

Are there limits to the definitional power of the users of the image? Hardly any! It can go so far as to mistake Vertumnus for other gods, confusing him with Iacchus and Phoebus (31–32). Here, however, a norm is formulated. Such confusion is characterized as illicit. *Furare speciem*, "I shall steal the appearance," implies a sharp condemnation. Thus, a limit to interpretation and ritual usage is set, even if counterfactually. This limit is not argued for on the basis of some "essence" or "nature" of the god, some identity delineated by theological discourse or a body of mythical narratives. The norm that is implied addresses ritual practice and the consequences of practices that endanger a user's ability to identify and differentiate between deities known through their names and iconography. Furthermore, the text itself excludes the possibility that the contents of the norm could be preserved. The following couplet (33–34), as printed here, succinctly expresses the permanent transition of divine activity and divine identity in the form of tutelage over a certain activity.[35] Equipped with

---

35. Thus I do not follow Cairns 2006 in his understanding of the transmitted (and probably corrupt) *Favor* or *Faunor* (v. 34) as *Favor* (282–83, with reference to Martianus Capella), or, pace Heyworth, as *Faunus* (Heyworth 2007b). The text as given succinctly expresses the permanent transition of divine activity and divine tutelage over an activity.

certain paraphernalia Vertumnus is a hunter; equipped with certain other paraphernalia he benignly supports the snaring of birds.

I have already dealt with the charioteer. Verses 35–40 offer further examples that might refer to historical evidence for the veneration of Vertumnus while also paying tribute to literary models.[36] I would like to point out that the statue "moves"; Vertumnus describes himself as a god in action. Consequently, the visible statue is but a snapshot, documenting a moment in a sequence of activities. And yet the god is modeled according to his statue; his appearance is extrapolated from that of the statue and its attributes as conferred in the form of votives. The sequence of verbs like "hunting," "catching," "fishing," "traveling," "bending," and finally "carrying amidst dust" evoke scenarios that transgress the idea of a statue caught in static poses and attitudes. Potential votives—objects such as a net, arrow, sunhat, fishing rod, tunic, crook, and basket—are the point of departure in each instance. The media to be imagined, however, are not statues and statuettes but paintings, such as might be found in private houses rather than open sanctuaries. This is, as I have to admit, a hypothesis built on the presupposition that Propertius refers to a real or at least plausible range of iconographies of Vertumnus that reach far beyond the average dedication.

Against the backdrop of this enormous range of definitions, enacted historically (that is, ritually, by means of gifts), the most statistically important construction of the god comes in an understatement: "Why, pray, should I add . . . ?" (41) Since, as I claim, Propertius is interested in the variety of appropriations of the god rather than in determining a normative "essence," this is pointed rather than ironic. It is telling that by transposing six verses (placing 13–18 after 44) from the beginning of the poem into this last field of competence (horticulture, detailed in 43–46), modern interpreters such as Stephen Heyworth add massive weight to what they imagine Propertius's emphasis should be: on an agricultural deity. Our hidden models of how ancient religion functioned are far from innocent! Propertius himself makes an argument, if I might say so, for the mutual constitution of ritual activity and the supposed competence of the god in the deliberate ambivalence of verse 42, claiming "that the choicest gifts

---

36. In particular, Hor. *Sat.* 2.3.226–29; see Cairns 2006, 285.

of horticulture are in my hands." *In manibus . . . meis* could refer to fruits
dedicated to the god and laid on the statue's arms as well as to the god's
tutelage over fruits collected in the garden.

The final part of the poem presents us with the statue proper. Here,
what is most important is the increasing passivity of the speaker. Vertumnus is not credited with any agency in his many transformations. Gram-
matically he is merely the patient, using the passive voice *vertebar* (47).
The god's position shifts from center scene to the wings, from action to
observation. He is bound to his location with no ability to move, and he
must pray to the father of the gods—in the first and only genealogic remark of the text—to grant him even an interesting view *ante meos . . .
pedes*, "before my feet for all time" (56). The addition *per aevom* (55) even
removes the possibility of change over time. The speaker is entirely ab-
sorbed within the statue. The maple stump is a "poor god" (*pauper deus*,
60). The separation between god and statue, carefully established in the
poem's opening, is erased in the final six verses. It is unmistakably now the
statue, the object that is speaking, not the god. This too is in imitation of
inscriptional convention. In his edition, Heyworth suggests that we read
suberunt, "written underneath," instead of *superant*, "rest," in line 57. But
above all, these lines present a sophisticated mise-en-scène of the god's
lack of agency.

Appropriating Images

In most cases, ancient images of gods were artifacts, man-made objects
("fetishes" from Latin *facticius* via Portuguese *feitiço*).[37] Reflections on this
fact can be found from early Greek and Greco-Roman antiquity, from the
Judaism of the Second Temple, down into late antiquity and Byzantine
iconoclasm.[38] The early imperial text analyzed above presupposes such discourses, but it is not primarily interested in the topic of adequate representation. The transition from a roughly worked piece of wood to a bronze
statue indicates, in a positive light, civilization and, by a negative view, pure

---

37. Kohl 2003.
38. An overview can be found in Malik, Rüpke, and Wobbe 2007 or Bräunlein 2009.

luxury. In Numan Rome, as the introductory poem of the fourth book had already made clear to the reader, a "poor god" was also welcome.[39] But it should be clear by now that 4.2 is not an ekphrasis; we have no idea about what the statue looked like, even after careful, repeated readings. Rather, the text is interested in an antithetical idea: the neutrality of the sign with regard to its usage (*usus*, 63). This is not derogatory; the statue remains an index of divinity, open to religious usage on a broad scale. Certainly, it is a sign chosen intelligently (*docilem*, 63).

Propertius addresses the practices that appropriate such an image in individual religious activity. The votives or dedications (or, more broadly speaking, objects)[40] immediately accompanying prayer are the central tools of these practices. The text concentrates on rituals involving a statue in a small, open sanctuary, but Propertius also seems to include other items: movable statuettes or paintings installed elsewhere. All these objects, whether directly placed on the statue, before it, or at another place, are instruments in the ritual communication of individuals with the divine as they actively construe the properties of the divine addressee. The text is not interested in the details of such practices. Unfortunately, we learn no details of how a statuette was used in court (*ad lites*, 29) (though magical papyri suggest a wide range of possibilities).[41]

The individual ritual dealings with the image are very diverse appropriations of that deity. For an observer (and, in the language of the text, for himself) the god is the result (cf. *ab eventu*, 48) of such appropriations. Synchronically as well as diachronically these vary widely. In their contradictions and contingencies a unifying concept or "essence" of a god or even a cult is hardly discernible; the sign "Vertumnus" does not resist different construals. There are no—though there should be—limits to sanction transgressions. When Vertumnus is mistaken for Bacchus and Apollo, the language of polytheism, based as it is on the selection and combination of recognizable signs called "gods," is endangered. But there is nobody to enforce such limits; the conventions of representation and individual

---

39. This does not, however, mean that the poem deals with a mere second-rank god, as Luisi (2008, 416) claims.

40. For a general treatment, see Latour 2005; for ancient religion, Raja and Weiss 2015a and Raja and Weiss 2015b in particular.

41. See Graf 1996, 124–30.

appropriation are all that might interfere. If Vertumnus is given a plectrum, he looks like Apollo and evidently is addressed in the terms of Apollo's field of competence, even if he "is" not Apollo. Individual religious
competence is guided, but not effectively limited, by traditional conventions. Propertius offers an image of Roman polytheism as lived ancient
religion.[42]

The poem analyzes the identity of god and image. On the one hand,
the god claims an identity independent of situational appropriations and
even of his image. He implicitly claims an identity within different material shapes, including statuettes and paintings. In the fiction of the speech,
the god claims such an identity by remembering other and former images. However, he remains subject to them; he is bound to concrete appropriations. Similarly, Vertumnus's physical movements are located in
the imagination of observers, where the manifestation of the "present"
is extended into imagined sequences of actions. This precarious form of
existence is not improved by the medium of language and the instrument
of names. Clearly the text claims to be an inscription, materially present
beyond the act of reading. And yet even the god's name is open to widely
different interpretations. What appears at first to be certain knowledge is
later discredited as "lying rumor." The poem does not invite its readers
to search for a hidden factual or historical reference. There is no fixed
system of "Etruscan" or "Roman religion" to be discovered in the ruins
of fragmentary transmission, which would be able to end the game of
interpretation. Instead, the text lays open the rules that bind (or rather,
hardly bind) fruitful engagement with religious signs on this side of the
horizon of divine. That horizon is referred to only with the phrase "father
of the gods."

Propertius's poem does not demand that we generalize its observations,
but I will. The range of votives found in sanctuaries, the range of attributes
and names applied to the "same" gods indicate that being "Vertumnus"
was the rule rather than the exception. The text itself, at the very least,
permits the following generalization: ritual action is not defined by the essence of the god; rather, ritual action defines that essence.

---

42. This is not to say that Propertius protests against any reductionist public discourse, as
Coutelle (2005, 571–73) claims.

Epilogue: Embodied Gods

The argument presented above can be taken one step further. If lived ancient religion is concerned with action and experience, we should address the question of the god's particular experience of his own body, as Propertius presents it to his readers. Here, the notion of "embodiment" is of particular value.

Embodiment denotes the conjoining of materiality and corporeal experience, and as such occupies a central position in contemporary epistemology[43] and anthropology of religion. Pioneering scholarship of the twentieth century that fused phenomenology and cognitive science generated the concept of "embodied cognition" with its powerful impact on discourse on culture and religion. The concept stems from work of the French philosopher Maurice Merleau-Ponty (1908–1961); his phenomenology-driven musings on embodiment advocate the crucial priority of movement and gestures over mind, and the principal role of the body in perceiving environments and structuring the world. The performance of gestures, though they do not cover the whole range of bodily experiences, contextualizes natural entities and their bodies by conveying mental dispositions and enacting emotions, and shapes culturally informed meanings. The human body, along with the conditions of perception it entails, is what nuances subjectivity and places the individual self within culture and society, thus rendering it an "embodied self."[44] The notion of an "embodied agency" grounded in diverse somatized impulses discloses the social implications of the embodied self.[45] Particularly intriguing here is the extent of alterity issuing from individual operations of embodiment, that is, the set of differentiating, even self-defining processes that are activated by the emotional and gestural modes of an individual's body.[46] Recent theoretical work on the anthropology of religion has gone so far as to identify in embodied alterity the "phenomenological kernel of religion," itself a correlate of individual experience, perception, and expression.[47]

---

43. Weil and Haber 1999.
44. Noland 2009.
45. Lyon and Barbalet 1994.
46. Reynolds 2004.
47. Csordas 1994.

Ritual studies, even when concentrated on individual involvement and performance,[48] tend to direct their analysis toward rules and actual or imagined repetitions of sequences of action, as well as on wider societal, economic, or power contexts. The concept of embodiment has shifted the investigations of religious studies to individual involvement and meaning beyond the cognitive level, and has identified new evidence even in historical studies.[49] With regard to communication with invisible gods or spiritual beings in antiquity, ordinary religious action is much more frequently encoded in bodily movements. Given that memory is inextricably intertwined with sensorial mechanisms, emotions produced by sensory input in diverse social contexts are embedded in bodily experience. Thus, religious experience was stimulated by and registered in the form of sensations and movements as well as in postures assumed, for instance, in prayer or in processions, and religious experience is shared by the intersubjective coordination of bodily movements and reactions. Religious practices in the epoch under analysis were only rarely taught through formal religious instruction. It was much more frequently the case that knowledge of these was acquired through appropriation and imitation of movements that were stored in and enhanced by memory. Thus images of rituals or gods in corresponding gestures could evoke embodied knowledge.[50] Paraphernalia, including garments, wreaths, incense, and amulets, alter bodily status (with gender variances that demand attention) for an extended period of time.

The identity of Propertius's Vertumnus is almost totally defined by bodily experiences: from being clothed, to his memory of different actions, involving manual touch and movements, to the experience of being worked on by sickle or being cast in metal. This is significant within a larger poetic text that gives prominence to emotions, visions, bodily experience such as hunger and thirst, temperature, and colors. My final claim is that Propertius reflects here not only on actual religious practices but also on human experience through the lens of religion. In defining the god through the addition of dedications one must reflect upon one's own identity, or rather, one must reflect on one's alterity with regard to others, as defined through

48. Rappaport 1999; Bell 1992; Grimes 2011.
49. Coakley 1997; Bynum 1991.
50. Gordon 1979.

Slab depicting Isis and her characteristic rattle (*sistrum*) from the temple of
Apollo Palatinus, late first century BC. Museo del Palatino, inv. 379054 and 379641.
Photo by J. Rüpke, used by permission of Ministero dei Beni e delle Attività
Culturali e del Turismo, Soprintendenza Speciale per il Colosseo, il Museo
Nazionale Romano e l'Area archeologica di Roma.

instruments, bodily paraphernalia, movement, and being moved. It is the
god Vertumnus who, furthermore, also offers the possibility to reflect both
on the contingency of such experience as well as on the lasting effects of
certain bodily experiences, the constraints produced by them. His memory
of time immemorial makes him greater than human. At the same time, in
his wooden or bronze form he is much more constrained than his human
observers.

I must stop here; I am treading on difficult methodological ground. I
might plausibly claim that Propertius does present such reflections, but
I can hardly assert that these characterize the experience of every, or even
any, person discharging a vow or simply praying to the statue. Nevertheless, historical data is comprised in the very fact of the thinkable being
written down and read.

4

Testing the Limits of Ritual Choices

Evidence is also available for individual appropriation of religion and embodied practice outside of public arenas. We find confirmation of domestic or even nearly invisible religious practice in the same period of the latter half of the first century BC if, as mentioned in the previous chapter, we take into account the evidence for and the discourse on magic. Research on magic in the Greco-Roman world is a growing field, and it has become increasingly apparent that magic was not a phenomenon restricted to the social and spatial margins of the Roman Empire—to Egypt, or to the poor, for example—but that it permeated all levels of society and was fully a part of what is useful to address as "religion" in antiquity.[1] This is true regardless of the clear differences between the professional magic of Egyptian papyri and the popular traditions with their individual appropriations in the (not only Latin) West. In the late 1990s an excavation at Rome revealed

---

1. See Gordon 2013, 107.

several curse tablets and special apparatuses deposited in a fountain sacralized in multiple ways.[2] Likewise, ashes from the sacrificial pit behind the temple of Mater Magna in a joint sanctuary of Isis and Mater Magna in ancient Mogontiacum (modern Mainz) has brought to light twenty-four texts on lead tablets and evidence that many more had once been deposited there.[3] These texts reveal the widespread use of certain prayer techniques, the diverse occasions to which these were applied, the variety of deities invoked (among which were the most prominent deities of the local *panthea*), and the figurative language and reasoning frequently adopted.

Yet I will not address this type of evidence here. Within the framework of this book my investigation does not concern the details of magic, its techniques and materials, but the position that magic occupied within the range of religious options available to individuals in the Greco-Roman world. Under what circumstances did individuals have recourse to magical practices and specialists of magic? How did they frame this recourse? Did they feel a need to justify it, or did magic simply enlarge the range of options available for individual action?

For the most part, my approach to these questions will be strictly philological and historical. Starting from the terms and phenomena we tend to designate as "magic," I am interested in historicizing magic, that is, in investigating the theoretical concepts *and* pragmatics associated with magic in a specific society and period. I am interested in the "user perspective" of magic as an individual option in early Augustan Rome. As my approach is qualitative rather than quantitative, a single intelligent member of Roman society who is aware of the surrounding world will comprise sufficient material for study. Possible generalizations will be discussed toward the end of the chapter.

Roman Poetry as Evidence for Ancient Magic

For evidence, I will draw on longer and more complex texts than the usual curse tablets; I again turn to Propertius and his four books of elegy.

---

2. For the concept of sacralization, see Rüpke 2012f.
3. Rome: Piranomonte 2002. Mainz: Witteyer 2004a, 2004b, 2005; Blänsdorf 2005, 2008, 2009.

Propertius's first publication, the so-called Monobiblos, was composed around 29/28 BC. As discussed in the previous chapter, his poetic production continued until ca. 16 BC, when his last (fourth) book was finished and probably published. Thus he was a contemporary of the elegist Tibullus and of the epic and bucolic poet Vergil, both of whom died shortly before Propertius completed his fourth book, and of the lyric and iambic poet Horace, who died shortly thereafter. The theme of magic appears in various contexts in the poetry of all four of these authors. In some instances, characters in poems have quite extensive recourse to magic.

Georg Luck and Anne-Marie Tupet have dealt thoroughly with the descriptions of magic practices in these and other texts.[4] Whereas the research of the 1960s and 1970s was directed toward compiling examples of magical practices and understanding the techniques and logic of these, more recent philological treatments have concentrated on the poetic function of the passages concerned with magic—how a reference to magic, for example, may serve as a metaphor for the binding qualities of love in relationships, or how the formulation of claims and expressions of skepticism regarding magical practices are informed by the techniques of rhetoric.[5] In these discussions, however, the magic per se is usually heavily downplayed.[6]

Other work on ancient magic has been engaged in historicizing the cultural techniques classified by this ancient term. There is unambiguous evidence from as early as the sixth century BC for practices of binding (*katadeín, defixiones*) in different social relationships, in particular in the context of lawsuits. Likewise, examples of erotic magic can be found from the fifth century onward. Hellenistic literature offered full-fledged literary models of erotic magic and witches: Apollonius of Rhodes's *Argonautica* gives a detailed account of Medea in books 3 and 4, and Theocritus's *Idyll* 2 portrays a young woman engaged in magical incantations and rituals directed toward her former lover.[7] Thus, from the third

---

4. Luck 1962, 1992, 2000; Tupet 1976.

5. Cairns 1979, 140; Zetzel 1996 (hence Reinhard 2006, 208–9). Despite its prominence in the poems (see below), the topic of magic is absent from many monographs on Propertius. I will restrict myself to citing bibliography on points of controversy or to provide suggestions for further reading.

6. See, e.g., Hubbard 1974, 17–18. For a larger overview of the research on magic and its intellectual frameworks, see Gordon 2013.

7. In particular Ap. Rhod. 3.1026ff., 1191ff.; 4.123ff., 445ff., 1636ff. Dickie 2001, 99–104.

Snake on the exterior south wall of a latrine, Pompeii, caupona of Euxinus, I, 11, 11.
Photo by J. Rüpke, used by permission of Ministero dei Beni e delle Attività
Culturali e del Turismo, Soprintendenza Pompei.

century BC onward, Greek-reading Romans could draw on such texts
in addition[8] to Italic ritual traditions. The latter, however, are difficult to
trace. By the end of the republic the practice (attributed to the Marsians)
of appropriating a neighbor's crop by means of incantation and snake
charms had been subsumed into the conceptual sphere that encompassed
binding spells, the use of which is attested in southern Italy in Oscan
examples from the fourth century onward.[9] "Killing by poison," *venefi-cium*, must have encompassed practices addressed by terms derived from
Greek *pharmakon*.[10] In Plautus, the term *venefica* refers both to the sorcer-
ess and to the poisoner.[11]

---

8. See Papanghelis 1987, 48, on the importance of both strands.
9. Dickie 2001, 128–44.
10. Briefly discussed by Graf and Johnston 1999, 662–70, particularly 669.
11. Dickie 2001, 131.

The extensive treatment of magic in poems of the 30s and 20s BC is contemporary with (as far as we can see) sudden harsh policing moves. Agrippa had astrologers and sorcerers driven out of the city in 33 BC; Augustus banned the sorcerer Anaxilaos of Larissa in 28 BC.[12] Against this background, the case for historic reference versus the purely literary value of poetic descriptions need not to be argued solely on the analogy of smoke and fire: much talk, therefore real magic.[13] Obviously, poetic treatments constituted part of a wider public discourse that was engaged in cultivating a negative image of professional practitioners of magic.[14]

The image of the old, drunk, and savagely cruel witch, so prominently developed in the early Augustan love poems, seems to be an innovation in the ancient discourse about magic.[15] Given the growing danger of criminalization, as pointed out by Richard Gordon, the poets would not have had much interest in denying the fictitious character of their magic figures. Textual analyses should, therefore, pay special attention to the linguistic cues that signal the reality or implausibility of the characters and practices described, but even more so—as indicated above—to the more general framing of references to magic.

Magic in Propertius's Oeuvre

Magic is already prominent in Propertius's very first poem (1.1):

> ergo velocem potuit domuisse puellam: 15
>   tantum in amore preces et benefacta valent.
> in me tardus Amor non ullas cogitat artes,
>   nec meminit notas, ut prius, ire vias.
> at vos, deductae quibus est fallacia lunae
>   et labor in magicis sacra piare focis,   20
> en agedum, dominae mentem convertite nostrae,
>   et facite illa meo palleat ore magis!

---

12. Graf and Johnston 1999; Dio Cassius 49.43.5 (the date being confirmed by Broughton, MRR 2:415); Jerome *Chron.* a. 735 auc.

13. Cf. Dickie 2001, 178, who concentrates on the sheer number of literary and specifically declamatory instances.

14. Simón 2001.

15. Ogden 2008, 39–76, esp. 75–76. For the resulting portraits, particularly in the case of prostitutes, see Dickie 2001, 175–91.

tunc ego crediderim uobis et sidera et amnis
　　posse Cytinaeis[16] ducere carminibus.
et vos, qui sero lapsum revocatis, amici,　　　　　　　　　　25
　　quaerite non sani pectoris auxilia.
fortiter et ferrum saevos patiemur et ignes,
　　sit modo libertas quae velit ira loqui.
ferte per extremas gentes et ferte per undas,
　　qua non ulla meum femina norit iter.　　　　　　　　　　30
vos remanete, quibus facili deus annuit aure,
　　sitis et in tuto semper amore pares.
nam me nostra Venus noctes exercet amaras,
　　et nullo vacuus tempore defit Amor.

And hence he was able to tame that fleet-footed maiden:
　　prayers and good deeds like his work wonders in love.
But Love runs slowly in my case,[17] and devises no schemes,
　　and forgets to use the methods he once knew well.
So you, who have tricks to make the moon looking to be drawn down,
　　performing your magic rites on hallowed hearths,
here is your chance, come, change my mistress's heart,
　　eclipse the light of her cheeks, fainter than mine.
I'll believe in your claims then, that Thessalian spells have power
　　to drain the sea of its floods and stars of their light.
And you, friends, who at this late stage still urge me to stand,
　　find me something to help a heart that's sick.
I'd suffer the [torments by][18] knife or savage cautery bravely,
　　to win the freedom to talk as my fury craves.
Send me to some far out-post, over the ocean,
　　where none of her sex would know the route I took:
but remain in Rome, if the god is kind and has heard you,
　　be always carefully matched in a safe affair.
That Passion in me is the cause of nights of anguish,
　　my lack of Love is present every hour.[19]

---

16. Hertzberg for transmitted *Cythalinis* (obelized by Fedeli 1980); the reference to Thessaly or to a Colchian Medea is without doubt, but the precise form of the adjective—due to the lack of sufficient parallels—is uncertain.

17. Taken from J. Booth 2001, 64.

18. Cf. Bennett 1969, 33 on 3.24.11, who, surprisingly, does not extend the notion of torture—so clearly alluded to in the following verse (*libertas . . . loqui*)—to this passage (n. 10).

19. Translations of Propertius in this chapter are those of Hodge and Buttimore 1977, 17. Here, I have adjusted only their rendering of line 19.

The excerpt begins with the end of the story of Milanion, who won the hand of Atalanta, the daughter of Iasus.[20] *Preces* (line 16) clearly has a religious ring (the addressee is not stated, but should be understood as Aphrodite rather than Atalanta),[21] which is emphasized when Propertius (as the text clearly invites us to identify the speaker), next reflects on his situation in relation to the god Amor; in this case, the gods remain unpropitious, as was summarily stated in line 8 of this poem: *cum tamen aduersos cogor habere deos*, "even if I am forced to suffer adverse gods."

The idea of adversity is repeated at the end of the quoted passage. Hopelessness (and the cautionary advice that results from it) informs the end of the poem. This is a final commentary on the vain—as we see—appeal to unspecified magic specialists in lines 19 and following. *At* and *en agedum* clearly mark addresses or exhortations,[22] and these words also introduce the speech Propertius directs first to his friends and then to a generalized audience—addresses that do not include the gods, as should be noted. The forceful demand that the magic specialists ameliorate his situation is in clear contrast to the plea that he directs toward the rest of his audience, which is only that they find ways to deal with an inalterable situation. Magic was a last resort.[23]

The characterization of this magic is interesting. The specialists are fully credited with having (*quibus est*) a trick that makes the moon appear to be forced down and with the practice of painstaking, i.e., elaborate, rituals (*labor*).[24] They claim to be able to alter the movement of water and light with Colchian (likely a reference to Medea)[25] formulas or songs, but this claim needs proof. The speaker does not make any reference to the kind

---

20. See Cairns 2007, 1–7 for the Propertian version of the story.

21. J. Booth 2001, 65–66.

22. Fedeli 1980, 79 on *at*.

23. This interpretation is in opposition to the tendency to downplay magic in analyses of Prop. 1.1 as does, for example, M. Prince 2003. Prince argues that the prominent and differentiated treatment of magic is merely transgressive. Cf. Fulkerson 2002 for an appraisal of the magic subtext in Ov. *Her.* 13.

24. The perfect tense of the participle (*deductae*) is rightly stressed by Fedeli (1980, 79). I follow Cairns (2007, 8–9, who follows Shackleton Bailey) and Fedeli, in interpreting *fallacia* as expressing skepticism. However, this is not simply an inversion of the traditional Hellenistic motif of trusting magic in matters erotic (Fedeli 1980, 80). As the following interpretations will show, it is important to note that this doubt is not total and that it does not exclude experiment and tentative belief. For the alleged technique of the trick, see Hippolytus, *Refutatio Haeresium* 4.37 (quoted by Cairns, 2007, 8–9). For a suggestion based on modern North African magical practice, see Tupet 1976, 97–100, and (following Tupet) Harmon 1986, 1934: "hypnotic suggestion."

25. Above, n. 16.

of activity he wishes to be performed, but only to the desired outcome: that the beloved become paler than himself, that she be even more emotionally involved than he himself. The absence of ritual detail is in keeping with the lack of any indicator regarding the status, age, or sex of the specialists invoked.

Until this point I have not commented on the phrase *in magicis sacra piare focis* (line 20). Commentaries[26] are quick to point out that *sacra* must be an internal accusative, meaning "to perform rituals," "a purificatory sacrifice,"[27] or to emend the phrase. But the former would be unparalleled[28] and does not account for the juxtaposition of *magicis* and *sacra* at the center of the line. To expiate something always means to alter its status, either to cleanse an object or person from defilement or to undo an illegal or impious action. *Sacra piare* is an unmitigated paradox. Semantically it implies an opposition between magic and sacred ritual,[29] syntactically an alteration of sacred ritual, and pragmatically the coexistence of sacral and magical "systems." After all, the invocation *at vos . . . en agedum* follows directly on Propertius's complaint about the god Amor's unrelentingly negative attitude. This is not, as Margaret Hubbard claims, a formal device to balance the invocation of his friends,[30] but signals that he is willing to employ the last resort (without providing details or implying possible criminal action), even if he is hopeless. But finally, the only source of relief is poetry, the liberty to give vent to what anger dictates (line 28).[31] This conclusion is important for all of Propertius's poetry.

Agents and Patients

More often, the speaker is not the initiator or subject of the magic but its object, not agent but patient. The ardent lover is warned in 1.5.5–6 that

---

26. E.g., Camps 1961 ad loc.; Fedeli 1980, 80. The interpretation suggested by Hodge and Buttimore 2002, 68 (following Sandbach), "to expiate a religious offence," is impossible.

27. Thus Cairns 2007, 9.

28. As pointed out by A. E. Housman. The discussion of the passage by Tupet (1976, 350–51) does acknowledge Propertius's typical originality in wording, but does not address difficulties of meaning: "*accomplir correctement des rites.*"

29. Fedeli's statement (Fedeli 1980, 80) "il valore di tali sacrifici è fortemente limitato dall'espressione in *magicis focis*" at least recognizes the tension.

30. Hubbard 1974, 17–18.

31. Newman 1997, 465; similarly Lyne 1998, 165.

he will have to walk over "unknown fires"[32] and—presumably also without knowing—"drink poisons from all over Thessaly," which I interpret as an indication that he is crazed enough to persist in a painful romance. In 2.24.27 the insane lover ingests "foul poisons" (*taetra venena*); problems with the transmitted text leave open whether he does this "happily" (*libens*) or he merely "sips" (*libet*) them.[33] In 1.12, the unnatural intensity of Propertius and Cynthia's relationship, and its sudden dissolution, are attributed to divine or magical action: "I was an object of envy: Was it a god that overwhelmed me, or did some herb gathered on Promethean hills separate us?" (1.12.9–10)

In the opening poem of book 2 the lover again expresses the strength of his love by imagining himself the victim of poison attacks.

> seu mihi sunt tangenda novercae pocula Phaedrae,
> > pocula privigno non nocitura suo,
> seu mihi Circaeo pereundum est gramine, sive
> > Colchis Iolciacis urat aëna focis.
> una meos quoniam praedata est femina sensus,
> > ex hac ducentur funera nostra domo.

Though I be doomed to drink of the cup that the stepdame Phaedra brewed, the cup whereof her stepson [i.e. Hippolytos] was destined to take no hurt, or must die of Circe's herbs; or though for me the Colchian heat the cauldron on the fires of Iolcus, yet since one girl hath stolen away my senses, from her house only shall go forth my funeral train. (2.1.51–56)

The argument is then extended: "Medicine cures all the anguish of mankind; love alone loves not the physician of the sicknesses caused by it" (2.1.57–58).

The attacks described above never include the terms "magic" or "witch" (*saga*), though translations introduce such words liberally.[34] The same holds

---

32. See Fedeli 1980, 157 on the expression, who rightly rejects any reference more specific than that of fire treacherously hiding under ashes.

33. Hendry 1996.

34. Thus, I do not follow Fedeli (2005, 87) in his strict differentiation between the love magic of ll. 51–52 and the generic magic in the following lines. Papanghelis (1987, 31) rightly points out: "their common dominator is their being enchanting and deadly at the same time."

true for poem 2.4, which again describes at length the tribulations that the speaker suffers for his love.

> non hic herba valet, non hic nocturna Cytaeis,
> non Perimedaeae[35] gramina cocta manu;
> quippe ubi nec causas nec apertos cernimus ictus,
> unde tamen veniant tot mala caeca viast.
> ....
> nam cui non ego sum fallaci praemia vati?
> quae mea non decies somnia versat anus?

For such a case as mine avails no drug, no Colchian woman in the night, no, nor the herbs Perimede's hands distilled. For here we see no cause nor whence the blow is dealt; dark is the path whereby so many griefs come none the less. . . . For of what lying seer am I not the prey? What hag has not three times three pondered my dreams? (2.4.7–10, 15–16)[36]

Again, the poison is qualified by geographical and mythical terms, not by any specific contemporary practitioners, such as those Propertius openly designates in the last verses quoted. The same observation can be made of 3.6.25–30, which describes the details of a magic attack, though the term "magic" is absent. The situation of the passage is complex:[37] the speaker of the poem demands that his slave report the miseries of his (the speaker's) mistress and fantasizes that she complains about his infidelity. Thus he imagines her words, as she speculates on his reasons for abandoning her and as she disparages the female rival she supposes:

> non me moribus illa, sed herbis improba vicit
> staminea rhombi ducitur ille rota.

---

35. This correction is supportable (see also Papanghelis 1987, 33), but Tupet's arguments for preserving the manuscript tradition with *per Medeae* (Tupet 1976, 358–59) are not without force. The decision has no consequences for my purposes.

36. I do not follow the interposition of vv. 15–16 after 8 proposed by Birt and followed by Fedeli 2005, 165. The reasoning offered by the latter is revealing: "La trasposizione . . . appare necessaria perchè illogica sarebbe la loro collocazione in un contesto in cui non si parla più delle maghe." His argument assumes clear borders for the field of cultural practices termed "magic." Thus the modern observer excludes what he considers to belong to the (modern) field of medicine. Günther (1997, 49), supposing a much damaged book 2, hypothesizes that the original positions of 9–10 and 15–16 have been lost.

37. This contributes greatly to the dramatic vivacity of the poem (Fedeli 1985, 206–7).

illum turgentis ranae portenta rubetae
et lecta exsuctis anguibus ossa trahunt,
et strigis inventae per busta iacentia plumae,
cinctaque funesto lanea vitta viro.

Not by her conduct, but by herbs the wretch [the rival] has conquered me:
he [i.e. my former lover] is led captive by the rotating string of the rhombus.
He is drawn to her by the monstrous charms of the swelling bramble-toad
and by the bones she has gathered from dried serpents, by the owl-feathers
found on low-lying tombs, and the woolen fillet bound about the [wax figure of the] doomed man.[38]

Here, the imagined complaint is very precise and descends even to details
of ritual activities.[39] The initiator of this attack is identified, but the question of whether ritual specialists are involved or not is left open. Interestingly enough, the term "herbs" (*herbis*) introduces and generalizes the
nonherbal ingredients of the ritual practices. As stated above, I do not aim
to contribute to the reconstruction of rites and their logic—detailed here
in an interesting selection of standard practices, starting with the swirling
"magic wheel." It is clear both from the text quoted and from the following lines that these practices achieve a single end: the victim is sexually at-
tracted to the woman who has instigated these practices.

Funestus hints at the devastating consequences of such an attraction, but
it does not activate the association of herbs with poison that is so prominent in the passages quoted previously. As in the case of Odysseus as victim to Circe's enchantments, the application of herbs need not have deadly
consequences.[40]

The insights gained so far can help resolve an interpretative problem
in another poem, which in turn will illuminate the final passage I will

---

38. *Funestus* is difficult with *vir* and has lead to numerous conjections, e.g., *raptaque
funesto . . . toro* or *rogo* (see ed. Heyworth and S. J. Heyworth and Morwood 2011, 153). Tupet
(Tupet 1976, 367) favors *mero;* Fedeli 1985 obelizes the phrase (see 220–21). The transmitted text
is reproduced by Viarre 2005 with no comment.

39. For a lucid discussion, see Tupet 1976, 361–68; S. J. Heyworth and Morwood (2011, 151–
52) point to Hor. *Epod.* 5.17–24 as an important intertext.

40. Cf. Prop. 3.12.17: *et Circae fraudes, lotosque herbaeque tenaces*, stressing the binding quality
of the herbs.

discuss.[41] Poem 2.28 (which I take as a unity)[42] presents the beloved as dangerously ill.[43] The poem begins as a prayer, first to Jupiter, then to various goddesses; it repeatedly returns to this frame, but intermittently addresses the beloved as well. Her illness is so serious that a (never-named) human addressee is exhorted to be prepared for death or for a last-minute reversal (2.28.32), and the speaker contemplates, as a final resort, the simultaneous deaths of himself and his beloved (2.28.39–42).[44] Interposed is a statement about the conclusion of magical activities and the appearance of ominous sounds (35–38):

> deficiunt magico torti sub carmine rhombi,
>   et tacet[45] exstincto laurus adusta foco;
> et iam Luna negat totiens descendere caelo,
>   nigraque funestum concinit omen avis.

Now cease the wheels whirled to the magic chant, the altar fire is dead and the laurel remains quiet in the ashes. Now the moon refuses to descend so oft from heaven, and the bird of night sings ominous of death.

As the immediately following verses stress the unity of the lovers, the verses quoted cannot point to the dissolution of the magic that had caused the speaker's attraction to the beloved. Rather, it must refer to a magical ritual on the part of, or on behalf of, this woman in order to attract some third party.[46] This would fit with the statement that now even Juno, who protects conjugal bonds, pities her (33–34).[47] The pragmatic content of the verses

---

41. See Hubbard 1974, 55–56 for previous attempts at elucidation.

42. See Fedeli 2005, 779–80 for pertinent arguments.

43. Hence classified by Cairns (1972, 151–57) as among the "soteria."

44. For the importance of the association of love and death, see Papanghelis 1987.

45. Fedeli (2005, 801), following Canter, suggests the (easy) correction of the transmitted *iacet* to *tacet*. Cf. Prop. 4.3.58 and Harmon 1986, 1933 with further references.

46. Syndikus's interpretation (2006, 301) that the reference is to magic intended to heal the woman is untenable. Likewise Tupet's proposition that the references to magical practices are commonplaces ("*d'une façon très large*," Tupet 1976, 360), nothing more than characterizations of an atmosphere of anxiety, misses the point. It is, however, more or less followed by Fedeli 2005, who interprets the end of the wheel's spinning as an omen (800).

47. Verses 33–34 are frequently transposed; Günther (1997, 22–24) rightly preserves the continuity of verses 33–46, but transposes them after l. 2, bringing 28a (as a separate poem) to an end with l. 32.

would be: "Your infidelity toward me has also ceased." This would give a new aspect to her beauty, earlier identified as rousing the gods' envy (10). And it would also prepare the reader for the pun of the final line,[48] demanding that the woman not only pay Isis with vigils, but also dedicate ten nights of lovemaking to the speaker as votive offering: "I'll leave Rome, the place of sexual distractions" (as shown in 2.19 and there stressed by reference to sacrifices to Diana) "I'll end my sexual relationship with the other man by keeping celibate vigils for Isis, and I dedicate ten nights to you." This is the invalid's votive formula that underlies the structure of the poem.[49]

For our purposes, it is important to observe that there is no indication of the magical agent: Propertius evades the question of true agency by assigning it to inanimates (as subjects of the cessative verbs: *deficient, tacet, negat descendere*). Only in the final line of the excerpt is the grammatical subject identical with the pragmatic subject: the bird, whose singing illustrates the shift away from the topic of magic practices. The beloved is only implicitly responsible for this binding, but not physically harmful, magic.

Piety or Poison?

As a whole, the more explicit and longer treatments of magical practices are framed by references or addresses to deities. In 2.28 the plea for the beloved's life is framed entirely as a communication with named deities. In 3.24 and 25 (which, following Heyworth's reconstruction of the hyparchetype Π, I take together as a single poem), the dissolution of the bonds of love could not be produced by friends or a "Thessalian witch" (*saga*), but only by a deity such as *Bona Mens* (19–20). In book 4, it is Venus whom Propertius thanks for the death of a procuress who practiced magic (4.5). As we have seen in our analysis of 1.1, there is an opposition between magical and sacred ritual. Finally, in 2.28 the speaker opposes his own *sacrum carmen* to the *magicum carmen* that has ceased (43 vs. 35). Magic is an instrument that is present and powerful in love affairs and its application can

---

48. Pun: Fedeli 2005, 815.
49. Alessi 1985 has argued that the reason for Cynthia being "affected" (l. 1) is Jupiter's sexual interest in her rather than some illness. Such an interpretation would fit in the verses in question even better, but the textual clues that support this reading remain very subtle.

extend to use of poison, but otherwise it is not employed in matters of life and death. After all, Propertius had another resort: poetry.

We need not dwell on the rhetorical qualities of magic in reading Propertius.[50] In the first poem of book 1 and the last poem of book 3, he clearly states his conviction that the creation and singing of poems is a technique superior to magic:

> has tibi fatalis cecinit mea pagina diras:
> eventum formae disce timere tuae!

> Such curses fraught with doom are the burden of my song for thee: learn to dread the end that awaits thy beauty! (3.25.17–18 = 3.24.37–38)

These are the last two lines of book 3, and they deliberately deploy the language of curses to put an end to his love for Cynthia.[51]

How, in conclusion, should we move from literary to historical considerations? Of course, the texts we have discussed offer no hard evidence of actual magic practices. They are part of a contemporary discourse on magic, a discourse that addressed both transregional and local features. I propose that we reflect on the pragmatics, the application of magic as imagined by the poet within that discourse. To this end, we should first recall the deliberately public stance of his poems, in particular those that introduce or terminate books.[52] Magic is an important—albeit not predominant—theme.

Propertius presupposes a set of techniques, characterized by their high degree of ritualization, e.g., by the use of instruments or ingredients that do not appear in common or daily praxis. These are termed "magic" and they are clearly distinguished from—and placed in semantic opposition to—the realm of the gods and such practices as are termed "sacred." This separation is not born out by the evidence, which shows that gods were invoked in spells and that the continuum of verbal and visual devices in common ritual use ranged from spells to amulets such as gems.[53] Propertius, however,

---

50. Cf. above, n. 5 (Zetzel 1996).
51. Stressed by Fedeli 1985, 694.
52. See Lyne 1998, 161 and 168 on 1.1 and 2.12.
53. Gordon 2008, 715; 2011, 45.

is evidently interested in a conceptual distinction. Such magical techniques as he mentions seem to have been readily available, but the group of possible activities so defined is relatively limited; in the texts analyzed above, cursing is not mentioned as a magical practice, though we can compare it both with magic and with communication with the gods in the form of vows or sacrifices.

In Propertius's view, magical practices are genealogically, that is mythologically, related to the malicious use of poisons.[54] This aspect of magic is not a part of ordinary use; it is illustrated by mythical examples and is associated with far-distant mythical landscapes (Colchis, Thessaly). The use of magical herbs and instruments, unlike that of poisons, is not criminal, but confusion between the two is possible—and Propertius is always careful to keep this in mind. This should be interpreted as a commentary on contemporary, even legal, discourse: crimes might be punished, but this does not concern ordinary magic.

Only in his last book does Propertius clearly attribute magical knowledge and practices to a concrete (even if fictitious) person. The procuress of 4.5 is, however, a variously qualified specialist in love, and she is not reduced to a magician only.[55] In terms of agency, the status of the client or initiator and that of the specialist or contractor remains unspecified. Propertius does not participate in the creation of the Roman gothic image of the sorceress, which Daniel Ogden defines as a feature of Roman texts in general.[56]

Much clearer is the role of the object of magic: the victim is struck precisely; he or she suspects but does not know, and cannot defend himself or herself regardless of the attacker's apparent inferiority (in terms of gender, status, and morals).

Magic—as one could conclude this short review of the Propertian literary representation—is potentially ubiquitous. Its presence is identified by behaviors or turns of events that are contrary to social expectation. Of course, the peripheral, even illegitimate sexual relationships, including prostitution, that are the frequent topics of Propertius's poetry, are much

---

54. As clearly expressed in the term *toxica* (1.5.6); see Tupet 1976, 352–53.

55. The accusation of verses 5–20 is not borne out by the advice Acanthis offers to the girl. See 4.5.41–44 with O'Neill 1998, 61. In fact, the procuress is already dead, and it might be the male accuser who practices magic; ibid., 76.

56. Ogden 2008.

less effectively regulated by social sanctions and expectations. However, Propertius is not interested in creating a specific subcategory of "erotic magic" as opposed to anything else. Despite the limited nature of the evidence, I will attempt a summary. For Propertius, magic is neither antisocial nor the "religion of the others." The aims of magical practices might be reached by other techniques of sacralization, but magic is as legitimately open to him as it is to others.[57] However, the ingestion of potions is (according to the dominant sensualistic Roman worldview) the most plausible explanation for magic's effects, and this is uncomfortably close to the crime of poisoning. One must, therefore, be wary of admitting responsibility for such magic, or of naming one's contractors. Believing, practicing, remaining silent—these are exactly the conditions that are valid for all imperial practitioners and specialists of magic.[58]

For lived ancient religion, magic is an option. Given the existence of many alternatives (good manners, prayer and votives, poetry, and curses), it has an expressive value, often taking on the character of a last resort:[59] "I am fed up with how things normally work in the social and cultural patterns dominating daily life. Thus, I have recourse to the powers of nature and their specialists." As a consequence, speaking about the use of magic is something that is usually done with polemical reference to others rather than in self-description. By contrast, votives and literary curses are public, or at least tend to be.[60] The former, too, are highly expressive, and they were selected with a view to specific situations and circumstances, as the previous chapter has shown. Struggling with social order and convention, with the preferences and dislikes of others, with changing moods and circumstances, the Propertian individual tests the limits of his ability to change or adapt to an ultimately uncontrollable environment. For this purpose, he needs and develops the full range of available cultural resources. Magic included.

---

57. See, e.g., the list in Luck 2000, 204.
58. Gordon 2013.
59. Hübner 2008, 337.
60. See on literary curses, e.g., Watson 1991.

5

RECONSTRUCTING RELIGIOUS EXPERIENCE

Can the practices and experiences of lived ancient religion be identified beyond those that are described and imagined in a discourse that sought to denounce certain procedures as extreme? Working with the paradigm of civic religion, scholars have been content to identify the traces of religious tradition, shared social meaning, and ritual precepts—all well-researched areas of religious practices and beliefs in the ancient circum-Mediterranean world. However, new tools in dealing with evidence of a past culture are needed if we are to investigate individual appropriation of tradition, personal experiences and responses, the incoherencies of situational interpretation, isolated performances, and local and group-specific styles. If our interest extends beyond listing the myriad documents of individual performance consisting of votives, inscriptions, anonymous depositional remains (all of which are deeply shaped by their usually formulaic and stereotypical character), the question of evidence becomes crucial. How can we identify individual appropriation and transformation, or the creative reassembling and consequent individual selections of elements of a tradition? How can we evaluate the impact of such individual modifications on the resulting shape of seemingly stable "traditions"? How can we elucidate the interdependencies of the individual and the social in specific situations?[1]

Individual religious practice is contingent on both the intellectual and the embodied availability of traditions, and on their situational salience. Religious traditions include complex belief systems as well as simple sequences of ritual action, and it is, therefore, necessarily the case that learning and memory are involved in processes of individual appropriation. These are processes of acquiring knowledge through formal training or repetition, through casual exchange, and through need-driven inquiry.[2] Attention to these modes of acquisition is a necessary element of any historic reconstruction.

By the late republican and early Augustan period, a small minority of Romans were literate and had access to private copies of texts and the first public libraries, or were of such means and/or status that they were invited to recitals. To these individuals there were available, from the mid-first century onward, texts on religion, rich in ritual and theological detail.[3] These texts, when extant, have for centuries been used as the principal sources for the reconstruction of "Roman religion." Occasionally (and more intensively in recent years) they have been identified as offering a glimpse into the intellectual concerns and the cognitive dimension of late republican and early imperial religion. They have come to be regarded as theological enterprises in their own right, establishing their authors as figures of religio-historical importance equal to that of the holders of public priesthoods.[4] Following on my analyses of Propertius's poetic texts in the two previous chapters, I will again demonstrate that analysis of such texts can also yield solutions to the methodological problems associated with the investigation of lived ancient religion. Here, I am specifically interested in how these texts might illuminate their users rather than their producers, their usage rather than their production.

---

1. For case studies addressing the problem of religious individuality, see Rüpke and Spickermann 2012; Rebillard 2012; Rüpke 2013c; Rüpke and Woolf 2013. This chapter draws extensively on Rüpke 2015c.

2. On memory, see Halbwachs 1992; Connerton 1989; Le Goff 1992; Flower 2003; Oesterle 2005; Cubitt 2007; Benoist et al. 2009; Erll 2011; Dignas and Smith 2012; Cusamano et al. 2013; Rüpke 2012i.

3. See Rawson 1985 (for the period as a whole); briefly Ledentu 2004, 329–37.

4. Beard 1986, 1987, 1991; Feeney 1998; Rüpke 2012e.

Searching for the Readers

One of the most pressing problems in the sociology of ancient literature is the almost total absence of testimonies to readers and readers'
reactions—excepting some famous anecdotes, e.g., Cicero's response to
Varro, and Augustus as Vergil's audience.[5] Likewise, the few extant cases
of dense sequences of manuscript copies, which at least allow a glimpse
into the reactions of copyists through their modifications of the original
wording (and layout), are restricted to texts later classified as Christian.[6]
Thus, analysis is more usually limited to the texts themselves and to what
information about the reader can be elicited from them. Reader response
criticism has suggested different approaches to this task, particularly in the
last third of the twentieth century.[7]

The act of reading is a complex process. It confronts a reader's pre-
conceptions and expectations with a text that confirms or frustrates such
expectations, and that offers a sequence of representations and metarepre-
sentations (that is, representations of others' representations), information,
and judgments; it is only in extreme cases, such as magical papyri or Dada-
ism, that the text offers little more than sounds or images. Reading per-
petually forces readers—and for antiquity we must imagine hearers more
often than readers—to recalibrate their appraisal of the text.[8] In addition
to the perhaps various voices of explicit (i.e., narrated) or implicit narra-
tors, the text might also offer perspectives that serve as models or alternatives of reception, so-called narrated readers (or, as I stress, hearers). The
text might also construe an intended audience as a person of a certain age,
gender, social identity, or intellectual interest. Often, this might even be an
ideal reader with all the competences necessary to fully grasp the text. The
text as a whole, that is, as a sum of its challenges to connect its disparate
parts and to combine its different perspectives, would, according to Wolfgang Iser, produce an "implicit" or "implied reader."[9]

---

5. Cic. *Acad. Post.* 8–9; Donat. *Vita Vergilii* 31.
6. See, e.g., Haines-Eitzen 2012.
7. E.g., W. C. Booth 1983 (1961); Jauss 1977a, 1977b, 1982, 1987; Iser 1972, 1974, 1976, 1978;
overview: G. Prince 2009.
8. Iser 1994.
9. Ibid., 62–66.

For this brief exposition, I am not interested in dissecting the merits or the subtleties of the various accounts of such a reader's ontological status.[10] Obviously, the more implicit the reader, the more her character depends on the literary critic's interpretation of the text as a whole, to the point that she may become little more than the undeterminable intersection of all the loose ends of a text.[11] For the purpose of my analysis it suffices (and eases my burden) to say that literary communication in antiquity, religious communication included,[12] is much more tightly bound to established social relationships than the literary texts of the late early modern and modern period.[13] This is due both to the limited extent of literacy and to its concentration in the upper echelons of society.[14] This tie is also reinforced by the necessity of manual copying; distribution usually depended on friends (and friends of friends) rather than on the very limited commercial book market.[15] For the most part, reading took place in a network made up of strong *and* weak ties.[16] Again, we typically have no external evidence on the specific religious appropriations of the members, the nodes, that is, of such a network. To avoid the circularity in argumentation that comes with the presumption of desired implications, my analysis will concentrate on explicitly narrated figures. However, I will of course also collect other clues that point to an intended audience. This is what I will call "connected reader" in the following discussion.

Informing and Involving the Connected Reader: A Case Study

The methodological approach I have outlined will be applied to Publius Ovidius Naso's *Libri fastorum*, his commentary on the Roman calendar in

---

10. For criticism, see Genette 1994, 291–92.

11. Nünning 1993; radicalized by Willand 2014, in particular 265–97.

12. For the latter, see Rüpke and Spickermann 2009; Rüpke 2001.

13. Habinek 1998, in particular 103–21.

14. For discussion, see Harris 1989; Corbier 1991; Bowman and Woolf 1994; Curchin 1995; Hezser 2001; Derks and Roymans 2002; Lardinois 2011.

15. In general W. A. Johnson 2012. For circulation, see Starr 1987; Mratschek 2010; and Haines-Eitzen 2012, 24.

16. For a fruitful application of network theory to ancient religion, see Collar 2007, 2014; Eidinow 2011.

its graphic form of the *fasti*. This book was largely composed between AD 2 and 8, and may have been almost complete as early as AD 4, about a generation after Propertius.[17] Again, the audience for this text must be sought among the Roman elite. This is true despite the diverse critical voices discernible in several late republican and early Augustan texts, from Catullus and Vergil to Horace and Propertius. It was in the communicative and social space of the elite that such poetry was instrumental. These texts "became part of the Romans' social equipment and came to inform their view of the world," as Sander Goldberg has shown in his study on republican Roman literature.[18] Religious practices, institutions, and history also played a substantial role in this view of the world.[19]

Ovid's six books, covering the months of January to June, are, together with Propertius's fourth book of elegies (to which Ovid reacts)[20] the apogee of such "authoritative" poetry in the early principate. These texts are part of the cultural revolution that Andrew Wallace-Hadrill has demonstrated to be at the heart of the Augustan "restoration."[21] Accordingly, they were highly political statements.[22] From a broader perspective, however, the composition of these texts on Roman religion was also a part of the process of insular rationalization, which took place from the third century BC onward, and which—at least for religion—came to a halt in the Augustan era.[23]

Ovid's elegiac poems on an epic scale are particularly fruitful material for investigations of audience and narrator construction. The homodiegetic narrator (Genette's terminology for the narrator fully embedded in the principal narration)[24] is not omniscient, but is himself frequently in

---

17. For the title and genre, see Rüpke 1994. Contrary to common usage, I use the fuller title to combat the widespread misunderstanding of the poem as versified calendar. For a brief discussion of the date (which does not accept the earlier *terminus post quem*, to which I tend), see Littlewood 2006, xx.

18. Goldberg 2005, 207.

19. See in general Feeney 1998; for history, see Feeney 2007a; Rüpke 2012i, 165–73.

20. In particular Ov. *Fast.* 2.7–8; see Rüpke 2009d.

21. Wallace-Hadrill 2008, 236, 239.

22. See Wallace-Hadrill 1988; Barchiesi 1994; Feeney 1994; Herbert-Brown 1994; Fantham 2002.

23. Rüpke 2012e, where I claim that this process predates the first century, which is the period proposed by Moatti 1997. Feeney 2007b is right, however, to point out the numerous innovations of the second half of the first century BC.

24. See Genette 1980, 1988.

need of further information, or he reflects on competing explanations for a single phenomenon. As Joy Littlewood puts it, "Audience involvement is essential to Ovid's Fasti narrative, which is a personal exchange with literary Rome, the educated elite." The short, self-contained units of elegiac distiches are especially suitable to "colloquial dialogue."[25] Furthermore, the elaborate dedication of the *Libri fastorum* to Augustus in the first version (probably transposed to the dedicatory opening of the second book, on February, in the final version)[26] and the dedication to Germanicus in the second and final version (written from exile, AD 8–17) obviously call for the active appropriation of every single reader. Not only do these lines argue directly and forcefully for the importance of the poems' contents to the individual dedicatees and their supporters, but they also demand that all readers consider their importance more generally. Time and again these "connected readers" are directly addressed. The opening of the sixth book provides an example:

> Hic quoque mensis habet dubias in nomine causas:
> quae placeat, positis omnibus ipse leges. (6.1–2)[27]

> This month, too, has dubious causes for its name.
> All will be listed. Pick the one you like.[28]

The form of literary communication found in the *Libri fastorum* is a feature of antiquarian literature that had been developing at Rome since the second century BC. In the face of imperial expansion and rapid social and cultural change, antiquarian descriptions and systematizations of Roman rituals and institutions offered a way to construe a particular cultural identity beyond military dominance; it also offered a way to negotiate change and tradition. Augustus exploited this fully; innovations could, through such literature, be rooted in a vision of religious continuity and reaffirmation.[29]

---

25. Littlewood 2006, lxviii–lxix and lxxiv, quotations lxix and lxxiv.

26. I follow the thesis of Peter 1874, 10 (accepted, e.g., by Bömer 1958, 19; rejected by Miller 1991, 143–44 with no new arguments).

27. For the most part I follow the text of Alton, Wormell, and Courtney (Ovidius Naso 1985).

28. The translations of Ovid in this chapter are taken from Boyle and Woodard 2004, who render the colloquial style nicely.

29. See Rüpke 2012e, in particular 144–51.

As Wallace-Hadrill points out, "'Traditionalism' brought not inflexibility, but the basis for creative adaptation. Cultural identity invested in a remote past becomes not so much a program as an alibi."[30]

But there is more to it. It is my contention that description and prescription went hand in hand in this discourse. By tapping into different local, social, and even ethnic traditions, antiquarianism offered not only a fuller account of a common cultural heritage, but also a broad range of religious resources, practices, and beliefs for individual appropriation. This detailed and colorful image of religion does more than serve the narrow ideological function of providing identity for contemporaries; for us, it offers a glimpse into "lived ancient religion," even if it is difficult or even impossible to determine in every particular instance whether we are dealing with actual or merely imagined lived religion. In the latter case, given the communicative and social context of this type of imagination, it is, at the very least, an imagination closely controlled by contemporaries. This holds true for the information that is supplied about religious practices as much as it does for that which is implied about a connected reader's interest in these practices. Whereas previous research, with its interest in religious institutions, has concentrated on the former, this analysis, which aims to investigate lived religion, will concentrate on the latter.

Ovid did not invent a Roman calendar of festivals. His commentary is a reaction to a series of calendar reforms that started with the technical reform of the dictator Caesar, and that changed an age-old instrument of daily use, rendering it a prominent tool of political and dynastic propaganda. First found in the form of a large marble calendar in the sanctuary of the reformed priesthood of the Arval Brethren shortly after the battle of Actium, publicly displayed Roman *fasti* were quickly produced, proliferating in Rome as well as in central Italy and occasionally beyond.[31] Augustus used the calendar to represent his own achievements in the form of extended festival annotations, creating heightened awareness of the included rituals, an awareness that extended far beyond the actual participants. In turn, the local elites even of small villages, magistrates, and slave *collegia* were able both to display their loyalty by copying these calendars and to

---

30. Wallace-Hadrill 2008, 239.
31. See Rüpke 2011b for a reconstruction of the process, and Rüpke 1995 for a review of the preserved calendars.

inscribe themselves into this Augustan world in the form of annual lists of magistrates, likewise called *fasti*.[32] If it had been attractive to know about Roman festivals and the "Roman year," it now became imperative to know about the *fasti*, the specific graphic form of the Roman calendar. Ovid embraced this necessity as a creative challenge.[33]

Before any further details are addressed, the implications even of the generic identification of the poem, not only as a didactic text but also as a commentary, must be pointed out. The poem functions only if the connected reader is using a personal copy of the calendar to actively follow the chronology. The poem assumes that the reader does this, and it is a requirement without which it would be hard, at times impossible, to understand the text.[34] The locus classicus is Ov. *Fast.* 5.727–28: "The next place comes with four marks, which, read in order, / denote a sacred rite or the king's flight." The connected reader is, therefore, very active.[35] The abbreviations, brief notes, and names that are found on the calendar itself are the primary prompts for questions (and at times answers). Ovid introduced treatments of the rising and setting of constellations, thus necessitating other devices, "parapegmata,"[36] and requiring an even more active reader. Here, we find implicit in Ovid's treatment a criticism of contemporary calendars in the face of the growing popularity of astrology; according to his model, important astronomic data ought to be integrated into the *fasti*. This initiative was later adopted by popular forms of domestic calendars found throughout the Roman Empire.[37]

In terms of reader construction, the *Libri fastorum*'s main feature is the directly apostrophized reader in the second-person singular. This was a well-known technique for involving readers (or listeners), relinquishing the magisterial authority of the omniscient narrator to exert a subtler influence over readers' interests. In Ovid, the narrator's questions are attributed to the narrated reader, as if the narrator's answers are prompted by the interjections

---

32. Rüpke 1997a, 1997b; Wallace-Hadrill 2008, 246.

33. Rüpke 1994; see also Rüpke 2009d.

34. The arbitrary and incomplete introduction of some calendar indications in our editions since Rudolf Merkel's *editio maior* of the nineteenth century has obscured this fact.

35. It is not simply "authorial passivity" that invites "co-authorship" on part of the reader, as claimed by King 2004, 199.

36. Rehm 1949; Rüpke 1996a; Lehoux 2007.

37. Goessler 1928; Wagner-Roser 1987; Rüpke 2014c, 101–17. See also Stern 2012, 218.

of a present interlocutor. The questions raised by the narrated reader are identical to those raised by the narrator, who asks these questions and either simply answers them, or addresses them to more knowledgeable entities, sometimes human, but more often the deities concerned or the Muses.

Posing such questions was normally an honorable enterprise, but it can also have its risks, as is illustrated by the example of Ino. On her arrival in Italy, Ino shows an inquisitive attitude—like the narrator of the *Librorum fasti*. Her inquiry into the race of the Maenads (6.505) is not very well received; Saturnian Juno stirs up the Maenads by suggesting: "She is a spy and aims to learn our sacred rites" (6.511). Clearly Juno prepares for Ino a fate parallel to that of Pentheus.[38] And yet the phrasing of Ino's questions, as well as the forcefully critical characterization of Juno as *insidiosa* (6.508), suggest that Ovid is well aware of parallel situations of inquiry. His readers, too, might have known that this inquisitive author was, by the time of the publication, himself exiled—for whatever reason. Finally, stories about Soranus, who was allegedly executed for pronouncing the secret name of the tutelary deity of Rome, might already have been in circulation.[39]

Question and answer is the basic mode of discourse. It is usually a single narrator or reader who poses questions. The verb "to ask," *quaerere*, occurs twenty-nine times, but interestingly, only five times in the plural, *quaeritis*.[40] *Cur*, "why?" is the quintessential question, found forty-five times in the poem. Similarly inquired after are origins (*origines*, eleven times) and causes (*causa/causae*, ninety-one times). The distribution over the books is fairly even in all cases. Answers may be supplied even in the absence of explicit questions: in response to nothing more than the narrator's tacit astonishment, an old woman gives the "cause" for her naked feet (6.415). In the following, I concentrate on examples taken from book 6. I aim to offer an argument that combines economy with a careful contextual reading: I will select representative examples while attending closely to the image of the connected reader as it is drawn within the framework of a typical unit of reception.

---

38. Thus Littlewood 2006, 161.

39. The incident occurred in the early first century BC; its earliest attestations are Plin. *NH* 3.65 and Plut. *Quaest. Rom.* 61.

40. These are found only in the second half of the poem, from book 4 onward: 4.878; 5.1, 526; 6.195, 551. This might point to an imagination of (or even experience with) an audience of several listeners rather than of isolated readers.

Knowledge and Ritual Competence in Ovid's Readers

The connected reader, then, is one interested in reasons, which are—in keeping with previous antiquarian discourse—usually given in the form of stories about origins, mythical or historical. Aetiological myths are woven into the exchange of questions and answers. Religion is subject to interrogation, and it is not priestly lore but historical research that provides answers.[41] The religious data to be explained are frequently names. These names, however, are visual data; they are suggested only by being seen in the calendar, which in itself represents visible cult. Other *explananda* also present themselves visually: temples are prominently seen or "looking out,"[42] and occasionally statues or ritual procedures force themselves into the narrator's field of vision.

If narrator and connected reader share an interest in visual data, vision also marks a decisive difference between the two. Visual epiphanies are a privilege of the narrator. Surprisingly, this fact empowers the inscribed reader as much as it does the narrator. The narrator fully expects the reader to doubt the authenticity of his visions, as a few lines at the opening of book 6 make clear:

> facta canam? sed erunt qui me finxisse loquantur
> nullaque mortali numina visa putent.
> est deus in nobis? agitante calescimus illo;   5
> impetus hic sacrae semina mentis habet.
> fas mihi praecipue voltus vidisse deorum,
> vel quia sum vates, vel quia sacra cano.

> I will sing facts, but some will call them fiction
> and think no gods appear to mortal men.
> There is a god inside us; his movement makes us glow,
> His power owns the seeds of sacred thought.
> For me above all it's lawful to see a god's face,
> Since I'm a poet *or* sing sacred themes. (6.3–8)

Such visions are a continuous source of knowledge. It is, however, a knowledge that is questionable and at times contested. The concept of "vision" is

---

41. Wallace-Hadrill 2008, 240–42, 248.
42. See, e.g., 5.669: *templa spectantia*. Similarly 5.567–68 and 6.205.

even adapted to accommodate direct contact with that goddess whose very characteristic it is to be not represented by a statue and to remain unseen by men: Vesta (6.291). This particular form of poetic knowledge supplements the type of information that is generically attributed to "old annals" in two prefatory remarks.[43] Occasionally (ten times throughout the poem) the narrator "remembers" (*memini, commemini*) what he has seen or even learned (*didici*) earlier, and in one passage of book 6 this knowledge is even stated to have been acquired in his "childhood years" (6.417). Knowledge in religious matters is learnable.

An interest in knowledge is attributed to the connected reader: *e nostro carmine certus eris*—"from my song you will gain certain knowledge" is the promise made by the narrator when he talks about obscure Carna (6.104). (I again take my example from book 6, which is representative in these respects.) Such gods as are known with certainty constitute a discrete category in Varro's classification of gods (*di certi*). Religious data could, therefore, be subject to ignorance or error; the narrator both acknowledges that this is possible (6.255, 295) and aims to protect his readers from incorrect beliefs.[44]

In some instances, knowledge will suggest the course of future actions. For example, Ovid offers information about the character of days, whether they are better (*melius*) suited to marriage or warfare (6.221–22, 769), or whether they are characterized by meteorological conditions beneficial to sailing (6.715; similarly 2.453 and 4.625). With regard to religious activities, superior knowledge seems not to have had any consequences. About Semo Sancus Dius Fidius and the names to be used in his cult the narrator learns from Semo Pater that "whichever of them you choose, I'll have the tribute" (6.215).[45] The long discourse on the reason why the statue in Fortuna's temple—identified as Servius Tullius—is covered by togas remains without consequence, as the matrons are exhorted to not touch the heap of textiles (6.621).[46]

Such exhortations to perform cult are extremely rare. Religion as lived in Ovid is not characterized by the accurate reproduction of scripted rituals. The connected reader is not admonished to fulfill ritual duties, nor

---

43. 1.7 and 4.11: *annalibus eruta priscis*.

44. See 2.47 *ne erres;* 2.151 *ne fallare;* 2.453 *tu desine credere* (relating to meteorological phenomena); cf. 2. 531 *stulta pars populi*.

45. See Bömer 1958, 349–50 on the deities.

46. See Littlewood 2006, 173 on the historical problem.

Baking mold with scenes from the circus, used for bread distributed in context of
such games. First half of the fourth century AD. Römermuseum Theurnia.
Photo by J. Rüpke, used by permission of Landesmuseum für Kärnten.

is regular participation in public cult a didactic aim of the text. The very
few exceptions are, rather, admonitions to adopt the appropriate emotional
tone during ritual participation. The first such instance appears with Ovid's treatment of *Feriae Sementivae* (a movable feast, treated in January),
where rural peoples of various vocations and their animals are addressed
(1.663–96). The entire exhortation to *enjoy* leisure with a festive spirit is
formulated as an emotionalized prayer. The *Karistia* or *Cara Cognatio* on
February 22 offers the next example (2.617–38); here, Ovid encourages the
boni to dedicate incense and simple meals in a *harmonious* domestic ritual.
The language of this passage gradually shifts from description to exhortation. During the Vinalia of April 23, it is appropriate that prostitutes
(*volgares . . . puellae*) venerate Venus, a deity useful for many professions
(4.865–72). As befits prostitutes, they should demand the qualities necessary to their profession in an *insistent* manner; this is made clear by the
repetition of *poscite*. In contrast, the Quirites should celebrate Mars Ultor
with *solemn* games in the circus, not by scenic games (5.597–98). Matrons

should celebrate the Matralia, because it is their very special festival, with "*golden* cakes" (6.475–76). The *Quirites* should celebrate Fors Fortuna *joyfully* (*laeti*), and drunkenness is no cause for shame (6.775–78). The plurals used in these passages and the explicit indication of social groups is in sharp contrast with the usual address to a singular reader.

It is interesting to observe the differences between the description of the ritual of March 15, the festival of Anna Perenna, to that of the festival of Fors Fortuna. On the surface, the two seem to be similar occasions for excessive drinking on the banks of the Tiber. However, the first instance (3.523–42) is an activity of the *plebs*—the narrator, and others, are clearly distanced as observers.[47] Veneration of Fors Fortuna on June 24 is characterized as originating in the *plebs*, but it is the *Quirites* (all the people) that are instructed to take part in the merrymaking by a series of three imperatives and two jussive subjunctives.[48]

> ite, deam laeti Fortem celebrate, Quirites;
>   in Tiberis ripa munera regis habet.
> pars pede, pars etiam celeri decurrite cumba,
>   nec pudeat potos inde redire domum.
> ferte coronatae iuvenum convivia lintres,
>   multaque per medias vina bibantur aquas   680

> Go, celebrate with joy the goddess Fors, Quirites;
>   The Tiber's bank has her gift from the king.
> Rush on down, some on foot, some in a speedy skiff,
>   And don't be ashamed to return home drunk.
> Garland yourselves, boats, and carry parties of the young,
>   And let wine be drunk aplenty mid-stream. (6.775–80)

Here, the drunkard returning home is not an object of ridicule, dragged along by his old and drunken wife, as he was during the Anna Perenna

---

47. 3.539: *sunt spectacula volgi*; 3.541 *occurrit nuper (visa est mihi digna relatu) / pompa . . .*

48. Other references to this festival do not permit an unambiguous identification of the participants. When Cicero contrasts the joy of the *Tiberina descensio* with that of a victor and triumphator (Cic. *Fin.* 5.70) one would expect that he refers to an experience that was open to his audience. The problem, however, has never been discussed. Bömer (1958, 180–81) doubts that the rites of the Anna Perenna festival are "fester Bestandteil des öffentlichen Kultus," but does not notice the social demarcation suggested by Ovid.

festival in March (*senem potum pota trahebat anus*, 3.542). Instead, he is a fairly reliable witness:

> ecce suburbana rediens male sobrius aede   785
>   ad stellas aliquis talia verba iacit;
> "zona latet tua nunc, et cras fortasse latebit;
>   dehinc erit, Orion, aspicienda mihi."

> Look, a man returns from the shrine near the city
>   Unsober, and hurls these words to the stars:
> "Your belt hides now, and perhaps will hide tomorrow.
>   After that, Orion, I shall see it." (6.785–88)

Unlike the *plebs*, the *Quirites* include the connected reader.

There is an interesting movement on the part of the narrator here. At the end of book 6, the connected reader might be one who is not only intellectually interested in cult but is also reminded of his or her (women are addressed in some plural exhortations) social or, rather, political status and thereby be incited to participate actively in religious merrymaking. And yet, the evidence remains inconclusive. First and foremost, the audience constructed by Ovid is one that witnesses the narrator's admonitions directed toward various large social groups composed of other individuals.

It is only at the very close of the poem, reworked in exile to end precisely where it ends, after six months (half a calendar), that the role of the observer meets that of the religious performer. Ovid's reader is, most certainly, an embedded reader, who understands what he or she is reading within the historical context of the poem at large.[49] This reader can decipher the author's clues and discern the incongruity that is implied as the second voice of the inscribed narrator emerges, a voice indulgent in merrymaking ritual. The implication must be spelled out: both the implied narrator and the connected reader are fully present at Rome. This is written by an author who was not present and made no secret of the grief his absence caused him.

---

49. I have taken the concept of "embedded reader" from Boyd 2006, 172 (who adapts J. J. Winkler's analysis of Apuleius's mysteries novel to Ovid's *Metamorphoses*).

Antiquarians' Connected Readers and Individual Appropriation of Religion

Does the concept of a connected reader help us analyze ancient individual appropriation of religion? I maintain that it does. To argue this, I must systematize my findings and bolster them with further evidence. We observe, on the one hand, the very specific character of Ovid's connected readers, and on the other, the coherence of this (of course) authorial construction throughout six books of epic length (and a re-edition). These two facts present of themselves adequate arguments that we are justified in seeking in this text a portrait of Ovid's addressees and their concerns—as ideal readers, or even as individuals of a specific social disposition.

Ovid's commentary on the *fasti* addresses the local (Roman) reader and supports his (or, as I would add in the case of Ovid, her) dominant mainstream political identity. Although this is not surprising, it is also not a necessity of antiquarian literature. Callimachus did not restrict himself to Alexandrian readers in his geographically wide-ranging *Aetia*.[50] Propertius problematizes identities and involves his audience in journeys outside of Rome, for instance to Lanuvium (4.8).

Ovid does not presuppose a reader who is interested in ritual details for the sake of active participation or highly specific observation. Nevertheless a wide range of ritual practices are touched on, far beyond even the necessities of a commentary on the Roman *fasti*. This holds true for the complex rite performed by the old woman for dea Tacita (2.571–82)[51] as well as for the otherwise unattested rites for Vacuna (6.307–8).

Ovid does construe a reader who is, above all, interested in the Why and Whence. Of course, these are questions that are welcome to the narrator as they offer opportunities for storytelling. But even if the answers occasionally remain inconclusive or conflicting, the reader is supposed to regard such etymological or historical knowledge as something that can be "learned" and "remembered." Religious practice and symbols invite questions and can be explained. Answers are neither forbidden nor dogmatic. The narrator is quite aware that his own answers are questionable. Explanation is not inimical to religion, but a part of it.[52]

---

50. I am grateful to Tony Bierl for this point.
51. See McDonough 2004, 357–58.
52. See in particular Beard 1987, 1988, 1989, 1993; Scheid 1992, 1993.

Ovid's connected reader is understood to be interested in visible religion. He or she is made aware of temples and statues and temples without statues, and of the ritual use of otherwise undistinguished space. There is, however, no hint at the private usufruct of such ritual topography.

In place of a systematics of religion such as modern research frequently conceptualizes on the blueprint of Varro's *Antiquitates rerum divinarum*—a functionally ordered "pantheon"—gods and temples and the attributes of days are quite often shown to be the outcome of historical contingencies and decisions. This conforms to a trend visible in other contemporary authors.[53] Here, the narrator is interested in recent changes and the latest renovation of a temple rather than in a complete chronology. Clearly, religion is presented as a field of creative action for members of the political elite, the emperor in particular.

The connected reader is interested not only in major public festivals but also in domestic and local cult, even if neither annotations in the text of the *fasti* nor public architecture point to the latter's existence. Such domestic and local cult, too, is regulated by the course of the year and consists of disconnected events, in any of which participation was optional. Its performance on the part of the reader is not presupposed.

A specific cult is an opportunity, or even a duty for a specific social, gender, or age group. The connected reader is supposed to learn these specifics, and he or she is at most indirectly admonished to join in, never without arguments. The most forceful exhortations concern not highly specific cult practices, but events that involve many groups, if not everybody: even animals in the case of the *Feriae Sementivae*, even slaves in the case of Fors Fortuna. In all these instances it is most important for the audience to have a clear understanding of the emotional tone of the cult. This holds true for the organizers of the cult as well as for any participant.

Finally, it is not the modern *bricoleur au religion* that corresponds to the connected reader crafted by Ovid. Rather, it is an informed and sympathetic observer or bystander, embedded in a structured society, but free to exercise his or her own choices, knowing the possible limits of individual innovation as well as the appropriate affective regulation or deregulation when participating in traditional cult activities. Such a reader will have already reached the stage of the trained reader, able "themselves to find

---

53. Rüpke 2014b.

interesting matter and understand it," as Quintilian put it (*Inst.* 2.5.13). For his didactic poetry Ovid would certainly have accepted the aim that Quintilian formulated in the following sentence: "For what else are we about in teaching than ensuring that our pupils will not always require to be taught?"[54]

Surveys, interviews, and participant observation (the methods employed in research on lived religion today)[55] are not available to the study of ancient religion. There is an abundance of evidence for a limited range of individual religious activities, such as votives, tomb inscriptions, and the material remains of funerary rituals. For other types of activity, we must rely on occasional anecdotal evidence as it appears in ancient historiography or in letters. In many instances, however, we see infrastructure rather than usage, texts rather than testimonies of their reception. Here, however, the instigators of architecture or the authors of texts step in, revealing the reactions they anticipate and focusing audience attention in direct or subtle ways. Such testimonies have been used to learn from texts what one can no longer learn about authors otherwise. But it can also be used to gather evidence, not elsewhere attested, about the character of the audience. In this chapter, my primary interest was not in Ovid, but in the religious practices of his contemporaries, presupposing that the text contains some insights into contemporary appropriation of religion. Through the lens of the connected reader (who in most cases is the inscribed, narrated hearer), Ovid's *Libri fastorum* is neither the script for a complex but fixed ritual system (as the text has been usually interpreted) nor an individual's reflection on such a system (as in more recent interpretations). Instead, it documents a field of social action, shaped and reshaped by contingent individual and group action. It documents lived ancient religion.

----

54. Translated by D. A. Russell and M. Winterbottom (Oxford: Oxford University Press, 1972), 378.

55. E.g., Heimbrock 2007; Bergmann 2008; McGuire 2008.

6

Dynamics of Individual Appropriation

In the past there existed a general consensus among classicists that it was primarily the practice of rituals over a long period of time that determined what could be described as Roman religion. Mere use of the term "ritualism" conferred on this characterization an evaluative and comparative quality.[1] It was the merit of research in the 1980s and '90s to enlarge this view by emphasizing the role of religious discourses beyond ritual communication.[2] The work of Mary Beard and John Scheid[3] (who developed their positions partly in direct dialogue) is foundational, and this shift in emphasis obtained further expression in the contributions of the French project

---

1. See Wissowa 1912, 34; cf. Beard, North, and Price 1998, 11. For this position in the history of the discipline, see Scheid 1987.

2. For this concept, see Rüpke 2001.

3. E.g., Beard 1985, 1986, 1987, 1988, 1989. More generally: Beard 1991, 1998; Scheid 1990c, 1992, 1993, 1994, 1998b, 1999.

of the "Mémoire perdue"[4] and the monograph of Denis Feeney on "Literature and Religion at Rome,"[5] as well as in the handbook of Beard, North, and Price.[6] Previously, ancient evidence had typically been subject to interpretations based on the "evolutionist" anthropology of the late nineteenth and early twentieth century.[7] A decisive step was made in the application of the interpretive framework of cognitive anthropology, especially the thinking of Dan Sperber,[8] to Roman material. The essence of the innovation was the redrawing of conceptual boundaries: those ancient authors that dealt with Roman religion were no longer seen merely as observers of Roman religion, but as participants; ancient exegetics[9] was no longer the first link in a long chain of attempts to find the "correct" interpretation of rituals (a chain that extends to current research).[10] Instead, indigenous exegesis is a feature of the religious system itself, and inconsistency is a permanent trace of that system. According to Beard, North, and Price, the success of so-called Roman ritualism lies precisely in the fact that largely unchanged transmitted rituals were open to ever new and up-to-date interpretations. They were, therefore, equally adequate within very different social situations.[11]

Rather than simply appending literary discourse to the idea of a rather static civic religion and its rituals,[12] the perspective of lived ancient religion developed here is interested in such discourse in terms of its power to produce religious "traditions" and to mediate between traditions and individual appropriation.[13] Thus, the reevaluation of ancient interpretations can lead to a more complex understanding of rituals, overcoming the division between ritual (as traditional, stereotyped, senseless action) on one hand and exegesis (the contextually adjusted, noncommittal, and intellectual attribution of meaning) on the other. Two concepts stemming from ritual theory can be employed to this end.

---

4. Anonymous 1994; Mémoire perdue 1998.

5. Feeney 1998.

6. Beard, North, and Price 1998; but cf. James B. Rives's review (1998, 359), which calls for a more intensive analysis of the literary texts.

7. Cf. (within a larger disciplinary framework) Schlesier 1991, 1995.

8. Sperber 1975.

9. The term is programmatically developed in Scheid 1992 and 1993.

10. See Feeney 1998, 117, 127.

11. Beard, North, and Price 1998, 7.

12. See ibid.; Scheid 1999. The "new consensus" was criticized by Bendlin 2000.

13. For the problem, see Belayche 2007.

The first is performance.[14] An individual performance of a ritual was not merely a simple repetition of an eternally fixed formula, but rather the conscious attempt of a historical individual to do the ritual, to repeat a time-honored pattern, to perform it to and for others in a specific situation, in a particular place. Individual feelings and social expectations were communicated. Standard meanings were reproduced or modified. Writing, that is literature, might have been part of the performance. In Rome, as in Greece, it was exactly rituals that were the frame for important types of literary communication. This applies especially to the games (*ludi*), the number of which exploded in the third and second centuries BC. "Scenic games" (*ludi scaenici*) supplied a venue for drama, tragedy as well as comedy, and integrated these forms into ongoing societal communication.[15] Insofar as identifiable texts are concerned, this process marked the beginning of a Latin literature;[16] through the evidence of images on vases we are able to discern the long prehistory of dramatic genres in ritual—especially Dionysiac—contexts, reaching at least as far back as the fourth century BC.[17]

Both larger dramatic texts as well as prayer formulations and hymns composed for individual recital are among the most flexible and hence most communicative elements of a ritual's performance.[18] Texts, however, are not only a part of the actual performance but also a part of its context, part of the performer's and audience's knowledge. Communication about ritual performances can be a determining factor in the interpretation and modification of a ritual action, and an individual performance cannot be analyzed in isolation from communication about previous performances or about the norms of the ritual. The existence of a written script for the performance of the ritual is but one possible component in the communicative mechanism. This is not to say that performance is a feature only of rituals; the texts associated with ritual, too, were performed, through public or private recitation.[19]

---

14. See R. L. Grimes 2006.

15. See, e.g., Bernstein 2007, and for tragedy Lefèvre 2001.

16. See Rüpke 2012b, 65–100, for an attempt to contextualize this process within the restructuring of literary communication in Rome in the third and second centuries BC.

17. Wiseman 2000.

18. Succinctly stated by Hickson Hahn 2007; see the forthcoming analysis of Maik Patzelt, Erfurt.

19. See Habinek 1998, 101–21, for Latin literature.

The second concept, ritualization, further radicalizes this approach. Catherine Bell introduced the concept of ritualization as a means to analyze the relationship between ritual and everyday action: ritualization is conscious modification of everyday action.[20] Humphrey and Laidlaw followed her lead by demonstrating that among the West Indian Jaina, rituals are not inherently rituals but instances of individual action that become rituals only because the agent or the audience ascribes to them the quality of ritual.[21] But this ascription is itself the product of the conceptual framework of the participants, a framework that is not only produced by previous ritual experiences but also by communication, including—even within a semiliterate society—textual communication. However, whereas Humphrey and Laidlaw were interested in the contents of the communication, the resulting general attitude toward ritual, and the conceptualization of ritual, I am interested in the different ways tradition is communicated, innovations, and the interplay of these with individual dynamics and appropriations. That is, I am interested in the historical process of change in rituals.

Dramatizing Ritual Performance

Even the earliest preserved literary texts in Latin contain ritual descriptions. Ennius, for example, in one of the longest extant fragments of his historic epic the *Annales*, describes an *auspicium* performed by two augurs, the brothers Romulus and Remus, who were in competition for the leadership of the city yet to be founded:[22]

> Curantes magna cum cura tum cupientes
> regni dant operam simul auspicio augurioque.
> in Murco Remus auspicio sedet atque secundam
> solus auem seruat. at Romulus pulcher in alto   75
> quaerit Aventino, seruat genus altiuolantum.

---

20. Bell 1992.

21. Cf. Humphrey and Laidlaw 1994, where the term "ritualization" is substituted for "ritual," and "ritual" is identified as a specific type of unintentional action, one for which success is defined as the realization of a supposed model for the action (Humphrey and Laidlaw 1994, 88).

22. Ennius, *Ann.* 72–91. Skutsch 1985 (partly following the conjectures of Jocelyn 1971) = 77–96 Vahlen = Cic. *Div.* 1.108. See the discussion of the text in Wardle 2006 ad loc.

certabant urbem Romam Remoramne uocarent.
omnibus cura uiris uter esset induperator.
expectant ueluti, consul cum mittere signum
uolt, omnes auidi spectant ad carceris oras,   80
quam mox emittat pictis e faucibus currus,
sic expectabat populus atque ore timebat
rebus, utri magni uictoria sit data regni.
interea sol albus recessit in infera noctis.
exin candida se radiis dedit icta foras lux   85
et simul ex alto longe pulcherrima praepes
laeua uolauit auis. simul aureus exoritur sol,
cedunt de caelo ter quattuor corpora sancta
auium, praepetibus sese pulchrisque locis dant.
conspicit inde sibi data Romulus esse priora,   90
auspicio regni stabilita scamna solumque.

With great care, anxious and desirous of kingship, they turn their attention both to the auspicious watching of the birds and to interpretation. Remus sits alone on the Murcus and watches for a favorable bird. But Romulus the splendid observes from the high Aventine and watches for the high-flying ones.

They were competing to name the city—Roma or Remora—and all men were concerned about which of the two would be the leader. They wait, just as when the consul is ready to give the starting signal, all eagerly look to the gates of the starting boxes, [to see] how soon he might send the cars out of the colorful mouths. In such a way the people waited with fear for the outcome on their faces, [wondering] which of the twins would be granted the victory of the great kingship.

Meanwhile the moon [or "morning star"] has receded into the depths of the night. Now, shimmering daylight has appeared, struck by the beams, and at once, from very high, a magnificent and auspicious bird has flown on the left. And when golden sun rises, three times four holy bodies descend from the sky and sit down on promising and splendid places. Thus Romulus sees that kingship's dais and throne has been given to him, confirmed by the birds' sign.

(trans. Jörg Rüpke and Alice Brigance)

As I have argued elsewhere,[23] the *Annales* was probably recited in a symposium attended by *nobiles*. From the perspective of the critical historian,

---

23. Rüpke 2012i, 30–35.

the passage above offers us valuable information for reconstructing the ritual of the *auspicium* and attests auspication—if not for the year 753, at least
for the early second century BC. Here, in one of the oldest transmitted literary texts of Rome, we are struck by the highly artful description: of the
allegedly historical performance of a legitimizing ritual, and of a unique
auspicium. The twelve *vultures* is a detail also found in other, less favorable
variants of the narrative.[24]

The passage is one in a long series of Roman attempts to deal with a
Greek story, full of discrediting elements, about Rome's foundation. As
Jocelyn has shown,[25] Ennius inserted contemporary augural practices in
order to render the narrative more palatable to his Roman audience. Jocelyn's view is that of the literary critic, focusing on the perspective of the
text's producer. What of the perspectives of its recipients? As senators and
(ex-) magistrates, they were, presumably, satisfied by this dignified story
about their founders. They would also have been gratified by the literary showcasing of one of their central but rather intimate practices: the
practice of going out to observe birds before sunrise (*infera noctis*, 89) was a
public, yet hardly prominent, performance.

The political importance of the ritual is confirmed by the central place
it holds in the story of the twins' conflict. Emphasis, however, is placed
not on structure but on performance. Personal engagement and intention
are stressed: *curantes magna cum cura* (77), "being careful with great care"
opens the passage. Jocelyn has drawn attention to the lingering obscurity
of the expression *auspicio se deuouet* (79), a sort of magical self-sacrifice to
the ritual. I use the expression "magical" deliberately: this phrase captures
the utter isolation, the asocial vigil of the observer, whose political will is
public, as are the technical conditions for a positive outcome of the bird
watching formulated in the *legum dictio*,[26] but not the strength of his reso-
lution, which the ritual also tests. It is this feature of the ritual performance
that is explicitly open to individual modification. Augury, as it is shown
here, is part of the aristocratic competition that informs Roman politics
and aristocratic values: *certabant* (82). For the listeners and readers of the

---

24. Livy 1.7.1: Here, Remus observes six vultures, Romulus twelve.
25. Jocelyn 1971.
26. Thus I understand the specifications of what is expected by each.

text, ritual is not only a means of political competition but is also itself a dynamic element of such competition.[27]

Given the fact that augury is, in principle, open to everybody, the text reminds its aristocratic listeners of the loftiness of their individual practice. Without actually asserting the presence of the citizens, all of whom are interested in the outcome (*omnibus . . . viris*), an audience is introduced by way of the simile: *ueluti, consul cum mittere signum / uolt, omnes auidi spectant* (84–85). Expecting, looking, and seeing (*expectare, spectare, conspicere*) are deliberately conflated as activities of the protagonists as well as the observers, and the reader is granted a simultaneous view of both parties (stressed by the visual *ore*, 87). Thus the literary depiction enables the nightly auspicial *certamen* to be observed by a breathless multitude as if they were witnessing a race in the circus.[28] The ritual practiced in solitude is transformed into a highly communicative performance.

No extant sources indicate the influence of the Ennian texts on the practitioners of augury. However, the proliferation of the practice of *tripudium*, augury by chicken feeding, and its criticism (not least in the very text of Cicero that supplies our Ennius passage) demonstrate that the communicative aspects of the performance were central. It is by stressing the individual's part in its performance that texts such as the *Annales* dramatized Roman *auspicia* and stabilized it against negative evaluations.

Competition in the Record Book

My next example is drawn from a late ancient source, the *Saturnalia* of Macrobius.[29] The following passage is quoted from the *commentarii*, the records of the priesthood of the Pontifices, and it is quite probably the most precisely identifiable quotation from priestly books: it is part of the fourth annual volume of the notes of the Pontifex Maximus Quintus Caecilius Metellus Pius regarding his urban official affairs. Caecilius held the office

---

27. For the eastern Mediterranean, cf. Rizakis 2007.

28. On observing rituals, see Huet 2015.

29. Macrob. *Sat.* 3.13.10–12. For Macrobius's dating (the decade after AD 400), see Döpp 1978.

of Pontifex Maximus from 81–64 BC. Given his periods of absence from
Rome, the described event would belong to the year 70 BC.[30]

> Refero enim pontificis vetustissimam cenam quae scripta est in indice quarto
> Metelli illius pontificis maximi in haec verba: ante diem nonam kalendas
> Septembres, quo die Lentulus flamen Martialis inauguratus est, domus or-
> nata fuit, triclinea lectis eburneis strata fuerunt, duobus tricliniis pontifices
> cubuerunt, Q. Catulus, M. Aemilius Lepidus, D. Silanus, C. Caesar, <***>
> rex sacrorum, P. Scaevola sextus; Q. Cornelius, P. Volumnius, P. Albinova-
> nus et C. Iulius Caesar augur, qui eum inauguravit; in tertio triclinio Po-
> pilia, Perpennia, Licinia, Arruntia virgines Vestales et ipsius uxor Publicia
> flaminica et Sempronia socrus eius. cena haec fuit: ante cenam echinos, os-
> treas crudas quantum vellent, peloridas, sphondylos, turdum asparagos
> subtus, gallinam altilem, patinam ostrearum peloridum, balanos nigros,
> balanos albos; iterum sphondylos, glycomaridas, urticas, ficedulas, lumbos
> capruginos aprugnos, altilia ex farina involuta, ficedulas, murices et purpu-
> ras. in cena sumina, sinciput aprugnum, patinam piscium, patinam suminis,
> anates, querquedulas elixas, lepores, altilia assa, amulum, panes Picentes.

I refer to the long bygone banquet of the pontiff that is described in the
fourth volume of that supreme pontiff Metellus as follows: on Septem-
ber 22, on the day when Lentulus was inaugurated as Flamen Martialis,
his house was decorated, the triclinia of ivory were prepared. On two of the
triclinia reclined the Pontifices, Q. Catulus, M. Aemilius Lepidus, D. Sila-
nus, C. Caesar, the Rex Sacrorum [the name is missing], P. [Mucius] Scaevola coming sixth; [now the Pontifices minores are listed:] Q. Cornelius,
P. Volumnius, P. Albinovanus and the augur L. Iulius Caesar, who had inaugurated the Flamen. On the third bed the Vestal Virgins Popilia, Perpennia, Licinia, Arruntia, and his own wife, the Flaminica Publicia, and
Sempronia, his mother-in-law. This was the meal: before the main course,
sea urchin, raw oysters (as many as they wanted), giant mussels, mussels,
thrush under asparagus, fattened chicken, a bowl of oysters and giant mussels, black shellfish, white shellfish, again mussels, Venus mussels, stinging
nettle, fig thrushes, loin roast of goats and boar, fattened poultry coated with
breadcrumbs, again fig thrushes, two sorts of purple snails. For the main
course pork udder, head of boar, a bowl of fishes, a bowl of udder, ducks,
cooked crick ducks, rabbits, backed fattened poultry, wheat porridge.

---

30. Cf. Marinone 1970.

Despite its exceptional testimony, the quotation is not found in any modern collections of the fragments of priestly books. It seems to correspond too little to the expectations of philologists interested in the history of religion.[31] We find neither a close description of the inauguration nor one of the ritual constitution of the new priest performed by an augur; rather, we read of the sumptuous meal that the newly elected person offers to his colleagues, the *cena aditialis*, the inaugural meal. What is happening here?

The text registers those present by listing the names in a certain order. As evidenced in other texts,[32] strict attention was paid to seniority, as determined by the period of membership in a given college. Documenting the membership of a college and individual terms of office might have been among the most important interests of this type of text.[33] Religious change and modification are not immediately apparent objects of documentation. Yet it is the instantiation of an essentially variable part of the entire ritual that is described in minute detail. The text documents a nonsynchronic, culinary competition. Priestly meals had *potlatch* character: they were known for ostentatious extravagance and they were the stage for such lavish culinary innovations as established the peacock and the moray as foods of prestige.[34] Written records enabled these feasts to be publicized with a precision that rendered competition all the more fierce, and all the more worthwhile. However, the reduction of culinary luxury to the price paid for it, monetarization, so to speak, was not a desirable mode of documentation; such an approach belonged not to internal communication, but rather to satirical mockery and antiquarian sensation seeking.[35] To summarize my interpretation: precise documentation, especially of how the most variable elements of the ritual had been realized, opened an additional venue for rivalry within an aristocracy based on a competition for prestige.

We know little about the use and the circulation of the *commentarii* of the Pontifices Maximi.[36] They were not secret documents, nor were they

---

31. On the idea of priestly books, see the critical discussion of J. A. North 1998; Rüpke 2003b. Cf. Sini 1983.

32. As demonstrated by Taylor 1942.

33. See Rüpke 1993.

34. See Rüpke 1998a, 200–201.

35. See Sen. *Ep.* 95.41 for a "million-dollar meal"; for a discussion of this motif in different genres, see Rüpke 2015d.

36. Cf. J. A. North 1998; see also Scheid 1998c.

internal to the committee. This is demonstrated by the famous *tabulae dealbatae*, the whitened wood panels, which were displayed before the house of the Pontifex Maximus. At least the abstracts of the protocols copied onto these tables were addressed to a public audience, as is attested by the tradition of their supposed publication by Publius Mucius Scaevola.[37] As far as the records of Metellus Pius are concerned, current or future colleagues were also likely potential readers. (Antiquarians would constitute a further, secondary audience.) These men were at very least aware of the existence of these records. Writing raised the details of a particular ritual performance into the sphere of permanently documented ritual, which fact surely influenced the hosts of events such as *cenae aditiales*: competition could now be waged via a medium both more stable and more predictable than unsupported memory.

The lengthy record of ritual details is exceptional in the case of the meal described above, but not isolated. Comparable examples of documentation can be found for ritual performances in a very different field—performances that were, nevertheless, enacted by the same class of people. Appian's description of the triumphal procession of Pompey closely matches the pattern of the description of the pontiffs' meal:[38] here again, it is the actual performance, the details of the procession of 63 BC that are the subject matter. By contrast, scarcely anything can be learned about what scholars usually like to conceive of as serious, invariant ritual. The similarities between the *commentarii pontificum* and Appian's description show that such a selective view of rituals was not exclusive either to antiquarian accounts or to historiography.

Fictitious Rituals and Ritual Performance

Texts do not just comment on rituals and ascribe "meaning" to them; the producers of text could also invent rituals. In doing this, they were surely directed by their own ritual competence[39] and culturally received ideas about ritualization and the logic of ritual, but they must also have been prompted

---

37. See Frier 1979; Rüpke 1993.
38. App. *Mith.* 116–17.
39. See E. Thomas Lawson 1990; McCauley 2002.

by their personal agenda in writing history.[40] A text may, in such cases, be an element of the cultural environment for ritual action, or even, as I will demonstrate, for ritual invention. Religion, as it turns out, allowed less prominent traditional and juridical acts to be ritualized on a grand scale.

The text in question is a passage in Livy's *Roman History*.[41] It concerns the procedure for the Roman (and, Livy imagines, typically Latin) declaration of war on other peoples:

> Legatus ubi ad fines eorum uenit unde res repetuntur, capite uelato filo—lanae uelamen est—"audi, Iuppiter" inquit; "audite, fines"—cuiuscumque gentis sunt, nominat—; "audiat fas. ego sum publicus nuntius populi Romani; iuste pieque legatus uenio, uerbisque meis fides sit." peragit deinde postulata. inde Iouem testem facit: "si ego iniuste impieque illos homines illasque res dedier mihi exposco, tum patriae compotem me nunquam siris esse." haec, cum fines suprascandit, haec, quicumque ei primus uir obuius fuerit, haec portam ingrediens, haec forum ingressus, paucis uerbis carminis concipiend-ique iuris iurandi mutatis, peragit. si non deduntur quos exposcit diebus tri-bus et triginta—tot enim sollemnes sunt—peractis bellum ita indicit: "audi, Iuppiter, et tu, Iane Quirine, dique omnes caelestes, uosque terrestres uosque inferni, audite; ego uos testor populum illum"—quicumque est, nominat—"iniustum esse neque ius persoluere; sed de istis rebus in patria maiores natu consulemus, quo pacto ius nostrum adipiscamur."

> When the legate arrives at the frontier of those from whom restitution is de-manded, he covers his head with a fillet (the covering is of wool) and says:[42] "Hear thou, Jupiter, hear ye, boundaries of"—naming whatever nation they belong to—"let divine law hear! I am the official herald of the Roman people; I come lawfully and piously commissioned, let there be trust in my words." Then he sets forth his demands, after which he takes Jupiter to wit-ness: "If I unjustly and impiously demand that these men and these goods be surrendered to me, then never let me be a full citizen of my fatherland."[43] He recites these words when he crosses the boundary-line, again to the first person he encounters, again when proceeding through the town-gate, and

---

40. See Certeau 1988.

41. Liv. 1.32.6–10 and (below) 12–14. The translation is that of Beard, North, and Price 1998, vol. 2, nr. 1.4a.

42. Here, the text oscillates between a general formula and the description of a (pseudo-) historical event.

43. This is a form of self-cursing that strengthens the justification of the claim.

again when he enters the market-place. . . . If his demands are not met, at
the end of 33 days—for such is the customary number—he declares war as
follows: "Hear thou, Jupiter, and thou, Janus Quirinus, and all ye heavenly
gods, and ye terrestrial gods, and ye infernal gods, hear! I call you to witness that this people"—naming whatever people it is—"is unjust and does
not render just reparation. But regarding these matters we will consult the
elders in our fatherland, how we may acquire our due."

The subsequent declaration of war (32.12–14) ends with an elaborate ritual:

Fieri solitum ut fetialis hastam ferratam aut praeustam sanguineam ad
fines eorum ferret et non minus tribus pueribus praesentibus diceret: "quod
populi Priscorum Latinorum hominesque Prisci Latini aduersus popu-
lum Romanum Quiritium fecerunt deliquerunt, quod populus Romanus
Quiritium bellum cum Priscis Latinis iussit esse senatusque populi Romani
Quiritium censuit consensit consciuit ut bellum cum Priscis Latinis fieret,
ob eam rem ego populusque Romanus populis Priscorum Latinorum hom-
inibusque Priscis Latinis bellum indico facioque." id ubi dixisset, hastam in
fines eorum emittebat. hoc tum modo ab Latinis repetitae res ac bellum in-
dictum, moremque eum posteri acceperunt.

The usual procedure was for the fetialis to carry to the boundary of the other
nation a spear of iron or fire-hardened cornel-wood,[44] and in the presence
of not fewer than three adult males,[45] to say: "Forasmuch as the tribes of the
Ancient Latins and men of the Ancient Latins have committed act and offence against the Roman people, and forasmuch as the Roman people have
ordained that war be declared on the Ancient Latins, and the senate of the
Roman people has affirmed, agreed, and with their votes approved that there
be war with the ancient Latins, I, therefore, and the Roman people, declare
and make war on the tribes of the Ancient Latins and the men of the Ancient
Latins." Having said this, he would hurl the spear across their boundary.[46]

Of course, the alleged performance of the eighth century BC is a fiction.
But neither was the ritual described above ever practiced, as I have argued

---

44. It was considered "fact" in Augustan times that the use of iron was preceded by weapons
hardened by fire.

45. This was a basic rule for legitimizing witnesses in Roman legal procedures.

46. Cf. Gell. *NA* 16.4.1 (Cincius); for the relationship between Livy and Cincius, see Rüpke
1990, 104–5.

elsewhere.[47] Authorial "knowledge" of prehistory is established in the narrative by the integration of elements that are known from (much later) legal procedures, such as, for example, the necessary numbers of witnesses, and an intense atmosphere of ritualization is created by frequent use of repetition and symmetry.

The resulting "ritual" in Livy is a fictitious one, but it did not remain in the realm of the imaginary. The dynamics of individual appropriation went far beyond literary invention. This fictitious ritual was quoted ritually, that is, it formed the basis for a remarkable historical performance: in 32 BC, Octavian in his capacity as fetial priest and by throwing a spear, declared war against the *foreigner* Cleopatra and thereby marked the beginning of the decisive phase of the civil war against his *Roman* rival Mark Antony.[48] Ritualization set the tone for this conflict and its representation in the city of Rome, and it cloaked the dreadful fact of civil war in the symbolism of conflict with foreign peoples. The ritual was repeated at least one more time, in AD 178: Marcus Aurelius, in exact imitation of Augustus's procedure, declared war on the Scythians by throwing a spear at the *columna bellica* near the temple of Bellona.[49] The narrow time frame in which we find the earliest testimonies for Fetials throwing a spear—Cincius (difficult to date exactly) and Livy were both late first-century BC authors—and the Augustan ritual evince the entanglement of written text and performance. A textually circulated, fictitious ritual set the interpretive horizon for a ritual that was intended to exonerate the official war strategy of the charge of initiating civil war.

The fiction in its perfection allowed for greater complexity and coherency than a concrete ritual. At the same time, it also radically limited the latter's horizons of interpretation: Octavian, soon-to-be Augustus, wore a *paludamentum* (military cloak) when he threw the spear, thus identifying himself in fact as a soldier and situating his performance in an older tradition of military symbolism, which the antiquarian M. Terentius Varro had just recently presented in the treatise *Calenus*.[50] But this "frame"

---

    47. Rüpke 1990, 104–5.

    48. Dio Cass. 50.4.4–5.

    49. Dio Cass. 72.33.3. For the column and the fictitious territory of enemies in Rome, see Serv. (auct.) *Aen.* 9.52. The historicity of the founding event of the time of the war against Pyrrhus as claimed by Dio has been refuted by Latte (1960, 122, n. 3).

    50. The fragment is preserved in Serv. *Aen.* 9.52; see Wiedemann 1986; Rüpke 1987. Further evidence for the ritual is given by Jocelyn 1971.

disappeared completely from later interpretations in the period following the Augustan ritual performance.

Guiding Individual Appropriation of Religious Roles

An even closer interdependence between the textual representation of ritual and the performance of ritual was possible. In the sanctuary complex
of the priesthood of the Fratres Arvales, a few miles outside of Rome, the
members of the priesthood performed their rituals alongside walls that
were inscribed with the *acta*, the chronicles of these very rituals in previous years. As I will argue, such an enormous epigraphical effort was pursued in this remote place in an attempt to guide individual appropriation
of the priestly role.

We know almost nothing about the activities or composition of the
Arvales during the republican period, except that they must have existed.
From this total *obscuritas* they emerge in the Augustan era as a high-ranking
priestly group that typically seems to have counted the Augusti and their
designated successors among its members.[51] Nevertheless, with respect to
ritual, their activities in Rome were limited to a brief sequence of games
that were held annually in the city, while their regular cult was concentrated in an area outside the town, in the grove of Dea Dia. Even today, La
Magliana is the outermost border of the urban area.

The complex, in operation for over three hundred years, was by no
means attractive to a wider public, neither in terms of cult nor architecture. It was, perhaps, even intentionally closed to the public. The
construction of baths in Severan times marked the largest architectonic
expansion.[52] But all this is secondary to the epigraphical fact. The tran-
scriptions of the records of this priesthood onto stone provide what is possibly the largest coherent complex of inscriptions of the ancient Roman
world.[53]

---

51. Not only has John Scheid presented a new edition of the inscriptions (Scheid 1998b), but
he has also made them accessible as a central source for the reconstruction of Roman religion in
his monographs, prosopographies, and articles: Scheid 1990a, 1975, 1990b. Also, cf. Beard 1985.

52. See Broise and Scheid 1987; Scheid 1990a, 69–70, 95–172.

53. New edition and French translation by Scheid 1998a.

The following extract is representative of the material found in the shrine area itself:

> [Is]dem co(n)s(ulibus) nonis Aprilib(us) [L. Calpurnius L. f(ilius)] Piso magister collegii fratrum arualium nomine immolauit [in Capitolio ex] s(enatus) c(onsulto) ob supplicationes indictas pro salute Neronis Claudi Caesar(is) [Aug(usti) Germ(anici) I]oui bouem marem, Iunoni uaccam, Mineruae uaccam, Saluti [publicae uaccam,] Prouidentiae uaccam, Genio ipsius taurum, diuo Aug(usto) bouem marem. [In co]llegio adfuerunt C. Vipstan[i]us Apronianus co(n)s(ul), P. Memmiu(s) [Regulus, L. Sal]uius Otho Titianus, Sulpicius Camerinus.

> Under the same consuls, on the Nones of April [April 5], Lucius Calpurnius Piso, the son of Lucius, the *magister* of the college, sacrificed in the name of the Arval brethren on the Capitol on the basis of a *senatus consultum* because of the supplications announced on behalf of the health of Nero Claudius Caesar Augustus named Germanicus: a male cow to Jupiter, a female cow to Juno, a female cow to Minerva, a female cow to Public Health, a female cow to Providence, a bull to his Genius, a male cow for the divine Augustus. Present in the college were the consul C. Vipstanius Apronianus, P. Memmius Regulus, L. Salvius Otho Titianus, Sulpicius Camerinus.[54]

The excerpt is a part of the records for AD 60. It demonstrates the attention to details of the ritual performance (location, participants, text of the prayer) that is typical of the *acta* as a whole. The text was produced or edited directly after the event by a slave who was in charge of the records.[55] At the end of each year, the entire annual record would then be transcribed onto stone. The fixing of the ritual in writing gained ritual character itself: the use of stone tools in the sanctuary—essential for producing inscriptions on marble slabs—was cause for an expiation ritual.[56] Piece by piece, these texts embellished the walls of the buildings.

What purpose did this serve? The texts could hardly be intended to instruct new priests: rituals were typically recorded in summary fashion. Indeed, the famous *carmen Arvale*, a song text that is difficult, if

---

54. *Acta arvalia* 28 a–c, 10–16 Scheid.

55. Scheid quite rightly points out that, for pragmatic reasons, a codex must be assumed to have preceded the inscriptions (Scheid 1990a, 69).

56. See ibid., 56–57, 86–88 for details.

not impossible, to understand, was entrusted to the record literally for the first time at the beginning of the third century AD.[57] Thus, the epigraphical texts were present during the ritual, but were not suitable as scripts, as guidance for performing the ritual. Since a wide public was not expected, the necessity for a symbolic interpretation of the texts is widely agreed on.[58]

John Scheid seeks an explanation in the ownership of the location and its architecture by the deity Dea Dia, ritually underlined by the expiation rituals (*piacula*), which acknowledged the presence and attention of the deity. Accordingly, Scheid regards the texts as documentation, composed for the deity's benefit, of dutiful fulfillment of her cult.[59] As such, these *acta* would parallel dedicatory inscriptions in other sanctuaries. However, any formula or note to this purpose is lacking. There is no documentation of success or gratitude, no praise of the goddess, no vaunting her power to new visitors as in other sanctuaries. The placement of the epigraphs, making them not part of an inner sanctuary, but a constitutive element of the ensemble, does not support this thesis either.[60] The richness of detail and the exceptional abundance of the epigraphic corpus would, furthermore, remain unexplained. I would maintain, rather, that the epigraphs found not only their authors but also their primary public within the members of the priesthood itself.

But to what effect would the Arvals read the inscription? From the Augustan period onward—we have no traces of earlier epigraphic culture from this site—the performance of rituals, the whole activity of the priesthood, took place in an environment that was emphatically marked by the documentation, the scriptuality, of former performances of this ritual. The readers of the inscriptions were exactly the persons who also performed the documented acts. One cannot separate the one from the other. Once more: the records themselves are too brief to secure the invariability of ritual details. What they did secure was the ritual quality of new acts. These *acta* must have been viewed by the participants in each new ritual act, and the new act was thus defined as a repetition of strict sequences of previous

57. *AA* 100a. 32–38 Scheid.
58. Scheid 1990a, 67, with reference to Beard 1985, 137–44.
59. Scheid 1990a, 70.
60. Thus Scheid 1990a.

acts. That is, it attained the character of ritual. Thus the mere presence of the *acta* guaranteed a high degree of ritualization.

"Repetition," however, is valid only in a restricted way. The term needs two qualifications. First, the *Acta arvalia* documented different types of rituals. Each particular ritual became more narrowly defined by its differences relative to other performances and became a distinct part of a complex and therefore demanding ritual system. Even the production of the inscription was addressed through a ritual that offered to the goddess of the grove an expiatory sacrifice to atone for the iron tools that had been brought into her domain for the purpose of chiseling letters.[61]

The second qualification concerns exactitude of repetition. The text of the epigraph offered records of actual performances, not a timeless liturgical form. Differentiation was produced by lists of names of all the participants and by exact dating. Typically, it was the Arval brothers themselves that were named, but we also occasionally find minor officials listed: senatorial boys (*pueri*), freedmen (*kalatores*) or public slaves (*servi publici*) of various functions, e.g., the record taker (*a commentariis*). It was not "the priesthood of the Arvals," but single Arvals (or assistants) that performed the religious duties entrusted to this *sodalitas*. Only writing could preserve these distinctions over time. This interpretation is supported by the results of Mary Beard, who investigated the correlation between a decline (albeit slight) in the priesthood's prestige and an increase in the number of ritual details supplied; this correlation is most clearly visible in texts from the early third century.[62]

The underlying text of the inscriptions, the *commentarii* of the Arvals, corresponds approximately, both in form and in institutional status, to the *commentarius* of the Pontifex Maximus treated above. Publication did not alter the form or content of the text, but it did have a decisive influence on its pragmatics. The formulation of individual or gentilician demands, the repetitive—that is, ritual—character of acts was not merely potentially visible, but was present in the ritual space itself. No menu lists can be found in the *Acta arvalia*. The documentation was restricted to the presence of individuals at routine rituals and special occasions (*vota*) that demonstrated loyalty to the imperial dynasty. Why?

---

61. E.g., *AA* 59.2, 36–41; 94.3, 19–25; 95c Scheid and passim: *ob ferrum inlatum et elatum scalpturae et scripturae* . . . (or similar expressions).

62. Beard 1985, 131–35.

Modern research has often characterized the cult of the Arvals with reference to its archaic elements: the prohibition against iron, the incomprehensible and archaic language of the *carmen Arvale*.[63] The epigraphic embellishment of the complex, visibly no older than the Augustan era[64] and including dates only of the most recent past (i.e., the previous year), does not fit this image. What is apparent instead is the affiliation with a tradition, the growth of which is measurable in terms of marble slabs covered with protocols. It is striking that over time the focus of documentation (excepting the constant details of dates and attendance) even shifts from the variable to the fixed elements of rituals. Increasingly, the extensive citation of the prayers offered on various occasions (along with the corresponding combinations of gods invoked and sacrificial animals) that we find from the first century gives way to the extensive and stereotypical description of ritual details of the third century AD. We can even detect more specific interests in later inscriptions. A close investigation cannot ignore, for example, the extensive treatment of purification rites in the third century, an interest that might very well have been related to other contemporary religious developments.[65] Despite the fact that the rituals remained constant, the written documentation reveals a shift from expressions of imperial loyalty to theurgic concerns—and, presumably, a corresponding shift in how the participants perceived their role. The quality of the performance was altered by its public documentation. Here, the slow shift in religious traditions interacted with the individual Arval's appropriation of his religious role, while the marble letters documenting his activities guaranteed the dignity of this role. It is not fortuitous that a newly refounded, topographically marginalized priesthood produced the most extensive of all records of priestly activities.

Collective Performance Replaced by Individual Reading

Reading, then, informed ritual action. It could even replace actual ritual action. The development of the Roman calendar in the late republican

---

63. Latte 1960, 65–66; more detailed, Scheid 1997.

64. The oldest inscription contains fragments of the protocol of 21 BC: *AA* 1.1–4 Scheid = *CIL* 6.32338.

65. See P. Brown 1988.

and early imperial years attests a religious dynamic that allowed individual reading to supplement or replace collective performance, thus expanding the possibilities for individual appropriations of ritual traditions. This was enabled, to be exact, by the production of a graphical representation of a calendar that listed *all* the days of a year and organized them in a clearly structured way, in terms of months—a direct ancestor of our modern calendar.[66] In this, Roman calendars were unique in the ancient Mediterranean world.

The Roman calendar in the form of the *fasti* included a wealth of religious, or, more specifically, ritual information. Days that were (by analogy to plots of land) the property of individual gods and therefore restricted for human use *(feriae)* were marked with names and abbreviations that could easily be associated with corresponding ceremonial rituals. Additionally, the foundation dates of temples and their anniversaries were listed, usually involving larger ceremonies *in situ.*[67]

The relationship between this text and the performances needs elucidation. It might be surprising, but it should be remarked all the more: the relationship between the calendar and ritual is not normative. It is easy to *associate* the ritual, but actual ritual data form no part of the *fasti.* Nor should we assign to them a function comparable to that of the so-called Attic calendars of demes: the latter were simply lists of ceremonies and the particular days on which they occurred, specific to the deme concerned. They included statements of the appropriate sacrificial animals that were intended to regulate the corresponding financial duties of certain districts or persons.[68] By contrast, it is the uniformity of Roman calendars that is most astonishing: the preserved inscriptions differ only in size or quality of the stone, but not in content, regardless of whether they were situated in a temple, a building of an association, or a private house. We almost never find even a hint that there was a specific cult associated with such a place.[69]

---

66. For the history of the reception of the Roman calendar, see Rüpke 2006a.

67. See Rüpke 2011b. This type of documentation was probably nonexistent before the second century BC.

68. For a summary treatment, see Dow 1968; Whitehead 1986, 185–208; Parker 1996, 43–55.

69. For the following, more details are given by Rüpke 2011b, 8–18; the texts were edited by Degrassi 1963.

Fasti Verolani, January through March. Early first century AD. Photo by G. Radke.

This characterization is true of both Roman calendars and the copies found outside Rome. Of the approximately fifty copies that have been found (mostly in fragmentary state), almost one half are from the city of Rome, while the remainder come largely from Latium, Etruria, and Campania. The only exceptions in Italy are the so-called Fasti Guidizzolenses from the region of Brixia. The southernmost example, the Fasti Tauromenitani, belongs to the Augustan colony Tauromenium of Sicily. This is the only copy that has been found outside Italy.[70]

We assume the primarily local character of ancient societies, yet the ceremony list containing the *fasti* of Urbinum Metaurense in north Umbria is identical with the list of the *fasti* from Venusia. The dates mentioned are Roman dates, even in copies of obscure Italian municipalities. The inscriptions do not even *add* data regarding local or regional festivals or rituals. In all the extant copies there is only one example of such supplementation:[71] Verrius Flaccus, the author of the *Fasti Praenestini* and an Augustan scholar, adds two local events to the list of Roman activities. This, however, occurs in a calendar that is already unusual for other reasons: it is the only calendar that connects the reproduction of the Roman *fasti* with a continuing commentary on these *fasti*.

The temporal distribution of the calendars is significant. The oldest Roman *fasti* must have been created by around 170 BC. These would have supplied the blueprint for the painted wall calendar found at Antium.[72] The oldest marble version comes from the shrine of the Arvals in Rome, which might have been reorganized by Augustus around 30 BC. This calendar was created very soon after Augustus's victory at Actium.[73] Urban copies remained predominant in the following period; only few calendars from Latium, Etruria, or Campania date to the Augustan period. But by the rule of Tiberius, they had spread over all of central Italy—and then proliferation ceased.

The information conveyed in the calendars also parallels the expansion of the imperial cult. Already in the Augustan period, the calendar of

70. For the particularities of this calendar, especially the attempt to combine the Roman calendar with a local Greek lunisolar calendar, see Rüpke 1995, 133–38; Ruck 1996.

71. The local character of the *dies vern(arum)* in the *Fasti Antiates ministrorum* is doubtful. See Rüpke 1995, 144–45.

72. Ibid., 346–52, 366–67.

73. Ibid., 178.

festivals was filled with a vast quantity of imperial data, from birthdays and days of accessions to power, to weddings and victories and, last but not least, disclosures of conspiracies.[74] Usually, these new dates did not acquire abbreviated festival names but were marked by the addition of short explanations for the new legal character of the day: *feriae, quod eo die* . . . (for instance, "this day is a day of the gods, because on this day Caesar occupied Alexandria"). Such is the pattern for many of the dates. Within a few years, this manner of registration lent the *fasti* a specific profile.

As argued previously, such a calendar of urban, Roman dates cannot be a prescriptive text for cult in, for instance, Antium. Considering the (frequently considerable) distances between such places and Rome and the lack of precise information conveyed, it could not even have supplied useful information on Roman cults for travelers planning to go to Rome. The calendar is, rather, a medium for representing imperial festivities, days of victories, honors, births, and the like, irrespective of the actual location of the reader; that is to say, it is independent of performance. Reading such a text afforded awareness of a date, even on another day. In terms of the individual appropriation of an imperial and metropolitan ritual tradition by reading, it was probably not the isolated information on single days that was important, but rather, a careful or cursory reading of the complex text of the *fasti* in its entirety. Of course, even more significant would be the production of such a text—to pay for its engraving and to design a headline or to have further information added. This allowed individual expression of loyalty, consent, and assimilation to the Augustan system. To put it anachronistically, there was no need to participate in celebrations; it was enough to hang posters.[75] The act of displaying such a calendar was the most important performance, permanently remembered by the monument itself, and actualized by its reading. This opened a new perspective for imperial communication: rituals might be created in order to ensure their representation in calendars. Attempts to "occupy" and "redefine" certain dates[76] might have had just such a motive.

---

74. See Herz 1978.
75. See Rüpke 2011b, 124–39. For such processes of medialization, see Galinsky 1996.
76. See Herz 1978.

If the image of Roman religion as a ritual system is to be replaced by an attempt to understand ancient religious practices and ideas as lived ancient religion, textualized practices are of primary importance. Not only does the "record" offer us glimpses into varying contemporary views on the complexity and malleability of religious practices (as well as their intellectual and emotional characteristics), but the very production of text adds to this complexity: its consumption informs individuals' appropriation of traditional religious practices, and perhaps incites them to modify old practices, or even invent new ones. Thus, the perspective of lived ancient religion does not simply supplement a previous reconstruction of a ritual system; rather, it renders the description more historical and more dynamic. Those who were entitled to conduct *auspicia* were the same people listening to Ennius's *Annales*; ambitious pontiffs were familiar with the records of the Pontifex Maximus; civil war generals read Varro and Livy or their sources; the nobles of the uppermost or upward-oriented echelons of society who very occasionally adopted the ritual role of an Arval were the ones who were able to read the Arval records; Italians newly defining their relationship to Rome and the emperors studied or produced copies of the *fasti*. These texts were also composed with such an audience in mind—sometimes exclusively. Text and ritual were interdependent contexts for ritual performance and for the reception of text respectively. Hence they shaped religion with a potency greater than that of mere intellectual attribution of sense or the preservation and transmission of knowledge. The coupling of ritual and exegesis in traditional scholarship did not sufficiently capture this relationship.

Communication about ritual—in historical matters, specifically *written* communication about ritual—was an inseparable part of ritual. As a consequence, I have proposed a modification of the term "ritual," which tends to imply a normative, repeated structure of acts, a script, or an ontology independent of any instantiated action. The term "performance," by contrast, lays open a perspective on the actualization of ritual, not just on individual variants, but also on interpretations and individual motivations—individual appropriations that inform ritual action and are informed by communication about ritual. For a performance to be characterized as ritual, it was not important that the act was repeated stereotypically, but that the performers and/or observers were aware of or assumed such a character: *ritualization* rather than *ritual*. Only thus is the quality of ritual guaranteed for the dining pontifical committee; only thus the ritual quality of the Arval *acta* increases the dignity of the priests' actions; thus, even the isolated spear throwing of Octavian could be a ritual as well as an individual and highly original appropriation of military and religious traditions.

7

RELIGIOUS COMMUNICATION

The mechanisms analyzed in the previous chapters (exercise and de-limitation of choice, individual appropriation of tradition, use of images, and the interplay of discourse and action) are not exclusive to religion and religious ritual; they can also be found in other areas of cultural practice. What I take to be specific for religion in antiquity (as I describe it) is a form of communication that extends beyond the interchange of authors and readers. It is a communication that refers to or directly addresses agents who are frequently, but not inevitably, personalized and who are not within the circle of those who are unquestionably present or relevant to a given situation. These were superhuman agents, or perhaps formerly alive but now dead human agents. The human actor who introduced such agents and chose this mode of action, enlarged her or his own agency, either by forging an alliance with the divine or by reducing the agency of other human actors as a result of the superior capacities of the god(s) in determining a course of events. Such action, however, bears a social risk, as others might deny the relevance of the specific divine agent, or even of any divine agency. It is exactly the uncertainty about whether a *not* unquestionably plausible agent is introduced that accounts for the potential as well as powerlessness of religion. Such action also bears a religious risk, as the divine agent might not attend to the human address. Again, it is the uncertain outcome of this move that makes it seem either dangerous and potentially powerful or simply futile.[1] As in all human communication, the human initiator is obliged to make his or her addressee aware of the communication and to signal to and persuade the addressee of the relevancy of the communicative effort and message.[2] Religious communication, thus, is not concerned with correctness; rather, it is concerned with success and how to achieve it. It is the individual who is obliged to identify the most successful way to make the gods (to use a standard example) aware of the communicative intention and to make the contents of this communication (the message) relevant and, hence, hopefully successful. Additionally, the individual is responsible for making others—allies, enemies, or mere bystanders—aware that this is happening and might be successful. Originality might be a conspicuous way to make this plausible, but repeating methods that had proven successful in the past, in other words, falling back on shared cultural knowledge, on traditions, would surely be even better. In relation to the gods, it is not the isolated individual, but the individual in society, that is the subject of lived religion, even if companionship with the gods is chosen over human fellowship. It is this modeling that helps us understand the mechanism of a ritual practice that is both highly individual and, at the same time, merely an instance of mass production and seemingly uniform religiosity: vows and dedications.

Why do we speak of vows and dedications? Of course, these are the practices found in our sources: a human being was in need, he or she uttered a wish to a deity, promised something if help or relief were given, the situation improved, and thanks were gratefully given to the god. Ancient theoreticians conceive of this process in juridical terms: after the promise, the vower is *voti reus*, "accused with regard to the vow," that is, under obligation to it, and after fulfillment on the part of the god, even *voti damnatus*, "penalized by the vow."[3] Fulfillment on the part of the human is

---

1. Rüpke 2015b.
2. See Sperber and Wilson 1994; Wilson and Sperber 2002, 2012.
3. Serv. *Aen.* 4,699; Livy 7.28.4; see Rüpke 2004, 181.

expressed as *votum solvere*, "to discharge the vow," and *v(otum) s(olvit) l(ubens) m(erito)*, "s/he discharged the vow with pleasure as the god had earned it," is a formula that accompanied the resulting dedications. Dedications were also juridical actions: the very word *dedico* denotes a transfer of property, from the individual's estate to that of the god. Georg Wissowa, in the chapter of his handbook *Religion und Kultus der Römer* titled "The Fundamentals of Sacred Law,"[4] took pains to differentiate between this sort of private dedication and the transfer of public property to the gods to which he—in accordance with credible sources—ascribed the quality of *consecratio*. Now, all these distinctions function on the basis of the actors' knowledge about the gods and their property rights. But from where did they obtain this knowledge? Obviously not from religious instruction in school,[5] but rather from observing the procedures of others, for example, from reading *tituli* (the inscriptions affixed to dedicated objects). Perhaps a term like local "microtradition" might better characterize these procedures and serve to avoid the interpretive distortions that result from tallying instances of certain formulas and practices as if they were mutually independent. The distinctions of the object language are part of the reality in which they function.

Is this not true for every cultural system? I will not deny that I am very sympathetic to the linguistic turn and this type of constructivist stance, but such a generalization begs the essential question. We are dealing with a specific problem of the historical religion we are analyzing (even if this problem is not restricted to the religion of the Romans). The concepts of giving and property transfer function within a framework that is not as straightforward as it might seem. Representations of the divine were themselves emphatically deemed not divine, as ancient discourse about statues demonstrates.[6] To a large extent divinities were modeled on superior humans, but the divine superiors were not similarly tangible; rather, they might need to be manifested through *epikleisis*.[7] And yet, statues of the gods were clothed and combed, bound or flogged.[8] Of course, as a

---

4. Wissowa 1912 (repr., 1971), 380–409.
5. For exceptions, see Cancik 1973.
6. See Gordon 1979.
7. Gladigow 2005, 75–77.
8. Ibid., 64–67.

discipline the history of religion usually adopts a methodological agnosticism that disposes of many such problematic inconsistencies. There is no need, for example, to deal with the problem of why vowers who deprived the gods of their due were not subject to divine retribution. However, the problem of how to describe such apparent contradictions remains.

Obviously, the idea of a divine associate who expects recompense and that of divine property are highly loaded with assumptions about the divine; these must be held conceptually distinct, from practices such as gift (*donum*) or prayer (*preces*) or simply words (*verba*).[9] In the following analysis I will address these phenomena through the lens of "communication."[10] Unlike "system" or "culture" or "ius sacrum" (not an ancient concept), communication starts from the intersubjectively constituted individual. This is also true of "agency" (a concept helpful for understanding appropriation), but communication, more so than agency, points to interaction, and to the problem of understanding and of misunderstanding. Communication establishes structures and traditions, but these remain precarious, perhaps based on old or newly arising misunderstandings, and are subject to diverse individual appropriation.

Unfortunately, we cannot observe ancient religious communication. The human actors are long dead (even if their gods enjoy an increasing internet presence). Sadly, most of the material remains, the sources on the basis of which ancient religion can be reconstructed, were in fact used in religious communication, were parts of acts of communication, and were loaded with intentions, meanings, and emotions, much of which is lost to us.

A Model of Religious Communication

How, then, should we describe ancient religious communication? Essentially, there was a human sender and his or her divine recipient. The sender attempted to transfer a signal, intending it to be received as information or as a script for action. But how could it be determined that the

---

9. For the concept of "gift" in general, see still Mauss 1925; for prayer, Pulleyn 1997; Fyntikoglou and Voutiras 2005.

10. For the sociological background of the concept, see Rüpke 2001.

signal had arrived and had been understood? And how could the message be made relevant?

Concentrating on Roman standard procedures, there was a vast array of strategies. The choice of location, for example, was important.[11] A raised platform would improve performance, as would a sacred area or temple. Timing was also important: the calendar regulated the opening of temples, and special occasions were set aside for specific requests, such as a good harvest, disease-free crops, or successful business ventures.[12] Multichanneling was another strategy: words were enhanced by gifts. Sound was combined with smell, rising smoke with the downpour of liquids. In many instances word choice explicitly points to the agents' reflection on the communicative problem: *audi* is a common exclamation in Latin prayers, and *epêkoos*, "the god who hears," is an important Greek cult title from Hellenistic times onward.[13] Representations of ears might even be offered as a gift.[14] Standard procedures, tested and hallowed by tradition, or just reported to be effective,[15] were employed, and action was thereby ritualized.[16] Occasionally ritual specialists were deployed, but their role tended to remain restricted in Roman antiquity.[17] The professionalism of Egyptian magicians is in stark contrast to the do-it-yourself curse tablets of the West, as mentioned earlier.

As the desired response would be delayed, checks were introduced. Divination, frequently considered an exotic and marginal feature of ancient religions, was in fact central to many rituals.[18] In a form of metacommunication, oracles were addressed to improve ritual communication. Successful transmission of the signal during animal sacrifice was regularly assessed through scrutiny of the liver or other entrails.[19] Because animal

---

11. An overview is given in *ThesCRA* 4 (2005), "Cult Places," 1–361.

12. For the establishment of cultic calendars, see Rüpke 1995, 547–62 and 523–40.

13. Versnel 1981, 34.

14. Ibid., 36. This might be a specific appropriation or profiling of sanctuary space, which was thus marked out as holding greater importance—beyond that of the statue—for communicative processes. I am grateful to Valentino Gasparini, who inspired me to develop this idea (see Gasparini 2016).

15. Ando 2008, 13, argues for the importance of the empirical dimension of Roman ritual.

16. See C. Bell, e.g., Bell 1992.

17. See Rüpke 1996b.

18. See Belayche and Rüpke 2007 and Rosenberger 2013b for the centrality of divinatory practices, and Belayche et al. 2005a for an overview of Roman forms.

19. Gladigow 2000.

sacrifice was a very costly form of signaling, it was therefore as much a clear indicator of relevance to the gods as an arrogation of agency with regard to the fellow human beings who were involved as the indirect beneficiaries of the sacrificial meal. Again, the risky nature of the communication is apparent:[20] pains are taken to exclude disturbances and eliminate mistakes, and yet the very performance of such risk management construes the communication as risky. An inappropriate or incorrect utterance during the ceremony, an agent's ominous name, a slip of tongue or foot: communication could be imperiled in countless ways.[21]

The ritual communication described so far was generically furthered by materialization and monumentalization, thus conferring prominence on the message and indicating its relevance. It was surely reassuring to use the temples and statues built by others for one's own attempts at communication; this enhanced the plausibility of new communicative efforts in the eyes of both the agents and their observers.[22] In accordance with the strategies mentioned above, temples could be named as locations and statues as addressees. But these were not *ab initio* creations: they were not simply built and dedicated, but they were themselves the products of acts of communication. Temples in Rome were built in fulfillment of vows.[23] Statues and other images were the most visible signs of the presence of the gods. (Sometimes they even acknowledged a prayer by a small movement of their eyes.)[24] They often were objects of thanksgiving,[25] promised in a vow or added to a prayer. Thus, the production of the most visible form of the addressee is both a result of communication and the precondition for further successful, and less risky, communication. Understanding this communicative circle is important to the issue of *ex post* differentiation between so-called cult statues and dedicated images,[26] or between promised dedications and spontaneous gifts. These monuments, however, might suggest that religious resources were unlimited. The risks of inflationary

---

20. Rüpke in Belayche et al. 2005a, 83.
21. For an analysis of Pliny the Elder's description of this problem, see Köves-Zulauf 1972.
22. Mylonopoulos 2006 points to the "visual experience of myths in a framework of mimetic representation."
23. See Pietilä-Castrén 1987; Orlin 1997.
24. See Gordon 1979.
25. Van Straten 1981, in particular 81; cf. Boardman et al. 2004, 316.
26. See Scheer 2000 ("*Kultbild*" vs. "*Weihgeschenk*").

Monopteros temple in Tivoli, entrance with the door of 5.5 x 2.4 meters.
End of second century BC. Photo by J. Rüpke.

devaluation and indifference were therefore countered by reduction in and control over accessibility: the size of doors, enlarged central *intercolumnia*, or fences within the *cella* (the inner room of the temple) could open or restrict access to the most important symbol of divine presence.[27]

An initial conclusion can be drawn from these general observations regarding vows: ritual communication was not just a sequence of prayers, vows, thanksgiving, and—often directly appended—new prayers.[28] The materialization of this process was the construction of a religious infrastructure that made communicative efforts plausible and provided them a channel. Such infrastructure, however, could not prevent the proliferation of religious communication outside of the monumental and beautiful sanctuaries that had been financed by the political elite. Nor could it halt its spread outside of the city. Thus, we must direct our attention to "cheap"

---

27. Mattern 2006, 171–72, 175.
28. See, e.g., van Straten 1981, 74.

religion: the appropriation of nonelite spaces, and the forms of communication practiced in such spaces. For most people, monumental expression was economically unfeasible and not part of everyday ritual praxis. And yet the less costly votives that were available, terra-cotta statues for example, followed the same communicative rules.

Appropriating Religious Space

Written prayers, the wax tablets mentioned in some authors of the first and second centuries AD,[29] prolonged the presence of a prayer, and thus the duration of the ritual. Placing the text on the legs of the statue allowed the supplicant to transcend the temporal restrictions on presence and performance. In this case, writing could replace repetition, sometimes hinted at by exhortations on objects of dedications to repeatedly kindle lamps or replace or add coins.[30] The idea of "perpetuated action" might also apply to images and their performance of a "pictorial act."[31] In cases of asocial wishes, the writing of a prayer and its secret deposition—in a fountain such as that of Anna Perenna, in a sacrificial hearth such as the one at Mayence, or in a grave—might have served to avoid the social exposure of praying aloud, but above all these actions exercise the same techniques of appropriating a special place in perpetuated action, relying on speech as much as on graphic and representational elements, from unusual or distorted letters to the treatment of the material bearers of such texts.[32]

Without doubt, dedicatory tablets, the notices of thanksgiving that accompanied objects, had a similar function. They permanently attested the power and beneficence of a deity, even if the laudatory section of texts was usually brief, and formulas such as *ex voto* or *ex visu* would simultaneously have referred the objects to the processes of communication. These elements furthered individual acts of worship in open, public spaces; that is, they were religious communication centered on sacred areas.

---

29. Juv. 10.56; Apul. *Apol.* 54; Philostr. *Her.* 3.2; Versnel 1981, 32.
30. Van Straten 1981, 74. See also Derks and Roymans 2002.
31. Weiss 2015, 66–67 (for Egypt).
32. See Gordon 2015a.

Analysis of religious texts of this type has concentrated on other elements: the dedicants figure prominently. Frequently, self-descriptions were not restricted to a name, but also included information about status, or even a career description. An excellent example is found in a narrative from Aelius Aristides (*Hieroi logoi* 4.45–47) that I present in summary:

> After several performances of a chorus for Zeus, Aelius intended to dedicate a tripod made of silver, a "symbol of gratitude toward the god, but also as a memorial of the choroi," as he formulates. He produced a distich, running thus: "Poet, judge, and choreutes in one person, I dedicated this memorial to you, o lord, for the foundation of the chorus." The following two verses named the donator and claimed the dedication to be under the tutelage of the god. In a dream, however, the god sent another text: "Not unknown to any Hellene, Aristides has dedicated me—Aristides, the famous dirigent of eternally streaming words and a hero." In a discussion with the priests all participants agreed to set up the memorial in the temple of Zeus Asklepios. The tripod, adorned with three golden statues of Asklepios, Hygieia, and Telephoros, held the new inscription and a note that it was added as a consequence of a dream. In order to fulfill an older oracle, Aelius also set up another dedication for Olympian Zeus. He finished his narrative with the remark that he devoted himself to oratory, being convinced that his name would survive the centuries as the god had characterized his speech as "eternally streaming." (4.47)

The story offers a splendid illustration of the mechanisms of religious communication and the agency arrogated by religious action. In talking to the gods, people communicated with their fellow citizens, contemporary or yet to come. Motives might have been diverse, but hoping for a public honorific statue (even paid for by oneself) would have been futile for many, while the funerary *cursus honorum* would come too late for the more ambitious. Here, religious communication offered an alternative; there was here no need to find somebody else to put up a votive inscription with your name on it. Women would not be as inclined to engage in such activities, as there was no position of agency for them to arrogate: of the Isis officials in the city of Rome, twenty-one *sacerdotes* are known. Ten males and one female are known from dedicatory inscriptions set up by themselves; nine females and one male are known from tomb inscriptions.[33]

---

33. Rüpke 2006b.

At the same time, religious communication must be taken seriously in its religious dimension. The text of Aristides makes his diverse motives explicit, but shows that the communicative efforts were concentrated on the deity above all.[34] Mary Beard, by contrasting the standard practices of open polytheistic cult in ancient cities with those of more tightly organized groups, identified the naming in dedicatory inscriptions as the functional equivalent of membership lists.[35] But would signaling a stable relationship with a certain deity prevent the dedicants from addressing themselves to other deities? The many instances of multiple acts of communication and different addressees suggest that this was not the case. Aelius's discussion with priests and temple personnel led to a change in the addressee,[36] and the dedicated object itself referred to several deities. In the end, that change also induced him to produce a second memorial.

Another facet is added to our interpretation of dedicatory inscriptions: if we take the problems of communication and its many risks into account, the emphasis must have been on the successful completion of communication rather than on a special relationship with one god to the exclusion of others. The author presents herself or himself as a person that is capable of establishing a communicative link with a deity, of gaining an audience and receiving an answer. Far from self-evident, this is a noteworthy individual religious accomplishment, even if one's success was surely perceived as partially attributable to familial and social status. Such a person would also be able to address other gods with similar reliability and success, and hence the inscription prepared the social environment for such new communications. If we accept that ancient societies were not hierarchically but heterarchically organized, on the combined criteria of social and political power, it is to be assumed that religious authority was an independent type of power.[37]

Of course, in Aelius's narrative about the change of the epigram, the special feature is the oracular prompt. The prophecy was addressed to an author who was obsessed by language and immediately started training

---

34. See Rosenberger 2013a for the importance of divination; in general C. P. Jones 1998; Petsalis-Diomidis 2006, 2010.

35. Beard 1991.

36. See McLynn 2013.

37. Ehrenreich, Crumley, and Levy 1995; Smith 2011.

in order to fulfill the prophecy. A note on Aristides's tripod added the information *ex visu*, "from a vision." This again points to an intention to make the dedication an organic part of the communication between the dedicant and the god. It is the location that eliminates any ambiguity about the addressee: the tripod is directly associated with the large temple statue. Again, it is a particular trait of Aelius's text that the addressee is not explicitly named. There is, rather, an explicit deliberation about the addressee and the interpretation of the location.[38]

Aspects of the scene described by Aelius can be generalized: prayers are often addressed to the *di immortales* as a generic group. In many instances it is not necessary to specify a particular addressee; during public festivals there was no need to be especially concerned about each of the many deities that appear in prayers or as statues. Such laxness was not admissible for occasions—and I should like to stress the difference—as specific and individual as we suppose the situations leading to dedications to have been. Admittedly, formulas like *sive dea, sive deus* show the ancients at pains to determine the correct deity. But what would be the range of choices? It was not a list learned by heart from teachers or parents. Temples offered the most obvious choices, and at first glance it would seem that this must have significantly limited the options available to those who were not inhabitants of larger cities. Yet a single temple might offer space for the veneration of multiple deities; the phenomenon of the *synnaoi theoi* was widespread.[39] Dedicatory inscriptions from a given site often feature the names of deities other than the divine owner or owners of the site—which is sometimes difficult to establish given this situation. Thus, existing dedications further determined the range of plausible choices for a new communication or the identification of the divine collocutor in a successfully concluded communication. At times, the more general invocation of "all gods" or the explicit refusal to name a specific not unquestionably plausible agent might have helped counter the competing claims or challenges of bystanders.

The rhetorical connotations of "plausibility" seem to be very fitting. The problem is to name—that is, to construct—the divine addressee in a way that is as successful and plausible to oneself as it is to others. As an

---

38. Aristid. *Hieroi logoi* 4.45–46.
39. See Nock 1930.

Copy of the tomb stele of Vibius, son of Urbus, who died at the age of four and is presented with the Horus lock, indicating youth in Egyptian imagery. The stele was dedicated to the di manes by his grandmother Vibia. From Pulst, Kärnten, third century AD. Römermuseum Theurnia. Photo by J. Rüpke, used by permission of Landesmuseum für Kärnten.

earlier part of Aristides's narrative made clear,[40] people might meet others in temples, offer each other assistance, and reinforce each other's attempts. Hence, naming was a situational strategy, not an absolute one. There was, for example, no *need* to name one's parents on a family tomb area,[41] but perhaps this was a helpful reminder of the individual construction of their divine status. On the other hand, a neighboring inscription might have stressed that there is nothing to follow the life that has passed. The model of a religion restricted to a rule-based system called "cult" is not adequate to describe the cumulative outcome of such decisions.

Religious metacommunication, that is, communication between humans about communication between humans and gods, was not restricted to inscriptions. Narratives such as that of Aelius Aristides explored problems of establishing communication and hinted at alternatives. In other instances iconography replaced words. Even treatises we would call "systematic theology," such as Varro's handbook *Antiquitates rerum diuinarum*, participated in such metacommunication, the communication about ritual communication. I doubt, however, that this would have been more relevant to most religious actors than the inscriptions visible in temples.

Success and Decline

In the Roman Empire—and I am thinking particularly of those parts that did not have a long-standing Greek tradition of putting up inscriptions—the frequency of inscriptions increased consistently until the second half of the second century and the beginning of the third, reaching its height in the late Antonine and Severan epoch, and thereafter began a long decline. These patterns are discussed under the heading "epigraphic habit."[42] Thus, epigraphic habit has become a factor in the history of religion. But is it a religious factor?

Certainly, a predilection to use text was a religious factor in the period of increasing inscriptional frequency.[43] For cultures lacking in widespread

---

40. Aristid. *Hieroi logoi* 4.42–43.
41. I reinterpret the material presented by Laura Chioffi (Chioffi 1996).
42. Mrozek 1973; MacMullen 1982; Alföldy 1991; Eck 1995.
43. For the importance of a chronological approach toward provincial religion, see Woolf 1998 and 1994.

monumentalization or for those whose religious monumentalization was simply limited to centralized or even monopolistic structures, visible offerings accompanied by permanent inscriptions offered the possibility of an inexpensive communication with the gods. Rome's republican polytheism burgeoned with the dedications of new temples by victorious generals, while the polytheism of Germania inferior and superior spread through the deployment of cheap sandstone slabs on the margins of military and civilian settlements.[44] On the basis of my earlier hypothesis, permanently visible gifts indicated religious competence, and religion claimed an important share in visible public culture. "Being Roman"—I will vary an already proverbial opening[45]—meant to possess the religious competence to identify one's divine addressee among the group of those known to one's peers, or even to plausibly address one that was new.

Ancient theoreticians elaborated on this competence. In the Hermetic treatise "Asclepius" (the transmitted Latin text of which might go back to a third-century composite Greek original and even earlier parts), Hermes Trismegisthos praises human beings:

> "Nec inmerito miraculo dignus est, qui est omnium maximus. deorum genus omnium confessione manifestum est de mundissima parte natuare esse prognatum signaque eorum sola quasi capita pro omnibus esse. species uero deorum, quas conformat humanitas, ex utraque natura conformatae sunt; ex diuina, quae est purior multoque diuinior, et ex ea, quae intra homines est, id est ex materia, qua fuerint fabricatae, et non solum capitibus solis sed membris omnibus totoque corpore figurantur. ita humanitas semper memor naturae et originis suae in illa diuinitatis imitatione perseuerat, ut, sicuti pater ac dominus, ut sui similes essent, deos fecit aeternos, ita humanitas deos suos ex sui uultus similitudine figuraret." "Statuas dicis, o Trismegiste?"—"Statuas, o Asclepi. uidesne, quatenus tu ipse diffidas? statuas animatas sensu et spiritu plenas tantaque facientes et talia, statuas futurorum praescias eaque sorte; uate, somniis multisque aliis rebus praedicentes, inbecillitates hominibus facientes easque curantes, tristitam laetitiamque pro meritis." (23–24)

> "Mankind certainly deserves admiration, as the greatest of all beings. All plainly admit that the race of gods sprang from the cleanest part of nature and

---

44. See Spickermann 2003, 2008.
45. Rüpke 2006b.

that their [celestial] signs are like heads that stand for the whole being. But the figures of gods that humans form have been formed of both natures—from the divine, which is purer and more divine by far, and from the material of which they are built, whose nature falls short of the human—and they represent not only the heads but all the limbs and the whole body. Always mindful of its nature and origin, humanity persists in imitating divinity, representing its gods in semblance of its own features, just as the father and master made his gods eternal to resemble him."—"Are you talking about statues, Trismegistus?" [Asclepius asks.]—"Statues, Asclepius, yes. See how little trust you have. I mean statues ensouled and conscious, filled with spirit and doing great deeds; statues that foreknow the future and predict it by lots, by prophecy, by dreams and by many other means; statues that make people ill and cure them, bringing them pain and pleasure as each deserves."[46]

Such anthropological statements about all mankind are found only among the few who understand. The growing public importance of religion in the imperial period caused reflection on religion, an intellectual discourse[47] among these "few" as well as a growing demand for religious specialists. Certainly, Egypt went much further in both respects, and it is probably significant that I must turn to Greek or originally Greek texts to find elaborate examples of a phenomenon that otherwise does not appear before the development of a Latin, largely Christian, theology.

These reflections, even if implicit and less elaborate, in turn demanded representation. The relationships between the deity and the human protagonist needed explanations or intermediaries. Who put up the additional and explanatory note *ex visu* for Aelius's tripod? We do not know. As far as the main epigram is concerned, Aelius Aristides discussed matters with the specialists but features as the sole agent (apart from Asclepius) in his text. This was not a matter of course. A text from Lugudunum of the year AD 197 complicates our view:

[Pro] salute Imp(eratoris) L(uci) Septimi / [Seve]ri Pii Pertinacis Aug(usti) / [et] M(arci) Aureli Antonini Caes(aris) / Imp(eratoris) destinati et / Iuliae Aug(ustae) matris castror(um) / totiusque domus divinae /eorum et statu c(oloniae) C(opiae) C(laudiae) Aug(ustae) Lug(udunum) / taurobolium

---

46. Translated by Brian P. Copenhaver, 1992.
47. See Bendlin 2006.

Septimius Severus and his wife Iulia Domna depicted on the Arco degli Argentari,
a private dedication by the money changers of AD 204 in Rome leading onto the
Foro Boario. Photo courtesy of A. Hupfloher.

fecerunt / Septicia Valeriana et / Optatia Siora ex voto / [the text might stop
here, but the inscription continues:] praeeunte Aelio Antho sa/cerdote sacerdotia Aemi/lia Secundilla tibicine Fl(avio) Restituto apparatore Vire/io Her-
metione / inchoatum est sacrum IIII / Nonas Maias consumma/tum Nonis

eisdem / T(ito) Sex(tio) Laterano L(ucio) Cuspio / Ru[f]ino co(n)s(ulibus) / l(ocus) d(atus) d(ecreto) d(ecurionum).[48]

For the well-being of Imperator Lucius Septimius Severus Pius Pertinax Augustus and of Marcus Aurelius Antoninus Caesar and Imperator to be and of Julia Augusta, mother of the camp, and of all their divine household and for the state of the Colonia Copia Claudia Augusta Lugdunum, Septicia Valeriana and Optatia Siora performed a taurobolium on account of a vow—led by the priest Aelius Anthus, [accompanied by] the priestess Aemilia Secundilla, the flute-player Flavius Restitutus, and the servant Vireius Hermetio. The ritual was begun on May 4 and finished on the seventh of the same month, when Titus Sextius Lateranus and Lucius Cuspio Rufinus were consuls. The place [for the dedication] was given by decree of the city council.

Little discursive space remains for Septicia and Optatia to advertise their religious competence in this ceremony that is sponsored and organized by the decurions mentioned at the end of the text.[49] Specialists dominate the religious communication, standardizing both the constructions of addressees and the modes of access. The growing importance of organization and intellectualization of religion[50] exacted a price: dedicators were increasingly less willing to act on behalf of others, while specialists proved to have a specific and lasting relationship with the divine in the form of permanent religious roles as prophets, teachers, or monks. With the increase of organized religion, documentation of isolated acts of religious communication by epigraphic texts might have seemed less relevant.

A second factor must be addressed: monumentally written communication was a matter of societies that conceived of themselves as stable. The costs of the production must have been (perceived to be) offset by the expected duration of the religious and social configuration. Hence, the spread of inscriptions took a long time to permeate provincial societies, and socially volatile societies preferred short-term investments, performances for instance. Intensification and repetition of ritual, daily cult in the extreme, might even replace action that was "perpetuated," but also frozen. The popularity of religious narrative accompanied ritual but did not replace it.[51]

---

48. *CIL* 13.1754 = *ILS* 4134.
49. I am grateful to Wolfgang Spickermann for this example.
50. See Cameron 1991.
51. For the role of narrative in lived ancient religion, see *RRE* 1.3 (2015).

A third factor can be adduced: permanently visible offerings individu-
alized acts of successful religious communication against a backdrop of
continuous practice of religious communication by means of prayers, per-
ishable offerings, sacrificial meals, and participation in festivals (the frequency and intensity of which might have varied considerably).[52] The gods
involved in this type of religious communication need not be the same as
those singled out for votive address. The developments of the third and
fourth centuries might rightly be described as an intensification and ex-
tension of religion within society and its different "publics," and even as
simultaneously increased differentiation *between* and concentrated coherence *within* religious options—a sort of "confessionalization."[53] In this case,
the costly act of spelling out religious communications on stone might have
lost its appeal, even if thousands of objects deposited in sanctuaries and on
the tombs of martyrs continued to materialize individual appropriations of
shared places. Stressing the continuous relationship with a god while denying the importance of a mere partial form of the divine would lead to the
preference for other types of religious communication and its documentation, for example membership, participation, moral conduct, a whole way
of life. The famous dedications of the fourth-century pagans in the city of
Rome[54] or the inscribed objects commemorating *taurobolia* and concentrating on priestly offices[55] announced multiple memberships and competences.[56] And yet, even if the focus of the writing shifted and its quantity
decreased, the communicative technique itself remained important and
powerful. It was Bishop Damasus's epigrams and the *litterae Filocalianae*
(or *semifilocalianae*) that announced the rise of Christian epigraphy.

---

52. See Apul. *Apol.* 56, on which Fowden 2005, here 540.
53. Rüpke 2009c, 2010a, 2011d.
54. E.g., *CIL* 6.504 (with 6.30779) = *ILS* 4153 (Ulpius Egnatius Faventinus); *CIL* 6.500 = *ILS* 4148 (Caelius Hilarianus); *CIL* 6.1779 = *ILS* 1259 (P. Vettius Agorius Praetextatus).
55. E.g., *CMRDM* 23 = *CIL* 6.499 = *ILS* 4147; *CMRDM* 27 = *CCCA* 241b = *AE* 1953, 238; *CIL* 6.510 = *ILS* 4152 = *CIMRM* 520 = *CCCA* 242.
56. Rüpke 2011a.

Instructing Literary Practice in *The Shepherd of Hermas*

In this final chapter I will return to my earlier methodological approach: I will concentrate on a single text, *The Shepherd of Hermas*. I do not intend to examine it sentence by sentence, but rather to analyze its composition and development and to select for special attention a few passages that I consider to be key. Chapter 1 of this book was significantly guided by the sociology of religion, while subsequent chapters took a more hermeneutical approach, as I aimed, for the most part, to reconstruct ancient observers' reflections on contemporary lived religion. I have also addressed the producers of texts as part of this religion and examined their specific appropriation of contemporary religious practices, slowly shifting from the early Augustan to the imperial period, and from poetry to mass-produced texts, that is, inscriptions. Ending here with a text from the second century AD, I will continue my twofold approach to authored text, but will then revisit the sociology of literature and religion and examine the text for evidence of long-term processes of individualization, as described in the introductory chapter. The history of the reception of *The Shepherd of Hermas* offers at least a glimpse into long-term processes that might indicate a specific type of religious individuality and its development. The text invites such an inquiry, as it explicitly asks for reception, for hearing rather than reading, and later develops a structure that, as I will claim, attests to repetitive use. In general, *The Shepherd of Hermas* has usually been treated as a—more or less negligible—point in a history of dogmatics. We find it so described, for instance, in the recent *Oxford Handbook of Christian Study*.[1] I aim to incorporate it into our view of lived ancient religion as a document that is characterized by uncoordinated, parainstitutional, and even contrainstitutional appropriations.

I will begin by sketching out the text of *The Shepherd of Hermas* in broad strokes, after which I will dissect the text through the concepts of mediality, authorship and genre, and contents and strategy, only in order to then reconstitute it from the perspective of "religious practice." The author, I claim, is somebody who thinks in terms of reflective—that is, self-conscious and religious—individuality and offers others material for contemplation, inviting those who wish to follow his lead. The text, its reproduction, and its performance will be analyzed as an institution that furthered individuality, hence as part of a process of religious individualization. Again, as we will see, "institution" does not imply a normative religious order, but a contingent development of lived ancient religion.

The Shepherd of Hermas comes to us as a Greek text in papyrus fragments written from the third until the sixth century. The text (cut off at the end) was part of the *Codex Sinaiticus*, the fundamental Bible manuscript of the fourth century with the siglum Aleph. It is preserved completely in a fifteenth-century manuscript from Mount Athos. Medieval manuscripts supply two complete Latin translations, the so-called Vulgate, that probably date to the late second century.[2] Additionally, external testimonials begin to appear at the end of the second century. The canon Muratori, as we will see later, assigns the work to the brother of a Roman bishop Pius, traditionally dated to the second quarter of the second century. No further

---

1. Fitzgerald 2008, 796–97.
2. Thus the first translation might even have been written in Hermas's lifetime. See Tornau and Cecconi 2014, 8. Cf. Joly 1958, 63. The oldest manuscript pages of the Palatine version date from the eighth century (Joly 1968, 417), but it might have been translated around 400 (Tornau and Cecconi 2014, 9).

evidence is offered, and this ascription is therefore without historical value. All other deductions must be based on the text itself and remain, therefore, hypothetical. The existence of a Roman "bishop," in the middle of the second century is, however, certainly a fiction. For the sake of brevity I will treat some of the conclusions drawn from historical analysis of the text as fact, despite their hypothetical character. I have, in earlier publications, offered detailed arguments for my identification of the author of the text as a producer of salt, fully embedded in his culture; this portrait differs from that of the *communis opinio*.[3]

Presentation of the Text

A decade ago I would have introduced *The Shepherd of Hermas* as an early Christian but post–New Testament document, as a well-known representative of the "apostolic fathers," which became an object of theological interest only in the nineteenth and twentieth centuries. However, our chronological assumptions have recently become tenuous. As an extreme but thoroughly plausible example, I will briefly outline the recent conclusions of Markus Vinzent.[4] The demanding and theologically very trenchant Pauline letters are old; they date from the middle of the first century. However, they were rarely read—despite the very diverse interests betrayed by the pseudo-Pauline letters—before the Asian shipowner Marcion came to Rome in the middle of the second century. He made them the central component of a new post-biblical "canon," which was completed by the Gospel of Luke and the same author's "Acts." These historical narratives, certainly built on earlier collections of sayings, quickly found imitators and rivals, leading to a larger number of Gospels, four of which achieved canonical status (earlier with some, later with other ancient theologians) and, like *The Shepherd*, were included in the *Codex Sinaiticus*. According to such a model, the *Shepherd* might antedate rather than postdate these Gospels.

I have not myself done sufficient research to judge this hypothesis, but against such a backdrop (or similar, even earlier scenarios), we need not be surprised that no quotations of what later came to be called the New

---

3. Rüpke 1999, 2003a; see now also Rüpke 2013b, 2013e.
4. Vinzent 2011a, 2011b, 2014.

Testament are to be found in *The Shepherd*. Nor need we be surprised that Hermas does not speak of "Christ followers," of *Christianoi*, and that his Christology identifies Christ with "god," the "son of god" (89), that is, Jesus Christ, who (like the *logos*) remains unnamed, is a "spirit," a "name," and a special "angel" of the father who has granted all power to his son and adviser (59, 89).[5] Finally, by this hypothesis, we should not be surprised by how many authors quote *The Shepherd*.[6] Around AD 200 Irenaeus quotes *The Shepherd* in Gallic Lyon, Tertullian does so in African Carthage, Clemens in Egyptian Alexandria, and Origen in Palestinian Caesarea. Translations (beyond those in Latin) were completed in both the Sahidic and the Achmimic dialects of Coptic, in Ethiopian, and in Middle Persian. The complete lack of interest of the theologians of the fourth and fifth century seems, admittedly, at odds with this popularity. But for these writers, the text did not provide arguments pertinent to ongoing Christological debates. Nevertheless, despite these theological debates, the text continued to be read and copied throughout this period. In the fifth or sixth century it found its way, in fairly good shape, into the compilation of Pseudo-Athanasius.[7]

I will postpone discussion of the possible reasons for the text's popularity at the time of its genesis and the ensuing period to later, when I examine its contents in detail. For now, I note that one would, rather, expect the text to have had limited appeal on account of its intimidating length; in today's editions *The Shepherd* is well over one hundred printed pages. Thus it exceeds every other text collected in the canon of the New Testament since the end of the fourth century.

The structure of the text points to a rather complex developmental process in the emergence of a written text. Five sections can be distinguished; I will argue that these are not merely layers, but indications of a process of textual growth, the duration of which cannot be precisely determined.

1. A book of visions (*vis* 1–*vis* 4) of about twenty modern printed pages mark the starting point—historically as well as in the text as it is published today. Different revelatory figures converse with the first-person narrator and

---

5. See in general Brox 1991, 485–95; for the angelology, see Stuckenbruck 1995; Bucur 2007, 2009a, 2009b.

6. Cf., for instance, the poor reception of the Gospel of Mark in antiquity.

7. Joly 1968, 62, 417.

appear to him in visions that he experiences while he is awake or asleep. Finally, a heavenly book is dictated.

2. Introduced by the fifth vision (this numbering is already ancient), twelve "commandments" (*entolaí, mandata*) follow, forming a second stratum consisting of about twenty-five printed pages (*vis* 5–*mand* 12), that is to say, filling an average ancient scroll of eight hundred to one thousand lines of text. The revelatory figure and interlocutor is, for the first time, the eponymous "shepherd," a man dressed in goatskin, with a satchel on his back and a staff in his hand, who introduces himself as the future companion of the first-person narrator, who is now addressed as "Hermas." The section closes with a discussion of the problem of false prophets, thus indirectly questioning the reliability of the text itself.

3. In an expansion of the dialogical scene of the twelfth commandment, the revelatory figure transforms into an angel "of penitence," of whom, till now, no mention has been made. This angel reports eight parables, a text again on a scale of almost twenty-five printed pages (*mand* 12–*sim* 8). These parables are interpreted in a dialogue between Hermas and the angel. This stratum is more politically oriented than those previous: not only does it commence with the question of belonging to the true city, of true *civitas*, it also reflects on specifically Roman and Italic institutions and social life, as can be seen from the metaphors and terminology used.

4. Opening with the remark that the previous two passages have been written down, the angel of penitence offers a new parable, the ninth and most extensive of all (*sim* 9). Alone it covers almost twenty-five printed pages, another ancient book. So far as its contents are concerned, it returns to the image of a tower, already introduced in vision 3. The tower signifies the new church (*ecclesia*), the new community of the faithful. The text closes with the equation of the angel and the shepherd. It was probably this apposition that prompted a later editorial adjustment introducing the same equation into the fifth vision (the opening of the second layer of text).

5. The final stratum is again introduced with the remark that the previous parable has been written down. The angel speaks for the last time (*sim* 10). The place of revelation is Hermas's bedroom (in which occurred the prelude to the third vision and the fifth vision itself, the first appearance of the shepherd). This relatively short text (only about three printed pages) is obviously editorial and marked the end of the redaction of *The Shepherd* as a whole. Here, the further support of the shepherd is promised, as well as that of the virgins, that is, those virtues of the Ecclesia, beautiful women robed in white, that had urged on the building of the tower in *visio* 3 and *simile* 9. In the latter, these women had invited Hermas to stay overnight with them.

One could summarize *The Shepherd* as the text of a Roman Jew who cared for his own moral status and the moral status of his contemporary co-believers, who were already Christ-followers. He tried to convey visions of an ideal church. His audience was a steadily growing group of Jews into whose collective imagination this spirit, angel, and son had entered. Otherwise, this group appears to have been fully integrated into local Roman society, a society that held reasonable values and offered many attractions. It is within this context, judged by the author as a context of temptation, that Hermas reports his insights in the form of an apocalyptic text, as readers of the book of visions or the canon Muratori could not fail to detect. Genuine religious experiences[8] are combined with a strong will to communicate them.

Mediality

In speaking of religious experience and referring to the text in the singular, I have already indicated that I assume a single author rather than a later editor. It is this author whom the text invites us to identify with the first-person narrator. The text is a narrative but it is dominated, indeed, overwhelmed, by direct speech from the second textual layer onward. Here, the text becomes a dialogue punctuated by long monologues. A written revelation is reported in the very first textual layer, namely in *visio* 2. Merely copying the letters, however, as Hermas tells us, does not result in understanding. For this, two weeks of preparatory fasting and praying is required. Even then, an additional vision with textual supplements and further tasks is necessary. The medium of oral speech (fictitious orality, of course, imagined on the basis of the written text only) is, by comparison, much more flexible. Oral exchange permits requests for immediate clarification, and it even allows the interlocutors to "read between the lines."

A view of verbal communication as a means to interactively clarify problems, deepen understanding, and overcome mistaken judgments is encoded in the written revelations of Hermas. From its earliest layer onward the text is characterized by requests for clarification, interpretation of what had already been said, and even corrections of understandings attained

---

8. See Stone 2003 on the question of authenticity.

previously.[9] The speakers are important; their characterization becomes a significant part of the text. As I will explain presently, autobiographical details play a momentous role in the generic conventions of apocalyptic literature. Revelatory figures are described in detail: their appearance, companions, changes of facial expression, and attire. The growth of the text suggests a broadening process of communications not only in written form (writing is a distributive medium) but also orally. The text does not merely represent verbal communication: each subsequent textual layer, perhaps initially oral and later in written form, also is constrained by earlier remarks,[10] employs consistent metaphorical language, and refrains from introducing large amounts of new material (as purely written communication would allow one to do). It was the written form, however, and perhaps even the publication of the different textual strata, that permitted precise reference to previous layers. It was the written form alone that allowed for a text of a length that prohibits full recitation on a single occasion; recitation of the final version in its entirety would have taken more than four hours.

However, a written text offers the further advantage of communication "to all those that are chosen" (8.3),[11] especially in its earliest phase of circulation. The organization of those Greek-speaking, Judeo-Christian Romans (this very specific designation is intended to counter common misconceptions) can be reconstructed in its basic structures from the book of visions itself:

> The elderly woman came and asked if I had already given the book to the presbyters. I said that I had not. "You have done well," she said, "for I have some words to add. Then, when I complete all the words, they will be made known through you to all those who are chosen. And so, you will write two little books, sending one to Clement and the other to Grapte. Clement will send his to the foreign cities, for that is his commission. But Grapte will admonish the widows and orphans. And you will read yours in this city, with the presbyters who lead the church." (8.2–3)[12]

The first authority—and, if we like, patron, reader, and (co-) author— is the elderly lady who "adds words," which are apparently not just marginal

---

9. Leutzsch 1989, 13–19.
10. Thus Osiek 1999, 10, 13.
11. I employ the continuous numbering of recent editions in the following.
12. All translations of *The Shepherd* are from Ehrman 2003a.

notes. Only once she has done her job does she permit the book to be made public. And yet it is Hermas's task to see to the initial copying and distribution, which will then be continued through distinct channels: a certain Clement will make further copies and send the book out for the foreign trade, while Grapte will use it for the admonition of "widows and orphans," hence a female channel for women and children in need. The college of the presbyters, therefore, holds only limited ruling powers, which are not specified at all. They do not, apparently, regulate the relation between patron and author, nor do they have a say in the book's distribution in foreign cities, nor do they interfere with the instruction of women. The term "presbyter" seems here to be used synonymously with episcopes. This staff forms the forum in which Hermas will recite the written text, which has been revealed to him and thus, probably, also to his patron (8.3).[13] In his narrative of the first layer of the text Hermas opts for precision: the divine original is a letter, which is addressed to Hermas and which features his personal problems as a central theme. It is a letter that charges him with messages for third parties and, above all, the vituperation of a certain Maximus (7.1–4). The general meeting, perhaps referred to by the salutation "brothers," is not described in terms of an institution that plays an organizational role, and it is not clear whether recitation before the presbyters implied a request for permission to recite the text before a larger circle under presbyterial supervision. By virtue of being written, the text would become easier to control. But above all, the existence of the written form permitted further copying, more precisely, another two copies: the one that reached widows and orphans via Grapte, the second to engage Clemens in the distribution of the text by letter in other municipalities, therefore to create additional copies (8.3). We might recall that John's Apocalypse also presented itself as a letter. However, as in all such cases it was, finally, re-oralization alone that enabled the text to become known to larger groups of people. That is, it succeeded in transcending spatial, social, or gender boundaries.

Authorship and Genre

If one were to believe the canon Muratori, perhaps written, as the text itself claims, at the end of the second century (perhaps, however, much

---

13. See Vinzent 2014, 106–7.

later), Hermas would have been the brother of the Roman bishop Pius.[14] On the other hand, the prologue to the text in the Latin Vulgate tradition identifies Hermas as one of those to whom Paul sends greetings in Romans 16:14. Evidently, learned scribes attempted to locate the popular text within valued traditions. *The Shepherd* itself does not offer the slightest hint that it aimed to solve its naturally questionable reliability through any such reference to the author's genealogy or association with the letters of Paul. Of course, every visionary faces the problem of establishing his or her credibility.[15] I do not here question the authenticity of the visionary experience. Rather, I presuppose it, taking into account all the refinements of our current understanding of the idea and even of the very concept of "experience."[16] It was a widespread conviction in Mediterranean antiquity that visions by day or during sleep were credible forms of communication with superhuman authorities, and such visions were passively or actively appropriated in many instances. This appropriation at times included critical attitudes, tracking down the deceptions, the false or empty dreams that were like water in wine. Cicero presents the extreme positions in the form of two radically contradictory statements in *On divination*: occasional false dreams cannot discredit correct forecasts. This is the position developed in the first book.[17] The second book, however, offers an argument that can be summarized thus: given the large number of dreams, occasional correct forecasts must be accepted as lucky chances, as flukes, but they are no proof of the divinatory character of such dreams.[18]

Against this critical background, Hermas chose a double strategy. First, he produced his own reliability through ruthless autobiographical self-revelation. Hence the beginning of the whole text:

> The one who raised me sold me to a certain woman named Rhoda, in Rome. After many years, I regained her acquaintance and began to love her as a sister. When some time had passed, I saw her bathing in the Tiber river; and I gave her my hand to help her out of the river. When I observed her beauty

---

14. See below.
15. Rüpke 2003a, 2013e.
16. Csordas 1994; Jung 1999, 2006; Ricken 2004; Davies 2008; Taves 2009, Taves 2010; Martin, McCutcheon, and Smith 2012; Mastrocinque and Rüpke 2013; Rüpke 2013a.
17. Cic. *Div*. 1.60ff.
18. Ibid., 2.121–122.

I began reasoning in my heart, "I would be fortunate to have a wife of such beauty and character." This is all I had in mind, nothing else. (1.1–2)

Hermas was a released domestic slave by birth (*verna*) or a foundling, who managed to establish a family of his own and had conducted business with variable success, probably trading. Only later did he come to the more honest activity of sea-salt extraction.[19] On seeing his former owner and fellow believer Rhode emerging naked from her bath in the Tiber, he indulged in inappropriate (as he himself will point out later) erotic fantasies.[20] To imagine a sexual relationship with his former mistress was probably deeply offensive to his social environment.[21] At the same time, realizing this fantasy—the ultimate libertine achievement, to judge from its frequent emphasis in tomb inscriptions—would endanger his legitimate marriage.[22] Hermas's self-recrimination continues. His own children have fallen prey to corrupting influences (3.1). As an old-fashioned Roman *pater familias* he must also accept responsibility for their behavior before the God of Jewish tradition. The text (that is, the message) has an author, and this author is "transparent," honest to the point of confessing his own mistakes and admitting that others mistrust him. He is, therefore, credible. Thus laid bare, the author remains present not only as a narrator but also as a partner in dialogue, within which he exposes himself as fainthearted and lacking in understanding, and is again and again rebuked.

This first strategy seems almost antithetical to the second. Hermas furthered his communicative efforts by combining his emphasis on orality and authenticity with the conventions of the apocalyptic genre. In postexilic Judaism, particularly since the second century BC, texts were produced that presented themselves as the reports of outstanding biblical characters. These offered insights in the form of visions into the events of the last days of continuous history.[23] The pseudonymous nature of such "apocalyptic" texts was predetermined by the putative narrator: a biblical seer narrating in the first person was meant to be understood as the

---

19. For this reinterpretation of Hermas's description of his professional activities, see Rüpke 1999.

20. For a more extensive discussion, see Rüpke 2013e.

21. I am grateful to Barry Schwartz for suggesting this probable attitude (through a comparison to American slavery), which is consistent with ancient epigraphic evidence.

22. For the general observation, see Mouritsen 2005; see also Ehmig 2015.

23. See Collins 1987; K. R. Jones 2011; Yabro Collins 1988; Kippenberg 1990.

Tomb of the rich freedman and baker Eurysaces at the Porta Maggiore, Rome, depicting work in his bakeries and using mixing machines as architectural elements. Second half of the first century BC. Photo by J. Rüpke.

author, as is frequently indicated by the titles of such texts. Hence writing was a necessary feature; only as a written text, that is, as a book, could the story be preserved for the often enormous period of time preceding its rediscovery, its "apocalypsis." The necessity of written communication is regularly (as would not be otherwise necessary) reflected in the contents of the visions: the knowledge of the visionary often originates from heavenly books, the contents of which are communicated summarily or even word for word in his visions.[24] Hermas knew apocalyptic texts, as is shown by the only explicit quotation in the whole of *The Shepherd*; he quotes the apocalyptic Jewish text "Eldad and Modat" (7.4), a text that is unfortunately lost to us.

It is into this tradition and this sequence of texts that Hermas inserted himself. Many of the conventions and motifs of apocalyptic texts appear in *The Shepherd*: the rapture by a spirit and the visions of heavenly revelatory figures, who within one vision add further visions and explanations. A command is issued to pass on the texts, either orally or by circulating the text. In a recitation of the book of visions the words *apokálypsis* or *apokalýptein* would have been spoken with extraordinary frequency: they appear twenty-seven times in total.

The combination of the two strategies described above would have changed the audience's concept of apocalypse. Above all, it presented the heavenly hypotext as an immediate concern; it encoded a contemporary individual moral admonition, not a primarily eschatological one. This strategy was modified in the later layers of the text, but it was pursued in principle. From the second layer onward, it is not the key word "apocalypse," which continued the strategy, but the address to the visionary individual, the repeated imperative to create a written record. This became true to an even higher degree when, in the second vision, Hermas is promoted to the role of primary addressee of all revelations. This rendered the apocalyptic tone less obtrusive, but more general at the same time, as is shown by the scope of the reception.

Contents and Strategy

From the perspective of classic dogma-historical terminology, *The Shepherd of Hermas* deals with the possibility of a second penitence after baptism. But this is a view of our text that presupposes later problems,

---

24. Sometimes a heavenly journey is necessary. See Segal 1980; Dean-Otting 1984.

situations, and a theology of sacraments as a point of departure. Without this lens the text appears in another light.

One of the distinctive features of the *The Shepherd* is its interest in typology and classification. This is conspicuous in the discussion of virtues and sins that structures the commandments, the second layer of the text. However, the classification of members of the *ekklêsia* is even more striking and central. They are presented as different types of stones (*vis* 3, *sim* 9) or tested with branches (*sim* 8). It seems to be of central importance to distinguish between different types and gradations, or even specific "percentages," of strong or weak belief. In parable 8 this results in twenty-eight different grades of believer. Thus, the distribution of long branches of willow leads to the following results:

> From some he received sticks that were withered and eaten up, as if by a moth. The angel commanded those who gave him these kinds of sticks to stand to one side. Others handed over withered sticks, but they were not moth-eaten; he commanded these to stand to one side as well. Others handed them over half withered. These also stood to the side. Others handed over sticks that were half withered and split. These stood to the side. Others handed over sticks that were green, but split. These stood to the side. Others handed over sticks that were half withered and half green. These stood to the side. Others brought their sticks two parts green and the third part withered. These stood to the side. Others handed over sticks that were two parts withered but the third part green. These stood to the side. Others handed over their sticks that were almost entirely green, but a little part of their sticks was withered, at the end. But they were split. These stood to the side. The sticks of others were just a little green, but the remaining parts of the sticks were withered. These stood to the side. Others came in carrying green sticks, as they had received them from the angel. The majority of the crowd handed over sticks like this. The angel was extremely happy with these. And they stood to the side. Others handed over sticks that were green and budding. They stood to the side, and the angel was extremely cheerful about these. Others handed over sticks that were green and budding, but their buds seemed to be bearing fruit. The men whose sticks were found like this were extremely cheerful. The angel rejoiced over them, and the shepherd was extremely cheerful with him about these. (67.6–18)

Hermas was not concerned with the delineation of sharp borders. There are those within and those outside circle of fellows in religion; "peoples" (*ethnoi*) and apostates are on the outside (4.2), and the text is not interested in these. Rather, the problem that was central for Hermas lies in the gray areas. According to him, it is easy to come to belief, and it is easy then to gradually fall out of it again. But it is difficult to know where oneself or another stands exactly. *The Shepherd* captures the problem in the parable of the trees in winter. If you regard the trees without leaves you do not know which of them still lives (*sim* 3): "For just as the trees that shed their leaves in the winter all look alike, with the withered indistinguishable from the living, so too in this age it is not clear who the upright are and who the sinners, but they all appear alike" (52.3).

The same problem is expressed in the parable of the building of the tower (*sim* 9). The tower rapidly rises to an impressive size, but then repair becomes necessary, and "stones" must be reworked or removed—"stones" that in their different qualities represent the members of the community and their deficiencies (82.2, 83.3–5). Construction is interrupted, and the eschatological completion is delayed. What is missing here is a clarification of the community's limits. Whosoever are in the gray area must quickly change their minds; they require *metanoia*.

But what exactly is to be changed? Here Hermas remains astonishingly vague. In talking about marriage and separation, adultery is described as "to behave like the peoples" (29.9),[25] and to seek for advice from professional fortune-tellers is idolatry (43.4). But such behaviors as these could also be observed among the members of Hermas's own group.

"The deeds of the peoples" are the indicator of full apostasy (75.3), but this is not specified further either. Obviously the wealthy are foremost in occupying dangerous territory, and a simple businessman like Hermas must be classed among these. To act euergetically, to gain in prestige and thus to reap public glory, is just as reasonable as it is problematic. Hermas, I am tempted to conclude, tries to fight a traditional middle-class ethics with a new middle-class ethics.

Occasionally, this leads to surprising emphases. Of course greed, extramarital sexual relations, luxury, and splendid meals are associated with each other. But Hermas focuses on the physical results of excessive dining, on business contacts with heathens, and on uncharitably turning away beggars. He formulates a complex psychological model for this and illustrates

---

25. Ehrman (2003a, 247) translates "like the outsiders" *(toîs éthnesin)*.

it with the simile of the willow branches. I quote only a portion of the relevant material from the end of the eighth parable:

> Those who handed over sticks that were two parts withered and the third part green are those who have been faithful, but who also have grown wealthy and maintained a high standing among the outsiders. These have clothed themselves with great arrogance and become conceited; they have abandoned the truth and do not cling to those who are upright, but live with the outsiders. And this path has become very sweet to them. Still, they have not fallen away from God, but have remained in the faith, even though they do not do the works of faith. And so many of these have repented, and their dwelling is in the tower. But others have taken up residence, once and for all, with the outsiders. These have fallen away from God by being borne along by the vanities of the outsiders and acting like them. And so these are counted among the outsiders. Some of them were doubleminded and did not hope to be saved because of what they did. Others were doubleminded and created schisms among themselves. (76.1–4)

Straightforward economic problems are signs of a divine punishment for the rich; as a consequence they fall into the danger of apostasy (14.5). The *angelos tryphês*, the angel of luxury, is also an angel of deception; it is inherent to the active and irritable character of the businessman. A productive occupation, therefore, should be preferred to trade. Here, the social climber Hermas evidently reflects on his own situation.

However, Hermas is not interested in issues of social class, but in the individual and in psychology: the high-spirited (*eupsychos*) and the doubtful (*dipsychos*) emerge as important types in his analysis. "Turning around," *metanoia*, is an individual biographical process. This process does not remain abstract but neither does it become radical: the rich man should make charitable donations but should not give up his status, as is stressed in the very first parable (50). Again, the problem exists that one cannot recognize the believer by his generosity, his euergetism. Too much prayer and fasting is also harmful; it weakens the body (18.7). To fast is fine, but a moral life is better (54.3–5). One can give the savings of short-term fasting to the poor (56.7). To do more than necessary is praised as *leiturgeia* (56.2–3), a concept fully established in the embedding society.[26] And finally, the positive role

---

26. Andreau, Schmitt, and Schnapp 1978; Veyne 1988.

of knowledge remains. Ironically, Hermas is criticized again and again for his inexhaustible thirst for knowledge. Only the knowing finally knows whether "God is or not" (12.3). This is a clear religious distinction.

Unfortunately, not much is so clear in everyday life. The text itself opens with the extreme example of a sin of thought. Not even Hermas himself knows that he is thinking of adultery on seeing Rhode naked. The divine revelatory figure must draw Hermas's attention to this fact. The individual needs such a figure, needs a "shepherd," an "angel of justice," an "angel of penitence," because he or she is always endangered by "angels of malice" and the like. The latter wage war within the individual, which the individual cannot win without help. The sixth commandment details this:

> "Hear now," he said, "about faith. A person has two angels, one of righteousness and the other of wickedness." "And how, then, Lord," I asked, "will I know the inner workings of these, since both angels dwell with me?" "Listen," he said, "and you will understand these things. The angel of righteousness is sensitive, modest, meek, and mild. And so, when he rises up in your heart, he immediately speaks with you about righteousness, purity, reverence, contentment, every upright deed, and every glorious virtue. When all these things rise up in your heart, realize that the angel of righteousness is with you. These are the works of the angel of righteousness. Trust this one, therefore, and his works. See now also the works of the angel of wickedness. First of all, he is irascible, bitter, and senseless, and his works are wicked, bringing ruin on the slaves of God. And so, when this one rises up in your heart, recognize him from his works." "I do not understand, Lord," I said, "how to perceive him." "Listen," he replied. "When any irascibility or bitterness should fall on you, realize that he is in you. Then there is desire for many activities and numerous extravagant food and drinking bouts and many wild parties and various completely unnecessary luxuries, and desires for women and greed and a certain great haughtiness and arrogance, and everything that is closely connected to these things." (36.1–5)

This is more than an ethical message. The text also presents a strategy of communication and participates in such a strategy. The question of good and evil is not just an act of accounting and balancing, but a biographical process that can be narrated. "Turning around" is not a unique, dramatic event, but an ongoing struggle. The text illustrates and enacts this in its ever-new approaches to the same ethical problems. Just as the visionary stimulus was decisive for Hermas, the representation of this process, the narrated vision, could become the stimulus for Hermas's addressees.

Text as a Religious Practice

In its biographical dimension—in its movement through rooms, through time, and through social constellations—the text describes a religious practice. It formulates the mode of its reception through multiple references to distribution and writing. Writing the text is, therefore, described as part of the religious practice of the narrator and protagonist called "Hermas." This is not about a unique action. Although we do not have any testimonials for how long the author worked on the text as it is transmitted, a period longer than a year is affirmed in the book of visions (5.1). The text may in fact, in its different layers, reflect the work of several years and multiple attempts to convey the visionary insights, primarily, in the additions and corrections necessitated by the author's patron (but perhaps not by the presbyters—at least we do not hear of such). In subsequent layers, reworking is also suggested by theological modifications, the use of images, and in their interpretations.

The resulting text invited its audience to engage in individual religious practice and offered itself for appropriation by any of those in situations that are not described as entirely hopeless. It is significant for its reception that the book was recommended by the canon Muratori for private reading, not for recitation in an official ritual setting:

> We receive only the apocalypses of John and Peter, though some of us are not willing that the latter be read in church. But Hermas wrote the Shepherd very recently, in our times, in the city of Rome, while bishop Pius, his brother, was occupying the chair of the church of the city of Rome. And therefore it ought indeed to be read; but it cannot be read publicly to the people in church either among the prophets, whose number is complete, or among the apostles, for it is after [their] time. (Canon Muratori, lines 71–80)[27]

---

27. The translation is that of Ehrman 2003b, 333.

In the prologue to the Latin Vulgate, the text was also recommended as "in fact a useful book," with the added note that "many of the ancient writers use the testimonies, but [that] among the Latins it is almost unknown." Perhaps this was one of the reasons why this Latin translation was made; a Latin audience demanded Latin versions of current texts.

Neither biblical traditions nor reflections on martyrdom appeared in *The Shepherd*; audiences needed to wait for Ignatius of Antiochia and Polykarp of Smyrna for the latter.[28] What was offered instead was an ideal of individual moral responsibility and the admonition to attend to (personified) internal voices and to follow the correct one. For this work on oneself (a metonym that does not appear in *The Shepherd*) the text continually offered new images, parables, and knowledge. The repeated reading of the text was a religious practice. Such ancient texts, as John Dagenais's characterizes medieval manuscripts, "engage the reader, not so much in the unraveling of meaning as in a series of ethical meditations and of personal ethical choices."[29] Evidently, many accepted this invitation, as my brief review of the processes of distribution and translation has shown.

However, other individuals necessarily mediated between author and reader. The female patron mentioned at the beginning of the text, copyists and translators, book traders, and their customers and financiers. The offer made by the text was not only determined by demand but also by supply, by the readiness to copy the text so that it could be disseminated. This included adapting it to the audience, both through translation and stylistic adjustments; the text of the fourth-century *Codex Sinaiticus* was much more literary and less popular than that of the third-century *Michigan Codex*.[30] The text itself suggested that these activities, too, should be understood as religious practice, both for one's own benefit—such multipliers were also users of their texts[31]—and as a way to share one's time and means with the poor but trained listeners or even readers among fellow believers.

Hermas's visions are, in short, available to us as a phenomenon of a specific textual quality. Strategies of communication and the use of media,

---

28. Frend 1965; Bowersock 1995; Klausner 2005; Waldner 2015.
29. Haines-Eitzen 2012, 11; drawing on Dagenais 1994.
30. Joly 1968, 62.
31. See Haines-Eitzen 2000, 130.

concepts of authorship, and constructions of genre shaped each other in the historical context of the city of Rome in the middle of the second century and in the Roman Empire for at least another two centuries. In the expanding communicative space of the Hellenistic period and the principate, writing was regarded as a resource of power, and copying books could express allegiance, whether this took the form of copying Epicurus in Campania, rewriting the Bible at Rome, or copying Hermas in Oxyrhynchos. The copying of these texts did not aim primarily at public reading but allowed for and called for individual practice, for which it was important to have them in an easily accessible library, if not one's own. In terms of book culture, I do not see any significant distinction between Jews and Christians, or Greeks and Romans.[32] But I do think that one can detect chronological differences and developments: by the third century AD, the practices of reading and copying were much more widespread and important for religion than they were in the third century BC. Writing had become a tool and institution in the individualization of lived ancient religion.

---

32. Here I would disagree with Haines-Eitzen (ibid., 132).

Conclusion

I began this book with a lengthy reflection on concepts and their consequences for our perspective on premodern, in particular ancient, religion. In later chapters I hope I have demonstrated that lived religion and individual appropriations need not be sought at the margins of orthodox religious practices, in the niches of civic religion. These phenomena are identifiable at the heart of rituals like praying, vowing, dedicating, and reading. We have observed interesting individuals in their role as authors, but this is by no means a new approach. However, these authors, in very different ways, reflect on individual appropriation of religion among their contemporaries, and they offer these reflections to their readership or audiences. Whereas Propertius remains in the role of the distant observer of a traditional religious role (albeit not without criticism, as 4.1 makes clear), and Ovid follows him in this, Hermas urgently pursues distribution and thereby opens up new religious roles for his recipients. For him, religious individuality has become crucial.

I will not deny that a very old explanation for this exists: the classification of Hermas as a Christian. I have not taken that path. Neither the causes of Hermas's religious individuality nor its consequences are restricted to what are later claimed as features of a Christian genealogy: being a Jew, a Roman, a businessman, a citizen of the Roman Empire. Ancient distinctions of this nature cease to be of primary importance when we focus on lived ancient religion and the individual. What is necessary today is a history of ancient religion that is not compartmentalized into a number of confessional histories, of Jewish and pagan, Christian or Manichaean histories of religion. In my Townsend Lectures I have endeavored to present alternatives.

BIBLIOGRAPHY

Ahn, Gregor. 1993. "Monotheismus, Polytheismus: Grenzen und Möglichkeiten einer Klassifikation von Gottesvorstellungen." In *Mesopotamica, Ugaritica, Biblica*, edited by Manfred Dietrich and Loretz Oswald, 1–25. Neukirchen-Vluyn: Butzon & Bercker Kevelaer.

Alcock, Susan E. and Robin Osbourne, eds. 1994. *Placing the Gods: Sanctuaries and Sacred Space in Ancient Greece*. Oxford: Clarendon.

Alessi, Paul T. 1985. "Propertius 2.28: Unity without Illness." *Classical Journal* 81 (1): 39–48.

Alföldy, Géza. 1991. "Augustus und die Inschriften: Tradition und Innovation: Die Geburt der imperialen Epigraphik." *Gymnasium* 98:289–324.

Altheim, Franz. 1953. *Römische Religionsgeschichte*. Baden-Baden: Verlag für Kunst und Wissenschaft.

Ando, Clifford. 2008. *The Matter of the Gods: Religion and the Roman Empire*. Transformation of the Classical Heritage. Berkeley: University of California Press.

Andreau, J., P. Schmitt, and A. Schnapp. 1978. "Paul Veyne et l'évergétisme." *Annales (ESC)* 33:307–24.

Anonymous. 1994. *La mémoire perdue: A la recherche des archives oubliées, publiques et privées, de la Rome antique; Avant-propos de Claude Nicolet*. Série Histoire Ancienne et Médiévale 30. Paris: Publications de la Sorbonne.

Anonymous. 1999. "Inscribing Performance." In *Performance Culture and Athenian Democracy*, edited by Simon Goldhill and Robin Osborne, 341–58. Oxford: Oxford University Press.

Arvanitis, Nikolaos, ed. 2010. *Il santuario di Vesta: La casa delle vestali e il tenpio di Vesta VIII sec. A.C.–64 D.C.; Rapporto preliminare*. Pisa: Serra.

Arweiler, Alexander, and Melanie Möller, eds. 2008. *Vom Selbst-Verständnis in Antike und Neuzeit: Notions of the Self in Antiquity and Beyond*. Berlin: de Gruyter.

Asad, Talal. 1973. *Anthropology and the Colonial Encounter*. London: Ithaca Press.

———. 1983. "Anthropological Conceptions of Religion: Reflections on Geertz." *Man NS* 18:237–59.

Assayag, Jackie, Roland Lardinois, and Denis Vidal. 2001. *Orientalism and Anthropology: From Max Müller to Louis Dumont*. 2nd ed. Pondichéry: Institut Français de Pondichéry.

Athanassiadi, Polymnia, and Michael Frede, eds. 1999. *Pagan Monotheism in Late Antiquity*. Oxford: Clarendon Press.

Auffarth, Christoph. 1997. "Atheismus." *Neuer Pauly* 2:159–60.

———. 2009. "Mittelalterliche Modelle der Eingrenzung und Ausgrenzung religiöser Verschiedenheit." In *Europäische Religionsgeschichte: Ein mehrfacher Pluralismus*, edited by Hans G. Kippenberg, Jörg Rüpke, and Kocku von Stuckrad, 193–218. Göttingen: Vandenhoeck & Ruprecht.

Aupers, Stef, and Dick Houtman. 2008. "The Sacralization of the Self: Relocating the Sacred on the Ruins of Traditions." In *Religion: Beyond a Concept*, edited by Hent de Vries, 798–812. New York: Fordham University Press.

Barchiesi, Alessandro. 1994. *Il poeta e il principe: Ovidio e il discorso Augusteo*. Rome: Laterza.

Bassani, Maddalena. 2008. *Sacraria: Ambienti e piccoli edifici per il culto domestico in area vesuviana*. Antenor Quaderni 9. Rome: Quasar.

Bätz, Alexander. 2012. *Sacrae virgines: Studien zum religiösen und gesellschaftlichen Status der Vestalinnen*. Paderborn: Schöningh.

Baudry, Robinson. 2006. "Patriciens et nobles à Rome: D'une identité à l'autre?" *Hypothèses* 10 (1): 169–78.

Beard, Mary. 1985. "Writing and Ritual: A Study of Diversity and Expansion in the Arval Acta." *PBSR* 53:114–62.

———. 1986. "Cicero and Divination: The Formation of a Latin Discourse." *JRS* 76:33–46.

———. 1987. "A Complex of Times: No More Sheep on Romulus' Birthday." *Proceedings of the Cambridge Philological Society* 33:1–15.

———. 1988. "Rituel, texte, temps: Les Parilia romains." In *Essais sur le rituel*, edited by Anne-Marie Blondeau and Kristofer Schipper, 15–29. Louvain: Peeters.

———. 1989. "Acca Larentia Gains a Son: Myths and Priesthood at Rome." In *Images of Authority: Papers Presented to Joyce Reynolds on the Occasion of Her Seventieth Birthday*, edited by Mary Margaret Mackenzie and Charlotte Roueché, 41–61. Cambridge: Cambridge Philological Society.

———. 1991. "Writing and Religion: Ancient Literacy and the Function of the Written Word in Roman Religion." *Literacy in the Roman World*, edited by Mary Beard, 35–58. Ann Arbor, MI: Journal of Roman Archaeology.

———. 1993. "Looking (Harder) for Roman Myth: Dumézil, Declamation and the Problems of Definition." In *Mythos in mythenloser Gesellschaft: Das Paradigma Roms*, edited by Fritz Graf, 44–64. Stuttgart: Teubner.

———. 1998. "Documenting Roman Religion." In *La mémoire perdue: Recherches sur l'administration romaine*, 75–101. Rome.

———. 2007. *The Roman Triumph*. Cambridge, MA: Belknap Press of Harvard University Press.

Beard, Mary, John North, and Simon Price. 1998. *Religions of Rome*. Vol. 1, *A History*. Vol. 2, *A Sourcebook*. Cambridge: Cambridge University Press.

Belayche, Nicole. 2006. "Rites et 'croyances' dans l'épigraphie religieuse de l'Anatolie impériale." *Entretiens sur l'Antiquité Classique* 53 (Rites et Croyances dans les Religions du Monde Romain): 73–115.

———. 2007. "Religious Actors in Daily Life: Practices and Related Beliefs." In *A Companion to Roman Religion*, edited by Jörg Rüpke, 275–91. Oxford: Blackwell.

———. 2008. "Du texte à l'image: Les reliefs sur les stèles 'de confession' d'Anatolie." In *Image et religion dans l'antiquité gréco-romaine: Actes du colloque de Rome, 11–13 décembre 2003*, edited by Sylvia Estienne et al., 181–94. Collection du Centre Jean Bérard. Naples: Centre Jean Bérard.

———. 2011. "Entre deux éclats de rire: Sacrifice et représentation du divin dans le 'De sacrificiis' de Lucien." In *"Nourrir les dieux?" Sacrifice et représentation du divin*, edited by V. Pirenne-Delforge and F. Prescendi, 165–80. Liège: Centre Internationale d'Étude de la Religion Grecque Antique.

Belayche, Nicole, and Jörg Rüpke. 2007. "Divination et révélation dans les mondes grec et romain: Présentation." *Revue de l'Histoire des Religions* 224 (2): 139–47.

Belayche, Nicole et al. 2005a. "Divination romaine." *ThesCRA* 3:79–104.

Belayche, Nicole et al., eds. 2005b. *Nommer les dieux: Théonymes, épithètes, épiclèses dans l'antiquité*. Recherches sur les rhétoriques religieuses 5. Turnhout: Brepols.

Bell, Catherine. 1992. *Ritual Theory, Ritual Practice*. New York: Oxford University Press.

Bendlin, Andreas. 2000. "Looking beyond the Civic Compromise: Religious Pluralism in Late Republican Rome." In *Religion in Archaic and Republican Rome and Italy: Evidence and Experience*, edited by Edward Bispham and Christopher Smith, 115–35, 167–70. Edinburgh: Edinburgh University Press.

———. 2006. "Vom Nutzen und Nachteil der Mantik: Orakel im Medium von Handlung und Literatur in der Zeit der Zweiten Sophistik." In *Texte als Medium und Reflexion von Religion im römischen Reich*, edited by Dorothee Elm von der Osten, Jörg Rüpke, and Katharina Waldner, 159–207. Stuttgart: Steiner.

Bennett, Alva Walter. 1969. "Propertius 3.24: A New Approach." *Classical Philology* 64 (1): 30–35.

Benoist, Stéphane et al., eds. 2009. *Mémoires partagées, mémoires disputées: Écriture et réécriture de l'histoire*. Centre Régional Universitaire Lorrain d'Histoire, Site de Metz 39. Metz: Université Paul Verlaine-Metz.

Berger, Peter L., and Thomas Luckmann. 1967. *The Social Construction of Reality: A Treatise in the Sociology of Knowledge*. Garden City, NY: Doubleday.

Bergmann, Sigurd. 2008. "Lived Religion in Lived Space." In *Lived Religion: Conceptual, Empirical and Practical-Theological Approaches*, edited by Heinz Streib, Astrid Dinter and Kerstin Söderblom, 197–209. Leiden: Brill.

Bernstein, Frank. 2007. "Complex Rituals: Games and Processions in Republican Rome." In *A Companion to Roman Religion*, edited by Jörg Rüpke, 222–34. Oxford: Blackwell.

Bettini, Maurizio. 2012. "Properzio, Vertumno e i *mores* pubblici." In *Properzio fra tradizione e innovazione: Atti del convegno internazionale, Assisi-Spello, 21–23 maggio 2010*, edited by Roberto Cristofoli, Carlo Santini, and Francesco Santucci, 99–110. Centro studi poesia latina in ditici elegiaci 12. Assisi: Accademia Properziana del Subasio.

Bierl, Anton. 2001. *Der Chor in der alten Komödie: Ritual und Performativität (unter besonderer Berücksichtigung von Aristophanes' "Thesmophüriazusen" und der Phalloslieder fr. 851 PMG)*. Beiträge zur Altertumskunde 126. Munich: Saur.

Blänsdorf, Jürgen. 2005. "The Curse Tablets from the Sanctuary of Isis and Mater Magna in Mainz." *MHNH* 5:11–26.

———. 2008. "Die Defixionum tabellae des Mainzer Isis- und Mater-Magna-Heiligtum." In *Instrumenta inscripta Latina 2: Akten des 2. Internationalen Kolloquiums, Klagenfurt 2005*, edited by Manfred Hainzmann and Reinhold Wedenig, 47–70. Aus Forschung und Kunst 36. Klagenfurt: Geschichtsverein Kärnten.

———, ed. 2009. *Forschungen zum Mainzer Isis- und Mater-Magna-Heiligtum*. Vol. 1, *Die Defixionum tabellae des Mainzer Isis- und Mater-Magna- Heiligtums (DTM)*. Mainzer Archäologische Schriften 1. Mainz.

Boardman, John et al. 2004. "Dedications, Greek." *ThesCRA* 1:269–318.

Bodel, John. 2008. "Cicero's Minerva, Penates, and the Mother of the Lares: An Outline of Roman Domestic Religion." In *Household and Family Religion in Antiquity*, edited by John Bodel and Saul M. Olyan, 248–75. Oxford: Blackwell.

Bömer, Franz. 1958. *P. Ovidius Naso, Die Fasten*. Vol. 2, *Kommentar*. Heidelberg: Winter.

Bonnet, Corinne, Jörg Rüpke, and Paolo Scarpi, eds. 2006. *Religions orientales, culti misterici: Neue Perspektiven, nouvelle perspectives, prospettive nuove*. Potsdamer altertumswissenschaftliche Beiträge 16. Stuttgart: Steiner.

Booth, Joan. 2001. "Problems and Programmatics in Propertius 1.1." *Hermes* 129 (1): 63–74.

Booth, Wayne C. 1983. *The Rhetoric of Fiction*. 2nd ed. Chicago: University of Chicago Press.

Borgolte, Michael, ed. 2001. *Unaufhebbare Pluralität der Kulturen? Zur Dekonstruktion und Konstruktion des mittelalterlichen Europa*. Historische Zeitschrift Beihefte NF 32. Munich: Oldenbourg.

Bowden, Hugh. 2010. *Mystery Cults of the Ancient World*. Princeton and London: Princeton University Press / Thames & Hudson.

Bowersock, G. W. 1995. *Martyrdom and Rome*. Cambridge: Cambridge University Press.

Bowman, Alan K., and Greg Woolf, eds. 1994. *Literacy and Power in the Ancient World*. Cambridge: Cambridge University Press.

Boyd, Barbara Weiden. 2006. "Two Rivers and the Reader in Ovid, *Metamorphoses* 8." *TAPhA* 136:171–206.

Boyle, A. J., and R. D. Woodard. 2004. *Ovid, Fasti: Translated and Edited with an Introduction and Notes*. Repr. with corr. edn. London: Penguin.

Brakke, David, Michael L. Satlow, and StevenWeitzman, eds. 2005. *Religion and the Self in Antiquity*. Bloomington: Indiana University Press.

Bräunlein, Peter. 2009. "Ikonische Repräsentation von Religion." In *Europäische Religionsgeschichte: Ein mehrfacher Pluralismus*, edited by Hans G. Kippenberg, Jörg Rüpke, and Kocku von Stuckrad, 774–77. Göttingen: Vandenhoeck & Ruprecht.

Brelich, Angelo. 1969. *Paides e parthenoi.* Vol. 1, *Incunabula graeca* 36. Rome: Ateneo.

Bremmer, Jan N. 1983. *The Early Greek Concept of the Soul.* Princeton, NJ: Princeton University Press.

———. 2002. *The Rise and Fall of the Afterlife: The 1995 Read-Tuckwell Lectures at the University of Bristol.* London: Routledge.

Broise, Henri, and John Scheid. 1987. *Recherches archéologiques à la Magliana: Le balneum des frères arvales.* Roma antica 1. Rome: École française de Rome.

Brown, John Pairman. 1986. "The Templum and the Saeculum: Sacred Space and Time in Israel and Etruria." *Zeitschrift für die Alttestamentliche Wissenschaft* 98:415–33.

Brown, Peter. 1988. *The Body and Society: Men, Women and Sexual Renunciation in Early Christianity.* Lectures on the History of Religions n.s. 13. New York: Columbia University Press.

Brox, Norbert. 1991. *Der Hirt des Hermas. Übers. und erkl. von.* Kommentar zu den Apostolischen Vätern 7. Göttingen: Vandenhoeck & Ruprecht.

Bruce, Steve. 1999. *Choice and Religion: A Critique of Rational Choice Theory.* Oxford: Oxford University Press.

Bucur, Bogdan Gabriel. 2007. "The Son of God and the Angelomorphic Holy Spirit: A Reading of the Shepherd's Christology." *Zeitschrift für Neutestamentliche Wissenschaft* 98:120–42.

———. 2009a. "The Divine Face and the Angels of the Face: Jewish Apocalyptic Themes in Early Christology and Pneumatology." In *Apocalyptic Thought in Early Christianity*, edited by Robert J. Daly, 143–53. Grand Rapids, MI: Baker Academic.

———. 2009b. *Angelomorphic Pneumatology: Clement of Alexandria and Other Early Christian Witnesses.* Supplements to Vigiliae Christianae. Leiden: Brill.

Burck, Erich. 1966. "Zur Kompositon des vierten Buches des Properz." *WS* 79:405–27.

Butrica, James L. 1984. *The Manuscript Tradition of Propertius.* Phoenix Suppl. 17. Toronto: University of Toronto Press.

Bynum, Caroline Walker. 1991. *Fragmentation and Redemption: Essays on Gender and the Human Body in Medieval Religion.* New York: Zone Books.

Cairns, Francis. 1972. *Generic Composition in Greek and Roman Poetry.* Edinburgh: Edinburgh University Press.

———. 1979. *Vergil and Roman Elegy, Medieval Latin Poetry and Prose, Greek Lyric and Drama.* Papers of the Liverpool Latin Seminar 2 = Arca 3. Liverpool: Cairns.

———. 1984. "Propertius and the Battle of Actium (4.6)." In *Poetry and Politics in the Age of Augustus*, edited by Tony Woodman and David West, 129–68. Cambridge: Cambridge University Press.

———. 2006. *Sextus Propertius the Augustan Elegist.* Cambridge: Cambridge University Press.

———. 2007. *Papers on Roman Elegy 1969–2003.* Eikasmos, Studi 16. Bologna: Pàtron.

Cameron, Averil. 1991. *Christianity and the Rhetoric of Empire: The Development of Christian Discourse.* Sather Classical Lectures 55. Berkeley: University of California Press.

Camps, W. A., ed. 1961. *Propertius, Elegies: Book I.* Cambridge: Cambridge University Press.

Cancik, Hubert. 1973. "Römischer Religionsunterricht in apostolischer Zeit: Ein pastoralgeschichtlicher Versuch zu Statius, *Silve* V 3,176–184." In *Wort Gottes in der Zeit: Festschrift für K. H. Schelkle*, edited by Helmut Feld and Josef Nolte, 181–97. Düsseldorf: Patmos.

———. 1985. "Rome as Sacred Landscape: Varro and the End of Republican Religion in Rome." *Visible Religion* 4/5:250–65.

Cancik-Lindemaier, Hildegard. 1990. "Kultische Privilegierung und gesellschaftliche Realität: Ein Beitrag zur Sozialgeschichte der Virgines Vestae." *Saeculum* 41:1–16.

Casadio, Giovanni. 2006. "Ancient Mystic Religion: The Emergence of a New Paradigm from A.D. Nock to Ugo Bianchi." *Mediterraneo Antico* 9 (2): 485–534.

Certeau, Michel de. 1988. *The Writing of History.* Translated by Tom Conley. New York: Columbia University Press.

———. 2007. *Arts de faire.* Edited by Luce Giard. New ed. Paris: Gallimard.

Chioffi, L. 1996. "Iuppiter Propugnator, Aedes." In *Lexicon Topographicum urbis Romae 3: H-O*, edited by Eva Margareta Steinby, 155. Rome: Querza.

Cicala, Valeria. 2007. "Tradizione e culti domestici." In *Immagini divine: Devozioni e divinità nella vita quotidiana ei Romani, testimonianze archeologiche dall'Emilia Romagna*, edited by Jacopo Ortalli and Diana Neri, 43–55. Quaderni di Archeologia dell'Emilia Romagna. Florence: All'Insegna del Giglio.

Coakley, S., ed. 1997. *Religion and the Body.* Cambridge: Cambridge University Press.

Collar, Anna. 2007. "Network Theory and Religious Innovation." *Mediterranean Historical Review* 22 (1): 149–62.

———. 2014. *Religious Networks in the Roman Empire: The Spread of New Ideas.* Cambridge: Cambridge University Press.

Collins, John J. 1987. "Apocalypse: An Overview." *Encyclopedia of Religion* 1:334–36.

Connerton, Paul. 1989. *How Societies Remember.* Cambridge: Cambridge University Press.

Corbier, Mireille. 1991. "L'écriture en quête de lecteurs." In *Literacy in the Roman World*, edited by Mary Beard et al., 99–118. Ann Arbor, MI: Journal of Roman Archaeology.

Coutelle, Éric. 2005. *Poétique et métapoésie chez Properce: De l'Ars amandi à l'Ars scribendi.* Bibliothèque d'études classiques 44. Leuven: Peeters.

Cristofoli, Roberto, Carlo Santini, and Francesco Santucci, eds. 2010. *Tempo e spazio nella poesia di Properzio: Atti del convegno internazionale, Assisi, 23–25 maggio 2008.* Centro studi poesia latina in distici elegiaci 11. Assisi: Accademia Properziana del Subasio.

Csordas, Thomas J. 1994. *Embodiment and Experience: The Existential Ground of Culture and Self.* Cambridge Studies in Medical Anthropology. Cambridge: Cambridge University Press.

Cubitt, Geoffrey. 2007. *History and Memory.* Historical Approaches. Manchester: Manchester University Press.

Curchin, Leonard. 1995. "Literacy in the Roman Provinces: Qualitative and Quantitative Data from Central Spain." *AJP* 116:461–76.

Cusamano, Nicola et al., eds. 2013. *Memory and Religious Experience in the Graeco-Roman World*. Potsdamer altertumswissenschaftliche Beiträge 45. Stuttgart: Steiner.

Dagenais, John. 1994. *The Ethics of Reading in Manuscript Culture: Glossing the "Libro de buen amor."* Princeton, NJ: Princeton University Press.

Davies, Douglas. 2008. "Cultural Intensification: A Theory for Religion." In *Religion and the Individual: Belief, Practice, Identity*, edited by Abby Day, 7–18. Aldershot: Ashgate.

Dawson, Lorne L. 2006. "Privatisation, Globalisation, and Religious Innovation: Giddens' Theory of Modernity and the Refutation of Secularisation Theory." In *Theorising Religion: Classical and Contemporary Debates*, edited by James A. Beckford and John Walliss, 105–19. Aldershot: Ashgate.

Dean-Otting, Mary. 1984. *Heavenly Journeys: A Study of the Motif in Hellenistic Jewish Literature*. Judentum und Umwelt 8. Frankfurt a. M.: Lang.

Degrassi, Attilio, ed. 1963. *Inscriptiones Italiae 13: Fasti et elogia*. Vol. 2, *Fasti anni Numani et Iuliani, accedunt ferialia, menologia rustica, parapegmata*. Rome: Libreria dello stato.

Demoen, Kristoffel, and Danny Praet, eds. 2009. *Theois Sophistes: Essays on Flavius Philostratus' Vita Apollonii*. Mnemosyne suppl. 305. Leiden: Brill.

Dépelteau, François. 2008. "Relational Thinking: A Critique of Co-Deterministic Theories of Structure and Agency." *Sociological Theory* 26 (1): 51–73.

Derks, Ton, and Nico Roymans. 2002. "Seal-Boxes and the Spread of Latin Literacy in the Rhine-Delta." In *Becoming Roman, Writing Latin? Literacy and Epigraphy in the Roman West*, edited by Alison Cooley and Andrew Burnett, 87–134. JRA Supplementary Series 48. Portsmouth: Journal of Roman Archaeology.

Dickie, Matthew W. 2001. *Magic and Magicians in the Greco-Roman World*. London: Routledge.

Dignas, Beate, and R. R. R. Smith. 2012. Introduction. In *Historical and Religious Memory in the Ancient World*, edited by Beate Dignas and R. R. R. Smith, 1–11. Oxford: Oxford University Press.

Döpp, Sigmar. 1978. "Zur Datierung von Macrobius' Saturnalia." *Hermes* 106:619–32.

Dow, Sterling. 1968. "Six Athenian Sacrificial Calendars." *Bulletin de Correspondance Hellénique* 92:170–86.

Dumont, Louis. 1986. *Essays on Individualism: Modern Ideology in Anthropological Perspective*. Chicago: University of Chicago Press.

Eck, Werner. 1995. "'Tituli honorarii,' curriculum vitae und Selbstdarstellung in der Hohen Kaiserzeit." In *Acta Colloquii Epigraphici Latini: Helsingiae 3.–6. sept. 1991 habiti*, edited by Heikki Solin, Olli Salomies, and Uta-Maria Liertz, 211–37. Helsinki: Societas Scientiarum Fennica.

Edwards, Catharine. 1996. *Writing Rome: Textual Approaches to the City*. Cambridge: Cambridge University Press.

Ehmig, Ulrike. 2015. "Ausschlussverfahren: Eine Gruppe italischer Grabinschriften als Beispiel sozialer Überassimilierung in der römischen Kaiserzeit." *Epigraphica* 77 (1–2): 193–205.

Ehrenreich, Robert M., Carole L. Crumley, and Janet E. Levy, eds. 1995. *Heterarchy and the Analysis of Complex Societies*. Archaeological Papers of the American Anthropological Association. Arlington, VA: American Anthropological Association.

Ehrman, Bart D., ed. and trans. 2003a. *The Apostolic Fathers.* Vol. 2, *Epistle of Barnabas, Papias and Quadratus, Epistle to Diognetus, the Shepherd of Hermas.* LCL 25. Cambridge, MA: Harvard University Press.

———. 2003b. *Lost Scriptures: Books That Did Not Make It into the New Testament.* Oxford: Oxford University Press.

Eidinow, Esther. 2011. "Networks and Narratives: A Model for Ancient Greek Religion." *Kernos* 24:9–38.

Elsner, Jaś. 1995. *Art and the Roman Viewer: The Transformation of Art from the Pagan World to Christianity.* Cambridge: Cambridge University Press.

Emirbayer, Mustafa, and Ann Mische. 1998. "What Is Agency?" *American Journal of Sociology* 103 (4): 962–1023.

Emmet, Dorothy. 1966. *Rules, Roles and Relations.* Boston: Beacon.

Ennabli, Liliane, and John Scheid. 2007–2008. "Une lex sacra de Carthage relative au culte des Cereres? Nouvelles observations sur les fragments découverts dans la basilique de Carthagena." *Rendiconti Pontificia Accademia Romana di Archeologia* 80:37–75.

Erll, Astrid. 2011. *Memory in Culture.* Houndmills, Basingstoke: Palgrave Macmillan.

Fantham, Elaine. 2002. "Ovid's *Fasti*: Politics, History, and Religion." In *Brill's Companion to Ovid*, edited by Barbara Weiden Boyd, 197–233. Leiden: Brill.

Farney, Gary D. 2007. *Ethnic Identity and Aristocratic Competition in Republican Rome.* Cambridge: Cambridge University Press.

Fedeli, Paolo. 1980. *Sesto Properzi: Il primo libro delle Elegie; Introduzione, testo critico e commento.* Accademia Toscana di Scienze e lettere "La Colombaria": Studi 53. Florence: Olschki.

———. 1985. *Properzio: Il libro terzo delle Elegie; Introduzione, testo e commento.* Studi e commenti 3. Bari: Adriatica.

———. 2005. *Properzio Elegie libro II: Introduzione, testo e commento.* Arca. Cambridge: Cairns.

Feeney, Denis. 1994. "Si licet et fas est: Ovid's *Fasti* and the Problem of Free Speech under the Principate." In *Roman Poetry and Propaganda in the Age of Augustus*, edited by Anton Powell, 1–25. London: Bristol Classical Press.

———. 1998. *Literature and Religion at Rome: Cultures, Contexts, and Beliefs.* Cambridge: Cambridge University Press.

———. 2007a. "The History of Roman Religion in Roman Historiography and Epic." In *A Companion to Roman Religion*, edited by Jörg Rüpke, 129–42. Oxford: Blackwell.

———. 2007b. *Caesar's Calendar: Ancient Time and the Beginnings of History.* Sather Classical Lectures. Berkeley: University of California Press.

Feichtinger, Barbara. 1991. "Properz, Vates oder Haruspex? Zu seinem politischen und poetischen Selbstverstaendnis." *Classica et Mediaevalia* 42:187–212.

Fitzgerald, Allan D. 2008. "Penance." In *Oxford Handbook of Early Christian Study*, edited by Susan Ashbrook Harvey and David G Hunter, 786–807. Oxford: Oxford University Press.

Flower, Harriet. 2003. "'Memories' of Marcellus: History and Memory in Roman Republican Culture." In *Formen römischer Geschichtsschreibung von den Anfängen bis Livius: Gattungen, Autoren, Kontexte*, edited by Ulrich Eigler, 39–52. Darmstadt: Wissenschaftliche Buchgesellschaft.

Fowden, Garth. 2005. "Late Polytheism." In *The Cambridge Ancient History*. Vol. 12, *The Crisis of Empire, A.D. 193–337*, edited by Alan K. Bowman, Averil Cameron, and Peter Garnsey, 521–72. Cambridge: Cambridge University Press.

Fox, Matthew. 1996. *Roman Historical Myths: The Regal Period in Augustan Literature*. Oxford: Clarendon.

Francis, James A. 2012. "Late Antique Visuality: Blurring the Boundaries between Word and Image, Pagan and Christian." In *Shifting Cultural Frontiers in Late Antiquity*, edited by David Brakke, Deborah Deliyannis, and Edward Watts, 139–49. Farnham, Surrey: Ashgate.

Frend, W. H. C. 1965. *Martyrdom and Persecution in the Eary Church: A Study of Conflict from the Maccabees to Donatus*. Oxford: Blackwell.

Frier, Bruce Woodward. 1979. *Libri Annales Pontificum Maximorum: The Origins of the Annalistic Tradition*. Papers and Monographs of the American Academy in Rome 27. Rome: American Academy.

Fröhlich, Thomas. 1991. *Lararien- und Fassadenbilder in den Vesuvstädten: Untersuchungen zur "volkstümlichen" pompejanischen Malerei*. Mitteilungen des Deutschen Archäologischen Instituts Rom, Ergänzungsheft 32. Mainz: Zabern.

Fuchs, Martin. 1988. *Theorie und Verfremdung: Max Weber, Louis Dumont und die Analyse der indischen Gesellschaft*. Europäische Hochschulschriften Reihe 20, Philosophie 241. Frankfurt am Main: Lang.

———. 2015. "Processes of Religious Individualization: Stocktaking and Issues for the Future." *Religion* 45 (3): 330–43.

Fuchs, Martin, and Jörg Rüpke, eds. 2015. "Religious Individualisation in Historical Perspective." = *Religion* 45 (1): 323–29.

Fuchs, Stephan. 2001. "Beyond Agency." *Scoiological Theory* 19 (1): 24–40.

Fulkerson, Laurel. 2002. "(Un)Sympathetic Magic: A Study of *Heroides* 13." *American Journal of Philology* 123 (1): 61–87.

Füssel, Marian. 2006. "Die Kunst der Schwachen: Zum Begriff der 'Aneignung' in der Geschichtswissenschaft." *Sozial. Geschichte* 21 (3): 7–28.

Fyntikoglou, V., and E. Voutiras. 2005. "Prayer 6.b. Roman." *ThesCRA* 3:151–79.

Galinsky, Karl. 1996. *Augustan Culture: An Interpretive Introduction*. Princeton, NJ: Princeton University Press.

Gasparini, Valentino. 2016. "Ears." In *Contributi in honore di Coarelli*. Potsdamer altertumswissenschaftliche Beiträge. Stuttgart: Steiner. Forthcoming.

Genette, Gérard. 1980. *Narrative Discourse: An Essay in Method*. Ithaca, NY: Cornell University Press.

———. 1988. *Narrative Discourse Revisited*. Ithaca, NY: Cornell University Press.

———. 1994. *Die Erzählung*. Translated and with an introduction by Jürgen Vogt. Translated from the French by Andreas Knop. Munich: Fink.

Gibson, Roy K. 2007. *Excess and Restraint: Propertius, Horace, and Ovid's "Ars amatoria."* Bulletin of the Institute of Classical Studies Supplement 89. London: Institute of Classical Studies, University of London.

Gill, Christopher. 1988. "Personhood and Personality: The Four-Personae Theory in Cicero, *De officiis* I." *Oxford Studies in Ancient Philosophy* 6:169–99.

———. 2006. *The Structured Self in Hellenistic and Roman Thought*. Oxford: Oxford University Press.

————. 2008. "The Self and Hellenstic-Roman Philosophical Therapy." In *Vom Selbst-Verständnis in Antike und Neuzeit: Notions of the Self in Antiquity and Beyond*, edited by Alexander Arweiler and Melanie Möller, 359–80. Transformationen der Antike 8. Berlin: de Gruyter.

Gladigow, Burkhard. 2000. "Opfer und komplexe Kulturen." In *Das Opfer: Theologische und kulturelle Kontexte*, edited by Bernd Janowski and Michael Welker, 86–107. Frankfurt a. M.: Suhrkamp.

————. 2002. "Polytheismus und Monotheismus: Zur historischen Dynamik einer europäischen Alternative." In *Polytheismus und Monotheismus in der Religionen des Vorderen Orients*, edited by Manfred Krebernik and Jürgen van Oorschot, 3–20. Alter Orient und Altes Testament 298. Münster: Ugarit.

————. 2005. *Religionswissenschaft als Kulturwissenschaft*. Religionswissenschaft heute 1. Stuttgart: Kohlhammer.

Glinister, Fay. 2011. "'Bring on the Dancing Girls': Some Thoughts on the Salian Priesthood." In *Priests and State in the Roman World*, edited by James Richardson and Federico Santangelo, 107–36. Potsdamer Altertumswissenschaftlich Beiträge 33. Stuttgart: Steiner.

Goar, Robert J. 1972. *Cicero and the State Religion*. Amsterdam: Hakkert.

Goessler, P. 1928. "Ein gallorömischer Steckkalender aus Rottweil." *Germania* 12:1–9.

Goldberg, Sander M. 2005 *Constructing Literature in the Roman Republic: Poetry and Its Reception*. Cambridge: Cambridge University Press.

Gordon, Richard. 1979. "The Real and the Imaginary: Production and Religion in the Graeco-Roman World." *Art History* 2:5–34. Repr. in Richard Lindsay Gordon, *Image and Value in the Graeco-Roman World: Studies in Mithraism and Religious Art*, chap. 1. Variorum Collected Studies Series 551. Aldershot: Ashgate.

————. 2008. "The Power of Stones: Graeco-Egyptian Magical Amulets." *Journal of Roman Archaeology* 21:713–18.

————. 2011. "Archaeologies of Magical Gems." In *"Gems of Heaven": Recent Research on Engraved Gemstones in Late Antiquity c. AD 200–600*, edited by Chris Entwistle and Noel Adams, 39–49. British Museum Research Publication. London: British Museum Press.

————. 2013. "Cosmology, Astrology, and Magic: Discourse, Schemes, Power, and Literacy." In *Panthée: Religious Transformations in the Graeco-Roman Empire*, edited by Laurent Bricault and Corinne Bonnet, 85–111. Religions in the Graeco-Roman World 177. Leiden: Brill.

————. 2014. "Coming to Terms with the 'Oriental Religions of the Roman Empire.'" *Numen* 61:657–72.

————. 2015a. "Showing the Gods the Way: Curse-Tablets as Deictic Persuasion." *Religion in the Roman Empire* 1 (2): 148–80.

————. 2015b. "Temporary Deprivation: Rules and Meaning." In *A Companion to the Archaeology of Religion in the Ancient World*, edited by Rubina Raja and Jörg Rüpke, 194–206. Malden, MA: Wiley.

Graf, Fritz. 1996. *Gottesnähe und Schadenzauber: Die Magie in der griechisch-römischen Antike*. Munich: Beck.

Graf, Fritz, and Sarah Iles Johnston. 1999. "Magie III: Griechenland und Rom." *Der Neue Pauly* 7:662–70.

Grimes, R. L. 2006. "Performance." In *Theorizing Rituals: Issues, Topices, Approaches, Concepts*, edited by Jens Kreinath, Jan Snoeck, and Michael Stausberg, 379–94. Numen Book Series 114.1. Leiden: Brill.

———. 2011. *Ritual, Media, and Conflict*. New York: Oxford University Press.

Günther, Hans-Christian. 1997. *Quaestiones Propertianae*. Leiden: Brill.

———. 2012. "Properz und der Prinzipat." In *Properzio fra tradizione e innovazione: Atti del convegno internazionale, Assisi-Spello, 21–23 maggio 2010*, edited by Roberto Cristofoli, Carlo Santini, and Francesco Santucci, 27–46. Centro studi poesia latina in ditici elegiaci 12. Assisi: Accademia Properziana del Subasio.

Gurval, Robert Alan. 1995. *Actium and Augustus: The Politics and Emotions of Civil War*. Ann Arbor: University of Michigan Press.

Habinek, Thomas. 1998. *The Politics of Latin Literature: Writing, Identity, and Empire in Ancient Rome*. Princeton, NJ: Princeton University Press.

Hahn, Johannes. 1989. *Der Philosoph und die Gesellschaft: Selbstverständnis, öffentliches Auftreten und populäre Erwartungen in der hohen Kaiserzeit*. HABES 7. Stuttgart: Steiner.

Haines-Eitzen, Kim. 2000. *Guardians of Letters: Literacy, Power, and the Transmitters of Early Christian Literature*. New York: Oxford University Press.

———. 2012. *The Gendered Palimpsest: Women, Writing, and Representation in Early Christianity*. Oxford: Oxford University Press.

Halbwachs, Maurice. 1992. *On Collective Memory*. Edited and translated by Lewis A. Coser. Chicago: University of Chicago Press.

Harmon, D. P. 1986. "Religion in the Latin Elegists." *ANRW* 2.16.3:1909–73.

Harris, William V. 1989. *Ancient Literacy*. Cambridge, MA: Harvard University Press.

Heimbrock, Hans-Günter. 2007. "Reconstructing Lived Religion." In *Religion: Immediate Experience and the Mediacy of Research; Interdisciplinary Studies in the Objectives, Concepts and Methodology of Empirical Research in Religion*, edited by H.-G. Heimbrock and C. P. Scholtz, 133–57. Göttingen: Vandenhoeck & Ruprecht.

Hendry, M. 1996. "Guzzling Poison and Draining the Sea: A Conjecture on Propertius 2.24b.27." *Phoenix* 50 (1): 67–9.

Herbert-Brown, Geraldine. 1994. *Ovid and the Fasti: An Historical Study*. Oxford: Clarendon.

Herz, Peter. 1978. "Kaiserfeste der Prinzipatszeit." *ANRW* 2.16.2:1135–200.

Heyworth, S. J. 1986. "Notes on Propertius, Books III and IV." *CQ* 36:199–211.

———. 1995. "Propertius: Division, Transmission, and the Editor's Task." In *Papers of the Leeds International Latin Seminar 8: Roman Comedy, Augustan Poetry, Historiography*, edited by R. Brock and A. J. Woodman, 165–85. Leeds: Cairns.

———. 2007a. *Sexti Properti Elegos*. Oxford: Oxford University Press.

———. 2007b. *Cynthia: A Companion to the Text of Propertius*. Oxford: Oxford University Press.

Heyworth, S. J., and J. H. W. Morwood. 2011. *A Commentary on Propertius, Book 3*. Oxford: Oxford University Press.

Hezser, Catherine. 2001. *Jewish Literacy in Roman Palestine*. Tübingen: Mohr Siebeck.

Hickson Hahn, Frances 2007. "Performing the Sacred: Prayer and Hymns." In *A Companion to Roman Religion*, edited by Jörg Rüpke, 235–48. Oxford: Blackwell.

Hodge, Bob, and R. A. Buttimore. 1977. *The Monobiblios of Propertius: An Account of the First Book of Propertius Consisting of a Text, Translation, and Critical Essay on Each Poem. Carmina.* Cambridge: Brewer.

———. 2002. *Propertius, Elegies Book I: Text and Translation with a Critical Analysis of Each Poem.* Bristol: Bristol Classical Press.

Hofmann, Gert. 2004. "Performance und Poiesis: Kontinuität und Differenzierung des Rituals in der Tragödie." In *Theater, Ritual, Religion*, 179–95. Münster: LitVerlag.

Hubbard, Margaret. 1974. *Propertius.* London: Duckworth.

Hübner, Wolfgang. 2008. "Maghi e astrologi in Properzio." In *I personaggi dell'elegia di Properzio: Atti del convegno internazionale, Assisi, 26–28 maggio 2006*, edited by Carlo Santini and Francesco Santucci, 337–63. Centro studi poesia latina in distici elegiaci 10. Assisi: Accademia Properziana del Subasio.

Huet, Valérie. 2015. "Watching Rituals." In *A Companion to the Archaeology of Religion in the Ancient World*, edited by Rubina Raja and Jörg Rüpke, 144–54. Malden, MA: Wiley.

Humphrey, Caroline, and James Laidlaw. 1994. *The Archetypal Actions of Ritual: A Theory of Ritual Illustrated by the Jain Rite of Worship.* Oxford: Clarendon.

Hutchinson, G. O. 1984. "Propertius and the Unity of the Book." *JRS* 74:99–106.

———. 2006. *Propertius Elegies: Book IV.* Cambridge: Cambridge University Press.

Ibn, Warraq. 2007. *Defending the West: A Critique of Edward Said's "Orientalism."* Amherst, NY: Prometheus Books.

Iser, Wolfgang. 1972. *Der implizite Leser: Kommunikationsformen des Romans von Bunyan bis Beckett.* Theorie und Geschichte der Literatur und der schönen Künste Texte und Abhandlungen. Munich: Fink.

———. 1974. *The Implied Reader: Patterns of Communication in Prose Fiction from Bunyan to Beckett.* Baltimore: Johns Hopkins University Press.

———. 1976. *Der Akt des Lesens: Theorie ästhetischer Wirkung.* Munich: Fink.

———. 1978. *The Act of Reading: A Theory of Aesthetic Response.* Baltimore: Johns Hopkins University Press.

———. 1994. *Der Akt des Lesens: Theorie ästhetischer Wirkung.* 4th ed. Munich: Fink.

Janan, Micaela. 2001. *The Politics of Desire: Propertius IV.* Berkeley: University of California Press.

Jauss, Hans Robert. 1977a. "Theorie der Gattungen und Literatur des Mittelalters." In *Alterität und Modernität der mittelalterlichen Literatur: Gesammelte Aufsätze 1956–1976*, edited by Hans Robert Jauss, 327–58. Munich: Fink.

———. 1977b. *Ästhetische Erfahrung und literarische Hermeneutik.* Munich: Fink.

———. 1982. *Aesthetic Experience and Literary Hermeneutics.* Theory and History of Literature. Minneapolis: University of Minnesota Press.

———. 1987. *Die Theorie der Rezeption: Rückschau auf ihre unerkannte Vorgeschichte; Abschiedsvorlesung von Hans Robert Jauß am 11. Februar 1987 anläßlich seiner Emeritierung mit einer Ansprache des Rektors der Universität Konstanz, Horst Sund.* Konstanzer Universitätsreden 166. Konstanz: Universitätsverlag Konstanz.

Joas, Hans. 2013. *The Sacredness of the Person: A New Genealogy of Human Rights.* Washington, DC: Georgetown University Press.

Jocelyn, H. D. 1971. "Urbs augurio augusto condita: Enn. ap. Cic. Diu. 1. 107 (= Ann. 77–96 V²)." *PCPS* n.s. 17:45–74.

Johnson, W. R. 2009. *A Latin Lover in Ancient Rome: Readings in Propertius and His Genre.* Columbus: Ohio State University Press.

Johnson, William Allen. 2012. *Readers and Reading Culture in the High Roman Empire: A Study of Elite Communities.* Oxford: Oxford University Press.

Joly, Robert. 1958. *Hermas: Le pasteur; Introduction, texte critique, traduction et notes.* Sources chrétiennes 53. Paris: CERF.

———. 1968. *Hermas: Le pasteur; Introduction, texte critique, traduction et notes.* 2nd ed. Sources chrétiennes 53. Paris: CERF.

Jones, Christopher P. 1998. "Aelius Aristides and the Asklepieion." In *Pergamon: Citadel of the Gods; Archeological Record, Literary Description, and Religious Development*, edited by Helmut Koester, 63–76. Harrisburg, PA: Trinity Press International.

Jones, Kenneth R. 2011. *Jewish Reactions to the Destruction of Jerusalem in A.D. 70: Apocalypses and Related Pseudepigrapha.* Suppl. to the Journal for the Study of Judaism 151. Leiden: Brill.

Jung, Matthias. 1999. *Erfahrung und Religion: Grundzüge einer hermeneutisch-pragmatischen Religionsphilosophie.* Freiburg i. Br.: Alber.

———. 2006. "Making Life Explicit: The Symbolic Pregnance of Religious Experience." *Svensk Teologisk Kvartalskrift* 82:16–23.

Kaufmann-Heinemann, Annemarie. 1998. *Götter und Lararien aus Augusta Raurica: Herstellung, Fundzusammenhänge und sakrale Funktion figürlicher Bronzen in einer römischen Stadt.* Forschungen in Augst 26. Augst: Römermuseum.

Keith, Alison. 2008. *Propertius: Poet of Love and Leisure.* London: Duckworth.

Kindt, Julia. 2012. *Rethinking Greek Religion.* Cambridge: Cambridge University Press.

King, Richard. 2004. "Male Homosocial Readership and the Dedication of Ovid's *Fasti*." *Arethusa* 37:197–223.

Kippenberg, Hans G. 1990. "Geheime Offenbarungsbücher und Loyalitätskonflikte im antiken Judentum." In *Loyalitätskonflikte in der Religionsgeschichte: Festschrift Carsten Colpe*, edited by Christoph Elsas and Hans G. Kippenberg, 258–68. Würzburg.

Klausner, Samuel Z. 2005. "Martyrdom." In *Encyclopedia of Religion*, edited by Lindsay Jones, 5737–44. 2nd ed. Detroit: Macmillan Reference USA.

Klose, Alfred. 1910. *Römische Priesterfasten.* Trebnitz i. Schl.: Maretzke & Märtin.

Knoblauch, Hubert. 1999. *Religionssoziologie.* Berlin: Walter de Gruyter.

Kohl, Karl-Heinz. 2003. *Die Macht der Dinge: Geschichte und Theorie sakraler Objekt.* Munich: Beck.

Köpf, Ulrich. 1993. "Die Idee der 'Einheitskultur' des Mittelalters." *Troeltsch-Studien* 6:103–21.

Köves-Zulauf, Thomas. 1972. *Reden und Schweigen: Römische Religion bei Plinius Maior.* Studia et Testimonia Antiqua 12. Munich: Fink.

Krech, Volkhard. 2011. *Wo bleibt die Religion? Zur Ambivalenz des Religiösen in der modernen Gesellschaft.* Bielefeld: Transcript.

Lardinois, André, ed. 2011. *Sacred Words: Orality, Literacy and Religion = Orality and Literacy in the Ancient World 8.* Mnemosyne Supplements. Leiden: Brill.

Latour, Bruno. 2005. *Reassembling the Social: An Introduction to Actor-Network-Theory.* Oxford: Oxford University Press.

Latte, Kurt. 1960. *Römische Religionsgeschichte.* Handbuch der Altertumswissenschaft 5.4. Munich: Beck.

Lawson, E. Thomas. 1990. *Rethinking Religion: Connecting Cognition and Culture.* Cambridge: Cambridge University Press.

———. 2000. "Towards a Cognitive Science of Religion." *Numen* 47:338–49.

Ledentu, Marie. 2004. *Studium scribendi: Recherches sur les statuts de l'écrivain et de l'écriture à Rome à la fin de la République.* Bibliothèque d'Études Classiques 39. Louvain: Peeters.

Leeuw, G. van. 1939. *Virginibus Puerisque: A Study on the Service of Children in Worship.* Mededeelingen der Koninklijke Nederlandsche Akademie van Wetenschappen, afd. Letterkunde, NR 2.12. Amsterdam: Noord-Hollandsche Uitgevers Maatschappij.

Lefèvre, Eckard. 2001. *Plautus' Aulularia.* ScriptOralia 122. Reihe A: Altertumswissenschaftliche Reihe. Tübingen: Narr.

Le Goff, Jacques. 1992. *History and Memory.* New York: Columbia University Press.

Lehoux, Daryn. 2007. *Astronomy, Weather, and Calendars in the Ancient World: Parapegmata and Related Texts in Classical and Near-Eastern Societies.* Cambridge: Cambridge University Press.

Lentano, Mario. 2012. "Properzio e i valori privati del *mos maiorum*: Una lettura dell'elegia 4, 11." In *Properzio fra tradizione e innovazione: Atti del convegno internazionale, Assisi-Spello, 21–23 maggio 2010*, edited by Roberto Cristofoli, Carlo Santini, and Francesco Santucci, 111–38. Centro studi poesia latina in ditici elegiaci 12. Assisi: Accademia Properziana del Subasio.

Leutzsch, Martin. 1989. *Die Wahrnehmung sozialer Wirklichkeit im "Hirten des Hermas."* Forschungen zur Religion und Literatur des Alten und Neuen Testaments 150. Göttingen: Vandenhoeck & Ruprecht.

Littlewood, R. Joy. 2006. *A Commentary on Ovid: Fasti, Book VI.* Oxford: Oxford University Press.

Lowrie, Michèle. 2008. "Cornelia's Exemplum: Form and Ideology in Propertius 4.11." In *Latin Elegy and Narratology: Fragments of Story*, edited by Genevieve Liveley and Patricia Salzman-Mitchell, 165–79. Columbus: Ohio State University Press.

Luck, Georg. 1962. *Hexen und Zauberei in der römischen Dichtung.* Zürich: Artemis.

———. 1992. *Arcana Mundi: Magic and the Occult in the Greek and Roman Worlds; A Collection of Ancient Texts; Translated, Annotated and Introduced.* Philadelphia: Johns Hopkins University Press.

———. 2000. *Ancient Pathways and Hidden Pursuits: Religion, Morals, and Magic in the Ancient Worlds.* Ann Arbor: University of Michigan Press.

Luckmann, Thomas. 1967. *The Invisible Religion: The Problem of Religion in Modern Society.* New York: Macmillan.

Lüdtke, Alf. 2009. "Practices of Survival—Ways of Appropriating 'The Rule': Reconsidering Approaches to the History of the GDR." In *Power and Society in the GDR,*

1961–1979: The "Normalisation of Rule"?, edited by Mary Fulbrook, 181–93. New York: Berghahn Books.

Luisi, Aldo. 2008. "Le divinità Italiche nell'elegia di Properzio." In *I personaggi dell'elegia di Properzio: Atti del convegno internazionale, Assisi, 26–28 maggio 2006*, edited by Carlo Santini and Francesco Santucci, 405–22. Centro studi poesia latina in distici elegiaci 10. Assisi: Accademia Properziana del Subasio.

Lundgreen, Christoph. 2011. *Regelkonflikte in der römischen Republik: Geltung und Gewichtung von Normen in politischen Entscheidungsprozessen.* Historia-Einzelschriften 221. Stuttgart: Steiner.

Lyne, R. O. A. M. 1998. "Introductory Poems in Propertius: 1.1 and 2.12." *Proceedings of the Cambridge Philological Society* 44:158–81.

Lyon, M. L., and J. M. Barbalet. 1994. "Society's Body." In *Embodiment and Experience: Existential Ground of Culture and Self*, edited by Thomas J. Csordas, 48–66. Cambridge: Cambridge University Press.

MacMullen, Ramsay. 1982. "The Epigraphic Habit in the Roman Empire." *AJPh* 103:233–46.

———. 2010. "Christian Ancestor Worship in Rome." *JBL* 129 (3): 597–613.

Madsen, Richard. 2009. "The Archipelago of Faith: Religious Individualism and Faith Community in America Today." *American Journal of Sociology* 114:1263–301.

Malik, Jamal, Jörg Rüpke, and Theresa Wobbe, eds. 2007. *Religion und Medien: Vom Kultbild zum Internetritual.* Vorlesungen des Interdisziplinären Forums Religion der Universität Erfurt 4. Münster: Aschendorff.

Marinone, Nino. 1970. "Il banchetto dei pontefici in Macrobio." *Maia* 22:271–78.

Markschies, Christoph. 1997. "Innerer Mensch." *RAC* 18:266–312.

Marten, Marleen. 2015. "Communal Dining: Making Things Happen." In *A Companion to the Archaeology of Religion in the Ancient World*, edited by Rubina Raja and Jörg Rüpke, 167–80. Malden, MA: Wiley.

Martin, Craig, Russell T. McCutcheon, and Leslie Dorrough Smith. 2012. *Religious Experience: A Reader.* Critical Categories in the Study of Religion. Sheffield: Equinox.

Martin, John Jeffries. 2004. *Myths of Renaissance Individualism.* Basingstoke: Palgrave Macmillan.

Mastrocinque, Attilio, and Jörg Rüpke. 2013. "Religious Experience in the Roman World." In *Memory and Religious Experience in the Graeco-Roman World*, edited by Nicola Cusamano et al., 135–36. Potsdamer altertumswissenschaftliche Beiträge 45. Stuttgart: Steiner.

Mattern, Torsten. 2006. "Architektur und Ritual: Architektur als funktionaler Rahmen antiker Kultpraxis." In *Archäologie und Ritual: Auf der Suche nach der rituellen Handlung in den antiken Kulturen ägyptens und Griechenlands*, edited by Joannis Mylonopoulos and Hubert Roeder, 167–84. Vienna: Phoibos.

Mauss, Marcel. 1925. "Essai sur le don." *Année sociologique* n.s. 1:30–186.

———. 2002. *The Gift: The Form and Reason for Exchange in Archaic Societies.* Routledge Classics. 1925. Reprint, London: Routledge.

McCauley, Robert N. 2002. *Bringing Ritual to Mind: Psychological Foundations of Cultural Forms.* Cambridge: Cambridge University Press.

McDonough, Christopher Michael. 2004. "The Hag and the Household Gods: Silence, Speech, and the Family in Mid-February (Ovid *Fasti* 2.533–638)." *CP* 99:354–69.

McGuire, Meredith B. 2008. *Lived Religion: Faith and Practice in Everyday Life*. Oxford: Oxford University Press.

McLynn, Neill. 2013. "Aelius Aristides and the Priests." In *Priests and Prophets among Pagans, Jews and Christians*, edited by Beate Dignas, Robert Parker, and Guy G. Stroumsa, 52–79. Studies in the History and Anthropology of Religion 5. Leuven: Peeters.

Mekacher, Nina. 2006. *Die vestalischen Jungfrauen in der römischen Kaiserzeit*. Palilia. Wiesbaden: Dr. Ludwig Reichert Verlag.

Mémoire perdue. 1998. *La mémoire perdue: Recherches sur l'administration romaine*. Collection de l'École française de Rome 243. Rome: École française de Rome.

Miller, John F. 1991. *Ovid's Elegiac Festivals: Studies in the Fasti*. Studien zur Klassischen Philologie 55. Frankfurt a. M.: Lang.

Misch, Georg. 1969. *Geschichte der Autobiographie*. Frankfurt: Schulte-Bulmke.

Moatti, Claudia. 1997. *La raison de Rome: Naissance de l'esprit critique à la fin de la République*. Paris: Seuil.

Moebius, Stephan, and Christian Papilloud, eds. 2006. *Gift: Marcel Mauss' Kulturtheorie der Gabe*. Wiesbaden: Verlag für Sozialwissenschaften.

Mouritsen, Henrik. 2005. "Freedmen and Decurions: Epitaphs and Social History in Imperial Italy." *Journal of Roman Studies* 95:38–63.

Mratschek, Sigrid. 2010. "Zirkulierende Bibliotheken: Medien der Wissensvermittlung und christliche Netzwerke bei Paulinus von Nola." In *L'étude des correspondances dans le monde romain de l'antiquité classique*, edited by Janine Desmulliez, 325–50. Collection UL3. Travaux & recherche. Lille: Université Charles de Gaulle.

Mrozek, Stanislaw. 1973. "À propos de la répartition chronologique des inscriptions latines dans le haut-empire." *Epigraphica* 35:113–18.

Mueller, Hans-Friedrich. 2002. *Roman Religion in Valerius Maximus*. London: Routledge.

Mulsow, Martin. 2012. *Prekäres Wissen: Eine andere Ideengeschichte der Frühen Neuzeit*. Berlin: Suhrkamp.

Münzer, Friedrich. 1920. *Römische Adelsparteien und Adelsfamilien*. Stuttgart: Metzler.

———. 1937. "Die römischen Vestalinnen bis zur Kaiserzeit." *Philologus* 92:47–67, 199–222.

Musschenga, Albert W. 2001. "The Many Faces of Individualism." In *The Many Faces of Individualism*, edited by Anton von Harskamp and Albert W. Musschenga, 3–23. Leuven: Peeters.

Mylonopoulos, Joannis. 2006. "Greek Sanctuaries as Places of Communication through Rituals: An Archaeological Perspective." In *Ritual and Communication in the Graeco-Roman World*, edited by Eftychia Stavrianopoulou, 69–110. Kernos suppl. 16. Liège: CIERGA.

———, ed. 2010. *Divine Images and Human Imaginations in Ancient Greece and Rome*. Religions in the Graeco-Roman World 170. Leiden: Brill.

Naiden, F. S. 2013. *Smoke Signals for the Gods: Ancient Greek Sacrifice from the Archaic through Roman Periods*. Oxford Scholarship Online. New York: Oxford University Press.

Newman, John Kevin. 1997. *Augustan Propertius: The Recapitulation of a Genre*. Spudasmata 63. Hildesheim: Olms.

Nisbet, R. G. M., and Margaret Hubbard. 1970. *A Commentary on Horace: Odes I, II.* Oxford: Clarendon Press.

Nock, Arthur Darby. 1930. "ΣΥΝΝΑΟΣ ΘΕΟΣ." *HSCPh* 41:1–62.

Noland, Carrie. 2009. *Agency and Embodiment: Performing Gesture / Producing Culture.* Cambridge, MA: Harvard University Press.

North, John. 1994. "The Development of Religious Pluralism." In *The Jews among Pagans and Christians: In the Roman Empire*, edited by Judith Lieu, John North, and Tessa Rajak, 174–93. London: Routledge.

———. 1998. "The Books of the Pontifices." *La mémoire perdue: Recherches sur l'administration romaine*, 45–63.

Nünning, Ansgar. 1993. "Renaissance eines anthropomorphisierten Passepartouts oder Nachruf auf ein literaturkritisches Phantom? Überlegungen und Alternativen zum Konzept des 'Implied Author.'" *Deutsche Vierteljahrsschrift für Literaturwissenschaft und Geistesgeschichte* 67:1–25.

Obbink, Dirk. 1989. "The Atheism of Epicurus." *Greek, Roman, and Byzantine Studies* 30:187–223.

Oesterle, Günter, ed. 2005. *Erinnerung, Gedächtnis, Wissen: Studien zur kulturwissenschaftlichen Gedächtnisforschung.* Formen der Erinnerung 26. Göttingen: Vandenhoeck & Ruprecht.

Ogden, Daniel. 2008. *Night's Black Agents: Witches, Wizards and the Dead in the Ancient World.* London: Hambledon Continuum.

Oksala, Teivas. 1973. *Religion und Mythologie bei Horaz: Eine literarhistorische Untersuchung.* Commentationes Humanarum Litterarum 51. Helsinki: Societas Scientiarum Fennica.

O'Neill, Kerill. 1998. "Symbolism and Sympathetic Magic in Propertius 4.5." *Classical Journal* 94 (1): 49–80.

———. 2000. "Propertius 4.2: Slumming with Vertumnus?" *American Journal of Philology* 121 (1): 259–77.

Orlin, Eric M. 1997. *Temples, Religion and Politics in the Roman Republic.* Mnemosyne Suppl. 164. Leiden: Brill.

———. 2007. "Augustan Religion and the Reshaping of Roman Memory." *Arethusa* 40 (1): 73–92.

O'Rourke, Donncha. 2010. "Maxima Roma in Propertius, Virgil and Gallus." *Classical Quarterly* 60 (2): 470–85.

Osiek, Carolyn. 1999. *Shepherd of Hermas: A Commentary.* Hermeneia. Minneapolis: Fortress Press.

Ovidius Naso, Publius. 1985. *P. Ovidi Nasonis Fastorum libri . . . sex.* 2nd ed. Bibliotheca Scriptorum Graecorum et Romanorum Teubneriana. Leipzig: Teubner.

Pace, Enzo. 2009. "Religion as Communication." *Revue Internationale de Sociologie* 21 (1): 205–29.

Papanghelis, Theodore D. 1987. *Propertius: A Hellenistic Poet on Love and Death.* Cambridge: Cambridge University Press.

Parker, Robert. 1996. *Athenian Religion: A History.* Oxford: Clarendon.

———. 2011. *On Greek Religion.* Townsend Lectures / Cornell Studies in Classical Philology. Ithaca, NY: Cornell University Press.

Pelikan-Pittenger, Miriam R. 2008. *Contested Triumphs: Politics, Pageantry, and Performance in Livy's Republican Rome*. Berkeley: University of California Press.

Peter, Hermann. 1874. *De P. Ovidii Nasonis Fastorum Locis Quibusdam Epistula Critica*. Leipzig: Teubner.

Petridou, Georgia. 2015. "Emplotting the Divine: Epiphanic Narratives as Means of Enhancing Agency." *Religion in the Roman Empire* 1 (3): 321–42.

Petsalis-Diomidis, Alexia. 2006. "Sacred Writing, Sacred Reading: The Function of Aelius Aristides' Self-Presentation as Author in the Sacred Tales." In *The Limits of Ancient Biography*, edited by Brian McGing and Judith Mossman, 193–211. Swansea: Classical Press of Wales.

———. 2010. *Truly Beyond Wonders: Aelius Aristides and the Cult of Asklepios*. Oxford: Oxford University Press.

Petzl, Georg. 1994. *Die Beichtinschriften Westkleinasiens*. Epigraphica Anatolica 22. Bonn: Habelt.

Pietilä-Castrén, Leena. 1987. *Magnificentia Publica: The Victory Monuments of the Roman Generals in the Era of the Punic Wars*. Commentationes Humanarum Litterarum 84. Helsinki: Societas Scientiarum Fennica.

Piranomonte, Marina. 2002. *Il santuario della musica e il bosco sacro di Anna Perenna*. Milan: Electa.

Pirenne-Delforge, Vinciane, and Francesca Prescendi, eds. 2011. *Nourrir les dieux? Sacrifice et représentation du divin; Actes de la VIe rencontre du Groupe de recherche européen "Figura, représentation du divin dans les sociétés grecque et romaine." Université de Liège, 23–24 octobre 2009*. Kernos Suppl. 26. Liège: Centre international d'étude de la religion grecque antique.

Platt, Verity. 2011. *Facing the Gods: Epiphany and Representation in Graeco-Roman Art, Literature and Religion*. Cambridge: Cambridge University Press.

Pongratz-Leisten, Beate. 2011. "A New Agenda for the Study of the Rise of Monotheism." In *Reconsidering the Concept of Revolutionary Monotheism*, edited by Beate Pongratz-Leisten, 1–40. Winona Lake, IN: Eisenbrauns.

Prince, Gerald. 2009. "Reader." In *Handbook of Narratology*, edited by Peter Hühn et al., 398–410. Narratologia. Berlin: de Gruyter.

Prince, Meredith. 2003. "Medea and the Inefficacy of Love Magic: Propertius 1.1 and Tibullus 1.2." *Classical Bulletin* 79:205–18.

Pulleyn, Simon. 1997. *Prayer in Greek Religion*. Oxford: Clarendon.

Radke-Uhlmann, Gyburg. 2008. "Aitiologien des Selbst: Moderne Konzepte und ihre Alternativen in antiken autobiographischen Texten." In *Vom Selbst-Verständnis in Antike und Neuzeit: Notions of the Self in Antiquity and Beyond*, edited by Alexander Arweiler and Melanie Möller, 107–29. Transformationen der Antike 8. Berlin: de Gruyter.

Raja, Rubina, and Jörg Rüpke. 2015. "Archaeology of Religion, Material Religion, and the Ancient World." In *A Companion to the Archaeology of Religion in the Ancient World*, edited by Rubina Raja and Jörg Rüpke, 1–25. Malden, MA: Wiley.

Raja, Rubina, and Lara Weiss. 2015a. *The Role of Objects: Creating Meaning in Situations*. Religion in the Roman Empire. Tübingen: Mohr Siebeck.

———. 2015b. "The Role of Objects: Meaning, Situations and Interaction." *Religion in the Roman Empire* 1 (2): 137–47.

Rappaport, Roy A. 1999. *Ritual and Religion in the Making of Humanity*. Cambridge: Cambridge University Press.

Rawson, Elisabeth. 1985. *Intellectual Life in the Late Roman Republic*. London: Duckworth.

Rebillard, Éric. 2012. *Christians and Their Many Identities in Late Antiquity, North Africa, 200–450 CE*. Ithaca, NY: Cornell University Press.

Rehm, Albert. 1949. "Parapegma." *RE* 18 (4): 1295–366.

Reinhard, Tobias. 2006. "Propertius and Rhetoric." In *Brill's Companion to Propertius*, edited by Hans-Christian Günther, 199–216. Leiden: Brill.

Renberg, Gil. 2010. "Dream-Narratives and Unnarrated Dreams in Greek and Latin Dedicatory Inscriptions." In *Sub Imagine Somni: Nighttime Phenomena in the Greco-Roman World*, edited by Emma Scioli and Christine Walde, 33–61. Testi e studi di cultura classica 46. Pisa.

Reynolds, Jack. 2004. *Merleau-Ponty and Derrida: Intertwining Embodiment and Alterity*. Series in Continental Thought. Athens: Ohio University Press.

Ricken, Friedo, ed. 2004. *Religiöse Erfahrung: Ein interdisziplinärer Klärungsversuch*. Münchener philosophische Studien N.F. 23. Stuttgart: Kohlhammer.

Rives, James B. 1995. *Religion and Authority in Roman Carthage from Augustus to Constantine*. Oxford: Clarendon.

———. 1998. "Roman Religion Revived." *Phoenix* 52:345–65.

Rizakis, Athanasios. 2007. "Urban Elites in the Roman East: Enhancing Regional Positions and Social Superiority." In *A Companion to Roman Religion*, edited by Jörg Rüpke, 317–30. Oxford: Blackwell.

Rodriguez-Mayorgas, Ana. 2011. "Annales Maximi: Writing, Memory, and Religious Performance in the Roman Republic." In *Sacred Words: Orality, Literacy and Religion*, edited by A. P. M. H. Lardinois, J. H. Blok, and M. G. M. van der Poel, 235–54. Orality and Literacy in the Ancient World, vol. 8. International Conference on Orality and Literacy in the Ancient World, 8th, 2008. Leiden: Brill.

Rosenberger, Veit. 2013a. "Individuation through Divination: The *Hieroi Logoi* of Aelius Aristides." In *Divination in the Ancient World: Religious Options and the Individual*, edited by Veit Rosenberger, 153–73. Potsdamer Altertumswissenschaftliche Beiträge 46. Stuttgart: Steiner.

———, ed. 2013b. *Divination in the Ancient World: Religious Options and the Individual*. Potsdamer Altertumswissenschaftliche Beiträge 46. Stuttgart: Steiner.

Ruck, Brigitte. 1996. "Die Fasten von Taormina." *ZPE* 111:271–80.

Rüpke, Jörg. 1987. "Kriegserklärung und Fahnenweihe: Zwei Anmerkungen zu einem 'historischen Experiment.'" *AU* 30 (3): 105–7.

———. 1990. *Domi militiae: Die religiöse Konstruktion des Krieges in Rom*. Stuttgart: Steiner.

———. 1993. *Römische Religion bei Eduard Norden: Die "Altrömischen Priesterbücher" im wissenschaftlichen Kontext der dreißiger Jahre*. Religionswissenschaftliche Reihe 7. Marburg: Diagonal.

———. 1994. "Ovids Kalenderkommentar: Zur Gattung der libri fastorum." *Antike und Abendland* 40:125–36.

———. 1995. *Kalender und Öffentlichkeit: Die Geschichte der Repräsentation und religiösen Qualifikation von Zeit in Rom*. Religionsgeschichtliche Versuche und Vorarbeiten 40. Berlin: de Gruyter.

——. 1996a. "Quis vetat et stellas . . . ? Les levers des étoiles et la tradition calendaire chez Ovide." In *Les astres 1: Les astres et les mythes, la description du ciel*, edited by Béatrice Bakhouche, Alain Moreau, and Jean-Claude Turpin, 293–306. Publications de la Recherche Université Paul Valéry. Montpellier: Séminaire d'Étude des Mentalités Antiques.

——. 1996b. "Charismatics or Professionals? Analyzing Religious Specialists." *Numen* 43:241–62.

——. 1997a. "Geschichtsschreibung in Listenform: Beamtenlisten unter römischen Kalendern." *Philologus* 141:65–85.

——. 1997b. "Funktionen des Kalenders: Ansätze zu einer kulturwissenschaftlichen Analyse der religiösen Qualifikation von Zeit am Beispiel der römischen fasti." *Kodikas/Code* 20 (1/2): 87–102.

——. 1998a. "Kommensalität und Gesellschaftsstruktur: Tafelfreu(n)de im alten Rom." *Saeculum* 49:193–215.

——. 1998b. "Karl Otfried Müller als Editor." In *Zwischen Rationalismus und Romantik: Karl Otfried Müller und die antike Kultur*, edited by William M. Calder III and Renate Schlesier, 375–96. Hildesheim: Weidmann.

——. 1999. "Apokalyptische Salzberge: Zum sozialen Ort und zur literarischen Strategie des 'Hirten des Hermas.'" *Archiv für Religiongeschichte* 1:148–60.

——. 2001. "Antike Religion als Kommunikation." In *Gebet und Fluch, Zeichen und Traum: Aspekte religiöser Kommunikation in der Antike*, edited by Kai Brodersen, 13–30. Münster: Lit.

——. 2003a. "Der Hirte des Hermas: Plausibilisierungs- und Legitimierungsstrategien im Übergang von Antike und Christentum." *ZAC* 8:276–98.

——. 2003b. "Libri sacerdotum: Forschungs- und universitätsgeschichtliche Beobachtungen zum Ort von Wissowas Religion und Kultus der Römer." *Archiv für Religiongeschichte* 4:16–39.

——. 2003c. "Pantheon." In *Religion in Geschichte und Gegenwart: Handwörterbuch für Theologie und Religionswissenschaft*, edited by Hans Dieter Betz, 6:857. Tübingen: Mohr Siebeck.

——. 2004. *La religione dei Romani*. Translated by Umberto Gandini. Turin: Einaudi.

——. 2005a. "Römische Priester in der Öffentlichkeit." In *Senatores Populi Romani: Realität und mediale Präsentation einer Führungsschicht; Kolloquium der Prosopographia Imperii Romani vom 11.–13. Juni 2004*, edited by Werner Eck and Matthäus Heil, 283–93. Heidelberger Althistorische Beiträge und Epigraphische Studien 40. Stuttgart: Steiner.

——. 2005b. "Gottesvorstellungen als anthropologische Reflexionen in der römischen Gesellschaft." In *Grenzen des Menschseins: Probleme einer Definition des Menschlichen*, edited by Justin Stagl and Wolfgang Reinhard, 435–68. Veröffentlichungen des Instituts für Historische Anthropologie 8. Vienna: Böhlau.

——. 2005c. "Varro's *tria genera theologiae*: Religious Thinking in the Late Republic." *Ordia Prima* 4:107–29.

——. 2005d. *Fasti sacerdotum: Die Mitglieder der Priesterschaften und das sakrale Funktionspersonal römischer, griechischer, orientalischer und jüdisch-christlicher Kulte in der*

Stadt Rom von 300 v. Chr. bis 499 n. Chr. Potsdamer altertumswissenschaftliche Beiträge 12/1–3. Stuttgart: Steiner.

———. 2006a. *Zeit und Fest. Eine Kulturgeschichte des Kalenders.* Munich: Beck.

———. 2006b. "Organisationsmuster religiöser Spezialisten im kultischen Spektrum Roms." In *Religions orientales—culti misterici: Neue Perspektiven—nouvelle perspectives—prospettive nuove*, edited by Corinne Bonnet, Jörg Rüpke, and Paolo Scarpi, 13–26. Potsdamer altertumswissenschaftliche Beiträge 16. Stuttgart: Steiner.

———. 2007a. *Religion of the Romans.* Edited and translated by Richard Gordon. Cambridge: Polity.

———. 2007b. *Historische Religionswissenschaft: Eine Einführung.* Religionswissenschaft heute. Stuttgart: Kohlhammer.

———. 2008. *Fasti sacerdotum: A Prosopography of Pagan, Jewish, and Christian Religious Officials in the City of Rome, 300 BC to AD 499.* Translated by David M. B. Richardson. Oxford: Oxford University Press.

———. 2009a. *A Companion to Roman Religion.* 2nd ed. Blackwell Companions to the Ancient World. Malden, MA: Blackwell.

———. 2009b. "Antiquar und Theologe: Systematisierende Beschreibung römischer Religion bei Varro." In *Römische Religion im historischen Wandel*, edited by Andreas Bendlin and Jörg Rüpke, 73–88. Tübingen: Mohr Siebeck.

———. 2009c. "Religiöser Pluralismus und das Römische Reich." In *Die Religion des Imperium Romanum: Koine und Konfrontationen*, edited by Hubert Cancik and Jörg Rüpke, 331–54. Tübingen: Mohr Siebeck.

———. 2009d. "Properz: Aitiologische Elegie in Augusteischer Zeit." In *Römische Religion im historischen Wandel: Diskursentwicklung von Plautus bis Ovid*, edited by Andreas Bendlin and Jörg Rüpke, 115–42. Potsdamer altertumswissenschaftliche Beiträge 17. Stuttgart: Steiner.

———. 2010a. "Hellenistic and Roman Empires and Euro-Mediterranean Religion." *Journal of Religion in Europe* 3:197–214.

———. 2010b. "Wann begann die europäische Religionsgeschichte? Der hellenistisch-römische Mittelmeerraum und die europäische Gegenwart." *Historia Religionum* 2:91–102.

———. 2010c. "Representation or Presence? Picturing the Divine in Ancient Rome." *Archiv für Religionsgeschichte* 12:183–96.

———. 2010d. "Radikale im öffentlichen Dienst: Status und Individualisierung unter römischen Priestern republikanischer Zeit." In *Religiöser Fundamentalismus in der römischen Kaiserzeit*, edited by Pedro Barceló, 11–21. Potsdamer altertumswissenschaftliche Beiträge 29. Stuttgart: Steiner.

———. 2011a. "Individual Appropriation and Institutional Changes: Roman Priesthoods in the Later Empire." In *Politiche religiose nel mondo antico e tardo antico: Poteri e indirizzi, forme del controllo, idee e prassi di tolleranza; Atti del Convegno internazionale di studi (Firenze, 24–26 settembre 2009)*, edited by Giovanni A. Cecconi and Chantal Gabrielli, 261–73. Bari: Edipuglia.

———. 2011b. *The Roman Calendar from Numa to Constantine: Time, History and the Fasti.* Translated by David M. B. Richardson. Malden, MA: Wiley-Blackwell.

———. 2011c. *Aberglauben oder Individualität? Religiöse Abweichung im römischen Reich.* Tübingen: Mohr Siebeck.

———. 2011d. "Reichsreligion? Überlegungen zur Religionsgeschichte des antiken Mittelmeerraums in römischer Zeit." *Historische Zeitschrift* 292:297–322.

———. 2012a. *Religion in Republican Rome: Rationalization and Ritual Change.* Philadelphia: University of Pennsylvania Press.

———. 2012b. *Antike Epik: Eine Einführung von Homer bis in die Spätantike.* Nova Classica 1. Marburg: Tectum.

———. 2012c. "Lived Ancient Religion: Questioning 'Cults' and 'Polis Religion.'" *Mythos* n.s. 5 (2011): 191–204.

———. 2012d. "Polytheismus und Monotheismus als Perspektiven auf die antike Religionsgeschichte." In *Gott, Götter, Götzen: XIV. Europäischer Kongress für Theologie,* edited by Christoph Schöbel, 56–68. Veröffentlichungen der Wissenschaftlichen Gesellschaft für Theologie 38. Leipzig: Evangelische Verlagsanstalt.

———. 2012e. *Religion in Republican Rome: Rationalization and Ritual Change.* Philadelphia: University of Pennsylvania Press.

———. 2012f. "Sakralisierung von Zeit in Rom und Italien: Produktionsstrategien und Aneignungen von Heiligkeit." In *Heilige, Heiliges und Heiligkeit in spätantiken Religionskulturen,* edited by Peter Gemeinhardt and Katharina Heyden, 231–47. Religionsgeschichtliche Versuche und Vorarbeiten 61. Berlin: de Gruyter.

———. 2012g. "Flamines, Salii, and the Priestesses of Vesta: Individual Decision and Differences of Social Order in the Late Republic." In *Demeter, Isis, Vesta, and Cybele: Studies in Greek and Roman Religion in Honour of Giulia Sfameni Gasparro,* edited by Attilio Mastrocinque and Concetta Giuffrè Scibona, 183–94. Potsdamer altertumswissenschaftliche Beiträge 36. Stuttgart: Steiner.

———. 2012h. "Religion und Individuum." In *Religionswissenschaft,* edited by Michael Stausberg, 241–53. Berlin: de Gruyter.

———. 2012i. *Religiöse Erinnerungskulturen: Formen der Geschichtsschreibung in der römischen Antike.* Darmstadt: Wissenschaftliche Buchgesellschaft.

———. 2013a. "On Religious Experiences That Should Not Happen in Sanctuaries." In *Memory and Religious Experience in the Graeco-Roman World,* edited by Nicola Cusamano et al., 137–44. Potsdamer altertumswissenschaftliche Beiträge 45. Stuttgart: Steiner.

———. 2013b. "Two Cities and One Self: Transformations of Jerusalem and Reflexive Individuality in *The Shepherd of Hermas.*" In *Religious Dimensions of the Self in the Second Century CE,* edited by Jörg Rüpke and Greg Woolf, 49–65. Studien und Texte zu Antike und Christentum 76. Tübingen: Mohr Siebeck.

———, ed. 2013c. *The Individual in the Religions of the Ancient Mediterranean.* Oxford: Oxford University Press.

———. 2013d. "Introduction: Individualisation and Individuation as Concepts for Historical Research." In *The Individual in the Religions of the Ancient Mediterranean,* edited by Jörg Rüpke, 3–28. Oxford: Oxford University Press.

———. 2013e. "Fighting for Differences: Forms and Limits of Religious Individuality in the 'Shepherd of Hermas.'" In *The Individual in the Religions of the Ancient Mediterranean,* edited by Jörg Rüpke, 315–41. Oxford: Oxford University Press.

———. 2014a. "Ethnicity in Roman Religion." In *A Companion to Ethnicity in the Ancient Mediterranean*, edited by Jeremy McInerney, 470–82. Malden, MA: Blackwell-Wiley.

———. 2014b. "Historicizing Religion: Varro's Antiquitates and History of Religion in the Late Roman Republic." *History of Religions* 53 (3): 246–68.

———. 2014c. *Religion: Antiquity and Its Legacy*. London / New York: Tauris / Oxford University Press.

———. 2015a. "Das Imperium Romanum als religionsgeschichtlicher Raum: Eine Skizze." In *Ein pluriverses Universum: Zivilisationen und Religionen im antiken Mittelmeerraum*, edited by Richard Faber and Achim Lichtenberger, 333–51. Mittelmeerstudien. Paderborn: Schöningh.

———. 2015b. "Religious Agency, Identity, and Communication: Reflecting on History and Theory of Religion." *Religion* 45 (3): 344–66.

———. 2015c. "The 'Connected Reader' as a Window into Lived Ancient Religion: A Case Study of Ovid's *Libri fastorum*." *Religion in the Roman Empire* 1 (1): 95–113.

———. 2015d. "Römische Priestermähler." In *The Eucharist: Its Origins and Contexts; Sacred Meal, Communal Meal, Table Fellowship, and the Eucharist*, edited by David Hellholm and Dieter Sänger, 3:1527–37. Wissenschaftliche Untersuchungen zum Neuen Testament. Tübingen: Mohr Siebeck.

———. 2016a. *Religious Deviance in the Roman World: Superstition or Individuality*. Translated by David M. B. Richardson. Cambridge: Cambridge University Press.

———. 2016b. "Individualization and Privatization." In *The Oxford Handbook for the Study of Religion*, edited by Steven Engler and Michael Stausberg. New York: Oxford University Press. Forthcoming.

———. 2016c. "Knowledge of Religion in Valerius Maximus' Exempla: Roman Historiography and Tiberian Memory Culture." In *Aspects of Memory in Rome and Early Christianity*, edited by Karl Galinsky, 89–111. Oxford: Oxford University Press.

Rüpke, Jörg, and Wolfgang Spickermann. 2009. "Religion and Literature." *ARG* 11:121–22.

———, eds. 2012. *Reflections on Religious Individuality: Greco-Roman and Judaeo-Christian Texts and Practices*. Religionsgeschichtliche Versuche und Vorarbeiten 62. Berlin: de Gruyter.

Rüpke, Jörg, and Greg Woolf, eds. 2013. *Religious Dimensions of the Self in the Second Century CE*. Studien und Texte zu Antike und Christentum 76. Tübingen: Mohr Siebeck.

Said, Edward W. 1978. *Orientalism*. New York: Pantheon Books.

Salzman, Michele. 1999. "The Christianization of Sacred Time and Sacred Space." In *The Transformations of Urbs Roma in Late Antiquity*, edited by W. V. Harris, 123–34. Portsmouth, RI: Journal of Roman Archaeology.

Saquete, José Carlos. 2000. *Las vírgenes vestales: Un sacerdocio femenino en la religión pública romana*. Madrid: Fundación de estudios romanos.

Schäfer, Alfred, and Alexandru Diaconescu. 1997. "Das Liber-Pater-Heiligtum von Apulum (Dakien)." In *Römische Reichsreligion und Provinzialreligion*, edited by Hubert Cancik and Jörg Rüpke, 195–218. Tübingen: Mohr Siebeck.

Scheer, Tanja S. 2000. *Die Gottheit und ihr Bild: Untersuchungen zur Funktion griechischer Kultbilder in Religion und Politik*. Zetemata 105. Munich: Beck.

Scheid, John. 1975. *Les frères arvales: Recrutement et origine sociale sous les Julio-Claudiens.* Collection de l'École Pratique des Hautes Études, sciences religieuses 77. Paris: Belles Lettres.

——. 1987. "Polytheism Impossible or the Empty Gods: Reasons behind a Void in the History of Roman Religion." *History and Anthropology* 3:303–25.

——. 1990a. *Romulus et ses frères: Le collège des frères arvales, modèle du culte public dans la Rome des empereurs.* Bibliothèque des Écoles françaises d'Athènes et de Rome 275. Rome: École française.

——. 1990b. *Le collège des frères arvales: Étude prosopographieque du recrutement (69–304).* Saggi di storia antica 1. Rome: Bretschneider.

——. 1990c. "Rituel et écriture à Rome." In *Essais sur le rituel*, edited by Anne-Marie Blondeau and Kristofer Schipper, 1–15. Louvain: Peeters.

——. 1992. "Myth, Cult and Reality in Ovid's *Fasti.*" *PCPhS* 38:118–31.

——. 1993. "Cultes, mythes et politique au début de l'Empire." In *Mythos in mythenloser Gesellschaft: Das Paradigma Roms*, edited by Fritz Graf, 109–27. Stuttgart: Teubner.

——. 1994. "Les archives de la piété: Réflexions sur les livres sacerdotaux." In *La mémoire perdue: A la recherche des archives oubliées, publiques et privées, de la Rome antique*, 173–85. Série Histoire Ancienne et Médiévale 30. Paris: Publications de la Sorbonne.

——. 1997. "Arvales Fratres." *Der Neue Pauly* 2:67–69.

——. 1998a. "Les annales de pontifes: Une hypothèse de plus." In *Convegno per Santo Mazzarino: Roma 9–11 maggio 1991*, 199–220. Saggi di storia antica. Rome: Bretschneider.

——. 1998b. *Commentarii fratrum Arvalium qui supersunt: Les copie épigraphiques des protocoles annuels de la confrérie arvale (21 av.–304 ap. J.-C.).* With Paola Tassini and Jörg Rüpke. Roma antica 4: Recherches archéologiques à La Magliana. Rome: École française de Rome / Soprintendenza archeologica di Roma.

——. 1998c. *La religion des Romains.* Paris: Armand Colin.

——. 1999. "Aspects religieux de la municipalisation: Quelques réflexions générales." In *Cités, municipes, colonies: Les processus de minicipalisation en Gaule et en Germanie sous le Haut-Empire romain*, edited by M. Dondin-Payre and Marie-Thérèse Raepsaet-Charlier, 381–423. Paris: Sorbonne.

——. 2003. *An Introduction to Roman Religion.* Edinburgh: Edinburgh University Press.

——. 2013. *Les dieux, l'état et l'individu: Réflexions sur la religion civique à Rome.* Paris: Éditions du Seuil.

Schlesier, Renate. 1991. "Prolegomena zu Jane Harrisons Deutung der antiken griechischen Religion." In *Religionswissenschaft und Kulturkritik: Beiträge zur Konferenz The History of Religions and Critique of Culture in the Days of Gerardus van der Leeuw (1890–1950)*, edited by Hans G. Kippenberg and Brigitte Luchesi, 193–235. Marburg: Diagonal.

——. 1995. "'Arbeiter in Useners Weinberg': Anthropologie und antike Religionsgeschichte in Deutschland nach dem Ersten Weltkrieg." In *Altertumswissenschaft in den 20er Jahren: Neue Fragen und Impulse*, edited by Hellmut Flashar, 329–80. Stuttgart: Steiner.

Schmid, Alfred. 2005. *Augustus und die Macht der Sterne: Antike Astrologie und die Etablierung der Monarchie in Rom*. Cologne: Böhlau.

Schmidt, Francis. 1987. "Polytheisms: Degeneration or Progress?" *History and Anthropology* 3:9–60.

Schultz, Celia E. 2006. *Women's Religious Activity in the Roman Republic*. Chapel Hill: University of North Carolina Press.

———. 2012. "On the Burial of the Unchaste Vestal Virgins." In *Rome, Pollution and Propriety: Dirt, Disease and Hygiene in the Eternal City from Antiquity to Modernity*, edited by Mark Bradley, 122–36. Cambridge: Cambridge University Press.

Segal, A. F. 1980. "Heavenly Ascent in Hellenistic Judaism, Early Christianity and Their Environment." *ANRW* 2.23.2:1333–94.

Seiwert, Hubert. 2009. "Post-durkheimianische Religion? Überlegungen zum Kontrast moderner und vormoderner Religion im Anschluss an Charles Taylor." In *Mauss, Buddhismus, Devianz: Festschrift für Heinz Mürmel zum 65. Geburtstag*, edited by Thomas Hase et al., 99–114. Marburg: Diagonal.

Simmel, Georg. 1917. "Individualismus." *Marsyas* 1:33–39.

Simón, Francisco Marco. 1996. *Flamen Dialis: El sacerdote de Júpiter en la religión romana*. Madrid: Ediciones clasicas.

———. 2001. "La emergencia de la magia como sistema di alteridad en la Roma del siglo I d.C." *MHNH: International Journal of Research on Ancient Magic and Astrology* 1:105–32.

Sini, Francesco. 1983. *Documenti sacerdotali di Roma antica*. Vol. 1, *Libri e commentarii*. Università di Sassari, Fac. di Giurisprudenza, Seminario di Diritto Romano 2. Sassari: Dessi.

Skutsch, Otto. 1985. *The Annals of Q. Ennius*. Edited, with introduction and commentary. Oxford: Clarendon.

Smith, Christopher. 2011. "Citizenship and Community: Inventing the Roman Republic." In *State Formation in Italy and Greece: Questioning the Neoevolutionist Paradigm*, edited by Nicola Terrenato and D. C. Haggis, 217–30. Oxford: Oxbow Books.

Sperber, Dan. 1975. *Rethinking Symbolism*. Translated by A. L. Morton. Cambridge: Cambridge University Press.

Sperber, Dan, and Deirdre Wilson. 1987. "Précis of Relevance." *Behavioral & Brain Sciences* 10 (4): 697–710.

———. 1994. "Outline of Relevance Theory." *Links & Letters* 1:85–106.

Speyer, Wolfgang. 1989. "Das Verhältnis des Augustus zur Religion." In *Frühes Christentum im antiken Strahungsfeld: Ausgewählte Aufsätze*, edited by Wolfgang Speyer, 402–30. Tübingen: Mohr.

Spickermann, Wolfgang. 2003. *Germania Superior*. Religionsgeschichte des römischen Germanien 1. Tübingen: Mohr.

———. 2008. *Germania Inferior*. Religionsgeschichte des römischen Germanien 2. Tübingen: Mohr.

Spiro, Melford E. 1993. "Is the Western Conception of the Self 'Peculiar' within the Context of the World Cultures?" *Ethos* 21 (2): 107–53.

Starr, Raymond J. 1987. "The Circulation of Literary Texts in the Roman World." *CQ* 37:213–23.

Stausberg, Michael. 2001. "Kohärenz und Kontinuität: Überlegungen zur Repräsentation und Reproduktion von Religionen." In *Kontinuitäten und Brüche in der Religionsgeschichte: Festschrift für Anders Hultgård zu seinem 65. Geburtstag am 23.12.2001*, edited by Michael Stausberg, 596–619. Berlin: de Gruyter.

———. 2009. "Renaissancen: Vermittlungsformen des Paganen." In *Europäische Religionsgeschichte: Ein mehrfacher Pluralismus*, edited by Hans G. Kippenberg, Jörg Rüpke, and Kocku von Stuckrad, 695–722. Göttingen: Vandenhoeck & Ruprecht.

Stavrianopoulou, Eftychia. 2006. *Ritual and Communication in the Graeco-Roman World*. Translated by Antique Centre International d'Étude de la Religion Grecque. Kernos Suppl. 16. Liège: Centre International d'Étude de la Religion Grecque Antique.

Steinsapir, Ann Irvine. 2005. *Rural Sanctuaries in Roman Syria: The Creation of a Sacred Landscape*. BAR International Series 1431. Oxford: Hedges.

Stepper, Ruth. 2003. *Augustus et sacerdos: Untersuchungen zum römischen Kaiser als Priester* PawB. Stuttgart: Steiner.

Sterbenc Erker, Darja. 2013. *Religiöse Rollen römischer Frauen in "griechischen" Ritualen*. Potsdamer altertumswissenschaftliche Beiträge 43. Stuttgart: Steiner.

Stern, Sacha 2012. *Calendars in Antiquity: Empires, States, and Societies*. New York: Oxford University Press.

Stewart, Peter. 2003. *Statues in Roman Society: Representation and Response*. Oxford Studies in Ancient Culture and Representation. Oxford: Oxford University Press.

Stone, Michael E. 2003. "A Reconsideration of Apocalyptic Visions." *Harvard Theological Review* 96 (2): 167–80.

Stroumsa, Guy G. 2008. "The End of Sacrifice: Religious Mutations of Late Antiquity." In *Empsuchoi Logoi: Festschrift Pieter van der Horst*, edited by M. Misset-van de Weg, 29–46. Leiden: Brill.

Stuckenbruck, Loren T. 1995. *Angel Veneration and Christology: A Study in Early Judaism and in the Christology of the Apocalypse of John*. Wissenschaftliche Untersuchungen zum Neuen Testament, Reihe 2, 70. Tübingen: Mohr.

Sundén, Hjalmar. 1975. *Gott erfahren: Das Rollenangebot der Religionen*. Translated from the Swedish by Horst Reller. Gütersloh: Mohn.

Syndikus, Hans Peter. 2006. "The Second Book." In *Brill's Companion to Propertius*, edited by Hans-Christian Günther, 245–318. Leiden: Brill.

———. 2010. *Die Elegien des Properz: Eine Interpretation*. Darmstadt: Wissenschaftliche Buchgesellschaft.

Takács, Sarolta A. 2008. *Vestal Virgins, Sibyls, and Matrons: Women in Roman Religion*. Austin: University of Texas Press.

Taves, Ann. 2009. *Religious Experience Reconsidered: A Building-Block Approach to the Study of Religion and Other Special Things*. Princeton, NJ: Princeton University Press.

———. 2010. "Experience as Site of Contested Meaning and Value: The Attributional Dog and Its Special Tail." *Religion* 40 (4): 317–23.

Taylor, Lily Ross. 1942. "Caesar's Colleagues in the Pontifical College." *AJPh* 63:385–412.

Tornau, Christian, and Paolo Cecconi. 2014. *The "Shepherd" of Hermas in Latin: Critical Edition of the Oldest Translation Vulgata*. Texte und Untersuchungen zur Geschichte der altchristlichen Literatur 173. Berlin: De Gruyter.

Tupet, Anne-Marie. 1976. *La magie dans la poésie latine.* Vol. 1, *Des origines à la fin du règne d'Auguste.* Paris: Belles Lettres.

Turner, Victor, ed. 1982. *Celebration: Studies in Festivity and Ritual.* Washington, DC: Smithsonian Institution Press.

Tyrell, Hartmann, Volkhard Krech, and Hubert Knoblauch, eds. 1998. *Religion als Kommunikation.* Religion in der Gesellschaft 4. Würzburg: Ergon.

Van Andringa, William. 2009. *Quotidien des dieux et des hommes: La vie religieuse dans les cités du Vésuve à l'époque romaine.* BEFRAR 337. Rome: Ecole francaise.

van den Bruwaene, Martin. 1937. *La théologie de Cicéron.* Université de Louvain: Revueil de travaux publiés par les mebres des Conférences d'Histoire et de Philologie 2.42. Louvain: Bureaux du Recueil.

van Straten, F. T. 1981. "Gifts for the Gods." In *Faith, Hope and Worship: Aspects of Religious Mentality in the Ancient World,* edited by H. S. Versnel, 65–151. Leiden: Brill.

Versnel, H. S. 1981. "Religious Mentality in Ancient Prayer." In *Faith, Hope and Worship: Aspects of Religious Mentality in the Ancient World,* edited by H. S. Versnel, 1–64. Leiden: Brill.

Veyne, Paul. 1988. *Brot und Spiele: Gesellschaftliche Macht und politische Herrschaft in der Antike.* Translated from the French by Klaus Laermann and Hans Richard Brittnacher. Theorie und Gesellschaft 11. Frankfurt a. M. / Paris: Campus / Maison des Sciences de l'Homme.

Viarre, Simone, ed. 2005. *Properce: Élégies.* Paris: Belles Lettres.

Vinzent, Markus. 2011a. *Christ's Resurrection in Early Christianity and the Making of the New Testament.* Farnham: Ashgate.

———. 2011b. "Give and Take amongst Second Century Authors: The Ascension of Isaiah, the Epistle of the Apostles and Marcion of Sinope." *Studia Patristica* 50:105–29.

———. 2014. *Marcion and the Dating of the Synoptic Gospels.* Studia Patristica Suppl. 2. Leuven: Peeters.

Wagner-Roser, Silvia. 1987. "Ein römischer Steckkalender aus Bad Rappenau, Kreis Heilbronn." *Fundberichte aus Baden-Württemberg* 12:431–38.

Waldner, Katharina. 2015. *Für die Wahrheit sterben: Antike Martyriumserzählungen zwischen Religion, Politik und Philosophie.* Studien zu Antike und Christentum. Tübingen: Mohr Siebeck.

Wallace-Hadrill, Andrew. 1988. "Time for Augustus: Ovid, Augustus and the *Fasti.*" In *Homo Viator: Classical Essays for John Bramble,* edited by Michael Whitby, Philip Hardie, and Mary Whitby, 221–30. Bristol: Classical Press.

———. 2008. *Rome's Cultural Revolution.* Cambridge: Cambridge University Press.

Wardle, David. 2006. *Cicero on Divination: De Divinatione Book 1; Translated with Introduction and Historical Commentary.* Oxford: Clarendon Press.

Watson, Lindsay. 1991. *Arae: The Curse Poetry of Antiquity.* Arca 26. Leeds: Cairns.

Weil, Gail, and Honni Fern Haber, eds. 1999. *Perspectives on Embodiment: The Intersections of Nature and Culture.* New York: Routledge.

Weiss, Lara. 2015. "Perpetuated Action." In *A Companion to the Archaeology of Religion in the Ancient World,* edited by Rubina Raja and Jörg Rüpke, 60–70. Malden, MA: Wiley.

Welch, Tara S. 2005. *The Elegiac Cityscape: Propertius and the Meaning of Roman Monuments*. Columbus: Ohio State University Press.

Wescoat, Bonna D., and Robert G. Ousterhout, eds. 2012. *Architecture of the Sacred: Space, Ritual, and Experience from Classical Greece to Byzantium*. Cambridge: Cambridge University Press.

Whitehead, David. 1986. *The Demes of Attica 508/7–ca. 250 B.C.: A Political and Social Study*. Princeton, NJ: Princeton University Press.

Whitehouse, Harvey, and Robert N. McCauley, eds. 2005. *Mind and Religion : Psychological and Cognitive Foundations of Religiosity*. Cognitive Science of Religion Series. Walnut Creek, CA: Oxford: Altamira Press.

Whitmarsh, Tim, ed. 2010. *Local Knowledge and Microidentities in the Imperial Greek World*. Greek Culture in the Roman World. Cambridge: Cambridge University Press.

Wiedemann, Thomas. 1986. "The Fetiales: A Reconsideration." *CQ* 36:478–90.

Wildfang, Robin Lorsch. 2006. *Rome's Vestal Virgins: A Study of Rome's Vestal Priestesses in the Late Republic and Early Empire*. London: Routledge.

Wili, Walter. 1948. *Horaz und die augusteische Kultur*. Basel: Schwabe.

Willand, Marcus. 2014. *Lesermodelle und Lesertheorien historische und systematische Perspektiven*. Narratologia. Berlin: de Gruyter.

Wilson, Deirdre, and Dan Sperber. 2002. "Relevance Theory." *UCL Working Papers in Linguistics* 13:249–87.

———. 2012. *Meaning and Relevance*. Cambridge: Cambridge University Press.

Winiarczyk, Marek. 1990. "Methodisches zum antiken Atheismus." *RhM* 133:1–15.

Wiseman, Timothy Peter. 2000. "Liber: Myth, Drama and Ideology in Republican Rome." In *The Roman Middle Republic: Politics, Religion, and Historiography c. 400–133 B.C.*, edited by Christer Bruun, 265–99. Rome: Institutum Romanum.

Wissowa, Georg. 1912. *Religion und Kultus der Römer*. Handbuch der Altertumswissenschaft 5.4. Munich: Beck.

———. 1923. "Vestalinnenfrevel." *ARW* 22:201–14.

Witteyer, Marion. 2004a. "Verborgene Wünsche: Befunde antiken Schadenzaubers aus Mogontiacum-Mainz." In *Fluchtafeln: Neue Befunde und neue Deutungen zum antiken Schadenzauber*, edited by Kai Brodersen and Armina Kropp, 41–50. Frankfurt a. M.: Verlag Antike.

———. 2005. "Curse-tablets and Voodoo-dolls from Mainz: The Archaeological Evidence for Magical Practices in the Sanctuary of Isis and Mater Magna." *MHNH: International Journal of Research on Ancient Magic and Astrology* 5:105–24.

———, ed. 2004b. *Das Heiligtum für Isis und für Mater Magna*. Mainz: Zabern.

Woolf, Greg. 1994. "Becoming Roman, Staying Greek: Culture, Identity and the Civilizing Process in the Roman East." *PCPS* 40:115–43.

———. 1998. *Becoming Roman: The Origins of Provincial Civilization in Gaul*. Cambridge: Cambridge University Press.

Yabro Collins, Adela. 1988. "Early Christian Apocalyptic Literature." *ANRW* 2.25.6:4665–711.

Zetzel, James E. G. 1996. "Poetic Baldness and Its Cure." *Materiali e Discussioni* 36:73–100.

General Index

Page numbers in italics refer to figures.

Index of Passages

CPSIA information can be obtained at www.ICGtesting.com
Printed in the USA
BVOW08*0651061016

464028BV00003B/8/P